ER

Also by Lynette Rice

How to Save a Life

ER

THE ORAL HISTORY

LYNETTE RICE

ST. MARTIN'S
PRESS
NEW YORK

First published in the United States by St. Martin's Press,
an imprint of St. Martin's Publishing Group

EU Representative: Macmillan Publishers Ireland Ltd., 1st Floor, The Liffey Trust Centre, 117–126 Sheriff Street Upper, Dublin 1, D01 YC43

www.stmartins.com

The Library of Congress Cataloging-in-Publication Data is available upon request.

ISBN 978-1-250-39958-8 (hardcover)
ISBN 978-1-250-39959-5 (ebook)

First Edition: 2026

10 9 8 7 6 5 4 3 2 1

Contents

Author's Note

Taking a trip back to County General required more than just an HBO Max subscription to rewatch all those classic episodes. I interviewed more than sixty actors, writers, directors, executives, producers, and crew members to help assemble an oral history that highlights the drama's breakout moments, poignant departures, and extraordinary one-shots, or "oners," that made *ER* so unique. Not everyone from the massive cast was available to chat, so I relied on archival interviews from multiple sources, including some from my time at *Entertainment Weekly* and *Deadline*. A full list of the stories that I drew from is provided at the back of the book.

Cast of Characters

Actors

ANTHONY EDWARDS (Mark Greene, 1994–2008)
GEORGE CLOONEY (Doug Ross, 1994–1999, 2009)
JULIANNA MARGULIES (Carol Hathaway, 1994–2000, 2009)
NOAH WYLE (John Carter, 1994–2005, 2009)
SHERRY STRINGFIELD (Susan Lewis, 1994–96, 2001–2005, 2009)
ERIQ LA SALLE (Peter Benton, 1994–2002, 2009)
YVETTE FREEMAN (Haleh Adams, 1994–2009)
ELLEN CRAWFORD (Lydia Wright, 1994–2003, 2009)
LILY MARIYE (Lily Jarvik, 1994–2009)
LAURA INNES (Kerry Weaver, 1995–2007, 2009)
MAURA TIERNEY (Abby Lockhart, 1999–2009)
ALEX KINGSTON (Elizabeth Corday, 1997–2004, 2009)
LINDA CARDELLINI (Samantha Taggart, 2003–2009)
CHRISTINE HARNOS (Jennifer Greene, 1994–1998, 2001–2002)
GORAN VISNJIC (Luka Kovač, 1999–2008)
JOHN STAMOS (Tony Gates, 2005–2009)
SHARIF ATKINS (Michael Gallant, 2001–2006)
ERIK PALLADINO (Dave Malucci, 1999–2001)

MICHAEL MICHELE (Cleo Finch, 1999–2002)
MEKHI PHIFER (Gregory Pratt, 2002–2009)
CCH POUNDER (Angela Hicks, 1994–1997)
GLORIA REUBEN (Jeanie Boulet, 1995–1999, 2008)
PARMINDER NAGRA (Neela Rasgotra, 2003–2009)
MING-NA WEN (Jing-Mei "Deb" Chen, 1995, 1999–2004)
KELLIE MARTIN (Lucy Knight, 1998–2000)
PAUL MCCRANE (Robert Romano, 1997–2003, 2008)
ABRAHAM BENRUBI (Jerry Markovic, 1994–1999, 2002–2006, 2008–2009)
LAURA CERÓN (Chuny Marquez, 1995–2009)
YVONNE ZIMA (Rachel Greene, 1994–2000)
HALLEE HIRSH (Rachel Greene, 2001–2002, 2004, 2009)
MIKE GENOVESE (Officer Al Grabarsky, 1994–1996, 1998–2000)
TROY EVANS (Frank Martin, 1994, 2000–2009)
RICK ROSSOVICH (John "Tag" Taglieri, 1994–1995)
SHANE WEST (Ray Barnett, 2004–2009)
EMILY WAGNER (Doris Pickman, 1994–2009)
SCOTT GRIMES (Archie Morris, 2003–2009)
SALLY FIELD (Maggie Wyczenski, 2000, 2003–2006)
CLANCY BROWN (Ellis West, 1997–1998)
ALAN ALDA (Gabriel Lawrence, 1999)
KAT DENNINGS (Zoe Butler, 2005–2006)
MARY MCDONNELL (Eleanor Carter, 2001–2002)
JOE MANGANIELLO (Officer Litchman, 2007)
MARTHA PLIMPTON (Meg Corwin, 1999)
DAVID KRUMHOLTZ (Paul Sobriki, 2000, 2002)
BRADLEY WHITFORD (Sean O'Brien, 1995)
COLLEEN FLYNN (Jodi O'Brien, 1995)
JEFFREY DEAN MORGAN (Firefighter Larkin, 2001)

JULIANNE NICHOLSON (Jordan, 2004)
JAMES WOODS (Nate Lennox, 2006)
MICHAEL GASTON (Rick, 2008)
MATTHEW WATKINS (Reese, 1999–2001, 2009)
TRINIA WATKINS (Matthew Watkins's mom)

Executives

BOB DALY (Warner Bros. chairman and co-CEO, 1980–1999)
LESLIE MOONVES (Warner Bros. TV president, 1993–1995)
PETER ROTH (Warner Bros. TV chairman, 1999–2021)
DON OHLMEYER (NBC West Coast president, 1993–1999)
WARREN LITTLEFIELD (NBC Entertainment president, 1991–1998)
DAVID NEVINS (NBC vice president of prime-time series, 1994–1999)
PRESTON BECKMAN (NBC head of scheduling, 1991–2000)
JEFF SAGANSKY (CBS Entertainment president, 1989–1994)
JOHN LEVEY (Warner Bros. TV head of casting)
TONY THOMOPOULOS (Amblin Television president, 1991–1995)
LORI OPENDEN (NBC casting, 1985–1999)
PAM MORRISON (NBC publicity, 1996–1998)
BARBARA TRANCHITO (NBC publicity)
KEVIN REILLY (NBC vice president of drama development, 1992–1994)

Titles/Music

JAMES NEWTON HOWARD (composer, *ER* theme music, 1994–2009)
BILLY PITTARD (senior title designer, 1994–1995)
SUZANNE KILEY (principal title designer, 1994–1995)

Writers/Producers

John Wells (1994–2009)
Neal Baer (1994–2000)
Carol Flint (1995–1999)
Lydia Woodward (1994–2006)
Lance Gentile (1996–1998)
David Zabel (2001–2009)
Jack Orman (1997–2003)
Joe Sachs (2000–2009)
Lisa Zwerling (2005–2009)
Dee Johnson (2000–2005)

Directors / Executive Producers

Christopher Chulack (1994–2009)
Tommy Schlamme (1995–1997)
Jonathan Kaplan (1997–2009)
Mimi Leder (1994–2009)

Crew

Guy Norman Bee (Steadicam operator)
Rick Ladomade (special effects)
Lyn Paolo (costume designer)
Chris Haston (NBC photographer)

In Memoriam

Rod Holcomb
Paul Manning
Glenne Headly

Ernest Borgnine

Bob Newhart

Dearon "Deezer D" Thompson

Brian Lester

John Aylward

Red Buttons

Jon W. Fong

Rosemary Clooney

Vanessa Marquez

Frances Sternhagen

Beah Richards

Ray Liotta

Joey Marino

Jonathan Kaplan

Mike Salamunovich

Don Ohlmeyer

Robert Pietranton

Michael Crichton

1

Admissions

ER began its epic journey in Steven Spielberg's dead files. Michael Crichton had recently finished a 150-page script called *Emergency Department*, which he began writing in 1975, after he finished his third-year rotation at Harvard Medical School. His heart set on a big cinematic release, Crichton had sent the material off to the director of the recently acclaimed *E.T. the Extra-Terrestrial*. But Spielberg was far more interested in what else Crichton had in the works: a mysterious tale about dinosaurs and DNA. As Spielberg kept pumping Crichton for more details about what would eventually become *Jurassic Park*, the script based on Crichton's time working at Boston's Massachusetts General Hospital took a serious back seat. It was ultimately packed away in the dead files of the Amblin Entertainment offices—until

Tony Thomopoulos, Spielberg's then-head of TV, went digging in the archives in the early '90s for inspiration.

Tony Thomopoulos (Amblin Television President) It was in the dead files because nobody wanted to make it as a movie. Everybody had basically forgotten about it. When I read the script, I went to Steven and said, "I think this is going to make a great television series." I really saw it coming alive. "We should do this." Steven said, "Crichton is never going to agree to it, because he wanted it to be made as a movie." So I said, "Let me try. Let me go talk to Crichton." I set up lunch with him at the 16th Cafe in Santa Monica. It's no longer there. I spent two hours with him and convinced him that he would make more money in success from television than he would from a movie, and he would get much more recognition from it than he would from a movie. That argument persuaded him.

Meanwhile, a drama writer by the name of John Wells got a call from his reps at Creative Artists Agency saying that his experience on China Beach, *a 1988 drama for ABC about a Vietnam-era evacuation hospital, could make him the perfect candidate to launch* ER. *Eventually, Wells would assemble a group of writers who had either worked with him on* China Beach *(Lydia Woodward and Carol Flint, for example) or had a medical background (like Lance Gentile and Neal Baer). Christopher Chulack was later recruited to run the production. It took a bit of convincing, however, for everyone to realize that* ER *was something special. At that point in time, everyone's idea of a gritty hospital drama was* St. Elsewhere, *an NBC series from the '80s about a run-down teaching hospital in Boston. Starring Denzel Washington and*

Mark Harmon, the series from MTM Enterprises was considered groundbreaking for the way it told multiple stories about the lives of doctors and their patients in an inner-city hospital.

John Wells (Executive Producer) Steven Spielberg had said he wanted to direct it. Steven had worked in an emergency room as a kid in Phoenix or Tucson. As is his practice, he takes ownership of anything he might want to direct, which is how his name ends up on all this stuff over time.

Neal Baer (Executive Producer) I did *China Beach*, and then I went back to Harvard Medical School. In my fourth year, John sent me the *ER* script. He said, "What do you think?" And I said, "It's like my life, only it's outdated. We don't use glass IV bottles. We don't use chloramphenicol, the antibiotic, and we don't call all the nurses *Nurse*."

In fact, most of the nurses just . . . didn't have names at all.

John Levey (Warner Bros. TV Head of Casting) One of my first questions to John was, "Is the nurse on page 3 the same as the nurse on page 52?"

Lance Gentile (Producer) A lot of the medicine had to be tweaked. I was an ER doctor for decades and I really knew the world, and I thought I could contribute to it because I had the doctor's point of view that most people didn't. I also went to USC film school and had made a couple of movies.

Lydia Woodward (Executive Producer) I will admit that I read it and didn't get it. I mean, all that medicine on the page. I had no idea what the hell was going on. Who were these people? Oh my God, it was all coming at you. It was a very atypical medical show. At least on *St. Elsewhere,* which had a small ER component in the storytelling, someone would come into the ER, and then you would follow them up and stay with the patient in cardiology or whatever.

Though Spielberg launched his career at Universal, the studio didn't own the script for ER.

Tony Thomopoulos At that point in time, Amblin was not funded by Universal, and this script was not at Universal. The property was at Warner Bros. So we had to make the deal. There was a little bit of tension at that moment in time, but we were able to pull it off and we went into the television business with Warner Bros. rather than Universal.

Leslie Moonves (Warner Bros. TV President) It needed some factual changes. It had been written in the early '70s about a hospital in Boston. *St. Elsewhere* had taken place in Boston. They decided to change it to Chicago. In addition, there was some reference to a Boston Celtics basketball player by the name of Tommy Heinsohn. He was a famous basketball player and coach, but he played for the Celtics in Boston, so they had to change that. But the script wasn't by any means a mess.

John Wells It was a big, old, mimeographed script. Michael was a remarkably talented researcher. He was interested in a million things, but character development wasn't really his strong point. Michael and I got together for lunch, and we had a very frank conversation about what I thought were the shortcomings of the piece, and he was very receptive. We hit it off.

Christopher Chulack (Executive Producer) John is a good writer. I remember talking to his mom, Marge, and she would say she'd hear John come home from school and he'd be downstairs, and [she would] hear the typewriter going at midnight. He was just practicing writing scripts, and his mom was a teacher. I think she gave him a lot of discipline.

David Nevins (NBC Vice President of Prime-Time Series) Crichton decided to rewrite the script on two conditions. No network notes and Crichton would take one pass to update the medicine. He ended up doing a dozen passes of the script with John Wells. He just kept whittling it down.

Lance Gentile Michael Crichton was funny. He was very dry. First off, he's gigantic, right? He's like seven feet tall. I sat down next to him during a table read once. I said to him, "I like to think of myself as a poor man's Michael Crichton." He just looked at me all Michael Crichton-esque and I thought, maybe I shouldn't have made that joke.

"It was probably season I. Steven Spielberg had it in his mind that when he was a kid, he had a sick cat in Tucson, and he didn't know where they were in Arizona. He took the cat to the emergency room. So cut to our version, which was Noah Wyle giving mouth-to-mouth resuscitation to a German shepherd, and it was just like God bless Steven Spielberg. Just because it happened to somebody doesn't necessarily make it right for the show."

—ANTHONY EDWARDS

Warren Littlefield (NBC Entertainment President) Biggest author. Biggest director. They wanted a commitment [from the network for a half season, or thirteen episodes].

Leslie Moonves We first went to NBC because CBS had [the medical drama] *Chicago Hope* from David Kelley. [CBS Entertainment president] Jeff Sagansky called and was gracious and told me how good it was, but he was committed to Kelley. I don't think ABC responded. At a certain point, NBC said they weren't sure about thirteen episodes, but they'll give us a two-hour pilot. So, we went back and did the two-hour pilot with NBC.

One of the things that made ER *so appealing to NBC was that it soon had a big hole to fill at 10:00* PM *on Thursdays.*

Preston Beckman (NBC Head of Scheduling) *L.A. Law* was starting to fade out. We considered doing what NBC did in 2009—offer Jay Leno a 10:00 PM show five nights a week, because we just didn't feel like we had the goods.

Warren Littlefield As much as I respected a project that I developed with the feature film talent Barry Levinson, *Homicide: Life on the Street*, in the few times we tried it Thursdays at 10:00, it certainly wasn't a blockbuster. When I asked Don [Ohlmeyer] if he wanted a policewoman centerfold or *ER*, I got a reluctant okay to pursue the latter.

Lori Openden (NBC Casting) We were very excited because the people behind it were impressive. You don't do something with Steven Spielberg for television very often.

Christopher Chulack I remember John Wells calling me when I was on vacation in Hawaii. He says, "Hey, Chris, NBC picked up the *ER* show, and we're going to need a producer. NBC doesn't really like it, but it'll be fun. It'll be nine episodes and out." I was considered a line producer. I ran the production and hired a lot of crew and actually hired the directors. So, I came in and

I started from episode 1 and produced the show for fifteen seasons. Nine episodes turned out to be 331 episodes.

After receiving a promise by Littlefield that he would have the final word on casting and that the drama would likely end up on Thursdays at 10:00, Wells set out to find Mark Greene, Doug Ross, Carol Hathaway, John Carter, Peter Benton, Susan Lewis, and the rest of County General's emergency room staff.

John Wells I knew Rod Holcomb [the director] from *China Beach*, and he came on, and we started casting like crazy.

Leslie Moonves I sent George Clooney two scripts. I sent him *ER*, which had eight leads, and he would be one of eight. And then I sent him this other crime drama, which took place in San Francisco, and it was sort of a buddy crime thing with only two leads. His part would have been much bigger, but it was not nearly the quality of *ER*. To George's credit, he read the *ER* script, and he said, "This thing is great. I want to be in this." So we sent George to meet with John Wells. The other pilot, ironically, starred David James Elliott. Do you remember him from *JAG*? It wasn't very good, and it didn't go anywhere. We shot a pilot with him and some other guy, and it sort of fell apart. The rest is history.

Preston Beckman I did chuckle at George Clooney being in it, just because he seemed to be in everything. Every pilot season, he would show up in something. I wasn't chuckling dismissively. It was like, "Oh, there's George Clooney."

George Clooney (Doug Ross) It's not like people considered me this wonderful television actor. I have always done fine. But this is the show that got me out of that.

John Levey George was the actor that every show was looking for: a thirty-five-year-old, great-looking man with a sense of humor and a great, flirtatious sexuality. He says that I brought the script to him in a brown paper bag, like it was a dirty magazine, and that he read it. And then subsequently, we had a meeting in the head of casting's office. That meeting was attended by John Wells and Rod Holcomb and me. George was his incredibly charming, seductive, wonderful, warm, and lovely self. It happened to be shortly after the Northridge earthquake. He told a story about how in the middle of the night when the earthquake happened, he ran out into the backyard with his roommate and pet potbellied pig. They were buck naked from being woken up in their sleep. We all got quite a chuckle out of that story.

Anthony Edwards (Mark Greene) George was obviously incredibly charming and a perfect pediatrician, because who wouldn't fall in love with him while he was saving their child?

John Wells Anthony Edwards never considered doing television.

John Levey John Wells stopped by my office early in the process. Back in those days, we weren't digital. We had hard copies of photographs and résumés, and I was opening envelopes and putting pictures and résumés in piles on a file cabinet in my office. There were open shelves with labels saying which character it was. When John came in to say hello, he had just come from a budget or a production meeting upstairs. And it just so happened that Anthony Edwards's picture was on the top of the Dr. Mark Greene pile. I'm not a big believer in divine intervention, but maybe that's what happened. John took one look at him, and he said, "That's a good idea." He had been in *Top Gun* recently, but he had also changed so significantly. He had lost a lot of hair, and he was no longer quite the sexy leading man that he had been in *Top Gun*. But he later became, again, the heart and soul of the heroic brigade of doctors.

Lori Openden No one was against Anthony. We all knew he was Dr. Greene. That's not usually the way. Usually, they bring us three choices to the network, and we all discuss it and make a choice. But Anthony Edwards was alone.

Anthony Edwards I was not getting great roles in movies. But I was supposed to be directing this children's movie, so I told John Wells I probably can't do it. Then I went home, and my wife and my manager slapped me around and said, "This is Crichton and Spielberg. This is a big deal."

John Wells Noah Wyle was, like, thirteen years old and waiting tables. We brought him in because you were always supposed to bring two choices to the network, and we wanted the other guy. But he kept getting better and better, and then he got the part.

John Levey He came in, and it just so happened that Noah read on the one day that Michael Crichton was in the auditions with me, John, and Rod. I went out into the hallway as I always did to greet the actor. And he said to me, "Hey, John, I'm going to do the things you asked me to do, but I want to do something else." And I was like, "Oh God, this is a terrible idea." I said, "Well, what is it?" And he said, "There's that scene where Dr. Carter is drawing blood for the first time, and he keeps messing up and he keeps failing to get the needle in correctly." And I said, "Okay," reluctantly. I sat in the chair that was meant for him, and he wrapped a bandanna or maybe a rubber band around my bicep. He took out a retractable pencil, and he started to pantomime drawing blood on me. And he kept failing and trying again to get a new angle. And Mr. Crichton literally fell off the couch laughing. I think Noah got the job right then and there.

Noah Wyle (John Carter) I thought [John Carter was] the best part, because everybody else has to be a really good doctor and this guy is dropping trays of piss all over himself. But eventually, this guy could be the greatest doctor in the hospital. What a journey that would be.

John Levey John and I were flying to New York to cast something else. I don't remember what it was, but it was just as the process of *ER* was beginning. And funny enough, Sherry Stringfield was also in first class on this plane from Los Angeles to New York, and she had been on *NYPD Blue* at the time, where she was famously unhappy and had been asking to be released. John put me up to go over to her. I said, "Hey, Sherry. I'm John Levey, and John Wells is sitting over there, and we're doing the *ER* pilot, and we hear you might be available soon." She bashfully acknowledged that. Her agent at the time, who's now sadly gone, was a guy named Joe Rice. I spoke to him the next day, and she was indeed intrigued. We sent her the script, and she came in to read. She cut her own space in a beautiful way. She was such a lovely, wholesome kind of actress.

John Wells I had to call Steven Bochco and ask him if he was going to let her out of her contract or not. There was this long pause, and then he said, "I hope you know what you're getting into."

Sherry Stringfield (Susan Lewis) I read it and I went, "That's not a normal medical show. I haven't seen anything like that." And I was really intrigued by the character. I was like, "These are people I know." They were real people. It had that raw feeling.

John Levey She came in with that great, earthy Texas regular girl, kind of beautiful tomboy.

Sherry Stringfield I remember it like yesterday, being in the room, and right as I'm about to go on and I'm like, "Oh God, I am sweating. I'm breaking out in a total sweat." And I walk in the room, and it's, like, Michael Crichton center stage. I had read all of his books. This guy's the coolest dude ever. It was like twenty people, and I was like, "Oh, whatever." And then two hours later they were like, "Yeah, you got it."

Julianna Margulies (Carol Hathaway) If I was going to stay in LA, I needed a job. My agents told me I had to find something to showcase my talent. Casting directors didn't know me in LA the way they did in New York [where I did theater]. My financial status was not looking hopeful. A few days after my decision to go home, my agent called. They wanted me to audition for a new TV pilot written by Michael Crichton and produced by Steven Spielberg. The role wasn't big. It was a recurring part that had potential to grow if the chemistry was right with one of the leading men, George Clooney.

John Levey I was casting another show before the pilot of *ER*. It was a Western called *The Adventures of Brisco County, Jr.* Bruce Campbell was the star. I kept bringing Julianna Margulies into that, but somehow, they just didn't see her as part of a Western, but I loved her. I thought of her for *ER*, and I'm sure I brought in six or seven women to read for that part. And I remember that Rod Holcomb loved her immediately.

John Wells Julianna Margulies was just a day player. She agreed to do a small part because she was leaving town. She left town thinking she died in the pilot.

Julianna Margulies I wasn't that excited. My character died. I would be jobless at the end of the pilot. What are they paying anyway? I asked. Twenty thousand dollars. I dropped the phone.

I had never made that much money in my life. I couldn't believe it. I was about to make as much money in three weeks as my mother made in a year of teaching.

John Wells We didn't cast Eriq La Salle until three or four days ahead of the pilot.

John Levey At that time, Michael Beach was going to play Dr. Benton. And famously, Don Ohlmeyer said to us, "You have four-fifths of the best cast on television, and you can have Michael Beach if you want to, but I'm not sure." Moonves and Wells and I were walking down the hall of NBC, and they said, "Don't pick up his option. Don't pick up his option. Let's keep looking." Eriq was cast on day three of the shoot. They were already shooting, and they kept changing the production schedule because we didn't have Dr. Benton yet. And then Eriq came in, and I remember he was wearing scrubs. I've forgotten what color they were, and he was lying in the hallway stretching like he was an NBA basketball player.

Eriq La Salle (Peter Benton) In my mind, I was stretching like Baryshnikov.

Lori Openden Eriq La Salle was my special contribution, because we had a lot of trouble casting that part. The man had no sense of humor. He just has that face. There was not the easy charm that George Clooney or Noah Wyle had. Eriq did not. That was good for Dr. Benton.

John Levey I remember very distinctly that Eriq was a wow in the room at NBC and was approved. He was standing with the other actors who had tested in the parking lot of NBC when John and I came out. I kind of looked at him from twenty-five yards away and gave him kind of a thumbs-up. He thought I was just being polite. Later, Michael Beach had a very important role, playing Jeanie Boulet's husband. He infected her with HIV.

Eriq La Salle I knew I had a good audition. It took me a while to realize what his thumbs-up actually meant.

John Levey I talk about the balance of casting a pilot, and I liken it to making a mobile. You have George Clooney on one end as the sexy guy who is also heroic with children, and then you have Anthony Edwards at the other end of the spectrum, and then you have the innocence of Noah Wyle and the arrogance and great strength and intelligence of Eriq La Salle. Those are four distinct areas of character that are covered. They don't bleed into each other. They can create conflict, and they can create resolved conflict. We were very fortunate to have those four guys each inhabiting different spaces and creating different colors.

Warner Bros. shot the pilot in an abandoned hospital in East Los Angeles. The location was so appealing that Chicago Hope *decided to make its pilot there, too.*

Christopher Chulack John and Rod asked for a recommendation. I said Linda Vista Hospital in East LA. I was producing a show called *Home Front*. It was a period piece, and we shot at that hospital.

Ellen Crawford (Lydia Wright) I think it was the first hospital to have an AIDS clinic, but we were shooting in the basement and *Chicago Hope* was shooting on another floor. They were a little more traditional, while *ER* was written in a very unusual way. We didn't really see each other. Nobody wanted to build a set for either of our shows because we weren't tried shows. But I do remember at one point the makeup artist, who I don't think went on to do the series, saying, "Oh, *Chicago Hope* is a show to be on. It's got all the stars and Mandy Patinkin. That's probably the show that's really going to go."

Yvette Freeman (Haleh Adams) [The hospital] looked like it had ghosts. It also had old, smelly rooms downstairs. You weren't supposed to walk around, but I did.

Abraham Benrubi (Jerry Markovic) The abandoned hospital is still there, and they've turned it into an old folks' home, I believe, or a retirement home, I should say. Super creepy place. It was the kind of place where you can picture, like, *Jacob's Ladder* having been filmed where there's the squeaky wheel on the gurney.

Anthony Edwards I didn't understand the script when I first read it, but I knew it was real. We weren't going to explain medicine to people. We were just going to do it. In an emergency room, it's an emergency for everybody, whether you have a splinter in your finger or a heart attack. I have no idea how we made that pilot. I never knew what door I was going in or out. Our job was to make it look easy. If it looked hard, you were doing it wrong.

George Clooney It started with Tony, who was number one on that call sheet. He walked on the set and said, "Let's enjoy ourselves and let's have fun." Every single actor that came on was treated with respect.

The pilot opened with Lydia waking up Mark Greene from a deep sleep because Doug Ross had shown up drunk to the ER.

Ellen Crawford I remember when we were setting up the very first shot for the pilot, when you see my shadow against the wall [as I wake up Dr. Greene]. At one point, Rod Holcomb, who was the sweetest guy in the world, went, "Oh my God, her nose is enormous." And I went, "I'm sorry, but I didn't have time for surgery before we started shooting." He goes, "It's not you. It's the shadow. We must adjust the shadow."

George Clooney I fashioned the drunk stuff after my Uncle George. Al Pacino did a perfect impersonation of my Uncle George in *Scent of a Woman*, so I [had] to do a mellower version because otherwise everyone will say, "You're doin' Pacino."

Julianna Margulies There wasn't a lot written about my character. It's an actor's job to find her own backstory. She came into the pilot basically OD'd from pills. The research I did was on nurses.

Abraham Benrubi There wasn't much to my role in the pilot, to be honest. Jerry's in the very beginning and at the very end when the shift changes. So, there are a couple of moments, like a funny moment with a paramedic that everybody always teases me about where I ask him if he wants a cookie or a medal or something. It's just one of those weird TV details that people remember.

Ellen Crawford One of the most indelible performances I remember from the pilot was when a guy had lost his father and he's talking to Dr. Greene and he's angry. He's going to beat him up. Then he just collapses in his arms. It was so authentic and such a moving moment. That was a guest actor who had one brief scene. To me, that was what made *ER* so special, those nuggets. We went on like that.

Christine Harnos (Jennifer Greene) I happened kind of late in the pilot. It was one of those kooky stories where an assistant knew a friend of mine, blah blah, and then I went to see John Levey. I didn't meet Anthony Edwards until I was cast. I was working within a week of being cast. Initially, the arc of my character [as Greene's wife] was only for five episodes. In fact, I was on the show on and off for seven years. I knew that the marriage was in trouble. I was told it would probably end a lot sooner than it did. I believe the relationship was there to illustrate how tough it is, having a relationship with an ER doctor. And then when you are married to another professional, what happens? They probably got in the room to write and realized, "Oh, we can't just tie this up with a bow in five episodes. It's going to take a little longer to really get invested and be rooting for these people."

Noah Wyle Oddly enough, I was administering [an IV] to a character actor named Troy Evans, who appears in our pilot and then came back years later, to be Frank the desk clerk. We never made mention of the fact that he'd been my first patient, and yet it was that same character. That was my audition scene, that IV scene.

Abraham Benrubi Everybody was just normal humans. It wasn't a starstruck kind of thing until much later. Then we had fancy guest stars like Angela Bassett and those kinds of people.

Julianna Margulies We weren't known actors but for Anthony Edwards, and he was mostly known for *Top Gun*.

Noah Wyle This gesture [Wyle holds up two fingers to his chest] became a touchstone gesture because of Eriq's first day on the show. He was the last character cast. It was a sort of a midnight session on a Friday night where they finally pulled the trigger on his offer and he started work on Monday. And on the very first day of work, he had to deliver what we used to call a bullet, which is a huge, long monologue of medicalese as he gives my character a tour through the hospital. He was nervous, and it was his first day. He was prepared. But things happened, and one take led to the next take, led to the next take. Finally, we got up to about nineteen or twenty takes, and I saw the director and cameramen start getting really nervous, because we were running out of film. We were shooting at Linda Vista Hospital, and we probably wouldn't be able to get another shipment on that day. So we ran the last magazine of the film on basically the last take that we could shoot that day. He finally got the monologue down and it was the twenty-second take. And so the rest of us, being fairly competitive but good-spirited, we used to tease him about it taking twenty-two takes. And then the very next week, I got given a very long monologue, and I was so intent not to screw it up that I've memorized it so thoroughly that I have total recall of it and could perform it [now].

John Wells We turned the pilot around in a hurry because we got started late. We showed it to Les Moonves. He said, "You know, I thought I'd hate this thing, but I actually really like it."

The real drama came when the pilot was screened for executives for the first time.

Warren Littlefield Don Ohlmeyer had strenuous objections to the style and the content of the show. He thought there was too much blood and far too much technical dialogue. My leading memory of the screening at our NBC offices in Burbank is of Don Ohlmeyer storming out of the screening room halfway through the show. He came back in at the end but was still pissed off. Don asked in a loud and angry voice, "Why do we want to be in business with people who don't listen to us?" The room was very quiet until Lori Openden spoke up and said, "I loved it."

Lori Openden It was a conference room with a big television. Don Ohlmeyer and Warren Littlefield were there. It was very intimidating. Don was six feet, four inches and 280 pounds or something. He's gone now and I don't want to say a lot of bad things, but he was not easy to work for. He spoke first and didn't like it. After a boss like him says something like that, it's a little scary to go against it. I don't know where I had the guts, but I did, because I loved it so much. I said, "I can't believe I sat in the same room with you guys. I loved every minute of it." And then people started to talk. Some of the others said, "It's too many storylines. Maybe we can cut that back a little."

Preston Beckman Don was a big believer in big-tent television, and I think he saw a lot of things about the pilot that he probably felt were going to be confusing to the viewer, such as the camerawork, the blood, the dialogue. He used to use the phrase "degrees of difficulty" all the time. He was saying you are making it hard for people to enjoy the show. Not dumbing it down, but you're just making it spinach. There are a lot of executives who like to make spinach, where you're basically making it more difficult than you need to for someone to enter a show. If anything, he was probably advocating for the viewer against the development executives who sometimes like to be cute.

John Wells We were trying to show people that you don't have to understand what they're talking about to *know* what they're talking about. That was a very difficult concept to get across. We kept saying, "Look, there's an emotional undercurrent to all these scenes that the audience is going to understand. They don't really have to understand what a thrombosis is to understand what's happening in the scene."

Leslie Moonves There was a hamburger joint near Warner Bros. It's where everybody at Warner Bros. and NBC would go to lunch. I was having lunch there, and it was the day NBC was screening the pilot. Lori Openden walked in. I'm expecting her to come over and say, "Oh my God, it's the greatest thing since sliced bread." All she said was, "They didn't like it." I said, "Who's *they*?" She wouldn't say. She realized she had spoken too soon, and I was crazed. I didn't want to shoot the messenger. We were pretty startled.

Years after the fact, Ohlmeyer would later tell Entertainment Weekly *that "I had some reservations about whether the audience was ready for something that powerful. Sometimes you can have a show that is past your audience." He also remembered how there was "just an awful lot of medical mumbo jumbo." Ohlmeyer died in 2017.*

Leslie Moonves Don, who was a very dear friend of mine, rest in peace, wasn't afraid of anything. He'd put on anything. He was a cowboy. It just didn't strike him. He and I never had a direct conversation about it.

John Wells Michael Crichton's idea, which is what the show became, was that when you're in the ER, as a physician, you are overtaxed. No stories have real strong, obvious conclusions. What you think the outlook is going to be, isn't. And most importantly, people die. That was the real problem with NBC, is that they literally gave me a whole thing of research that said nobody wants to see anybody dead in a hospital. Michael's point and mine was that people actually know that people die in hospitals, and you're going to be more comforted if you're in a world that's real.

Lydia Woodward I remember John saying to me somewhere later in the season, when we were getting these kinds of rude comments from the network, and he was saying, "Oh, you think they're being rude now? You should have seen what they did to Michael Crichton." And this was to Michael Crichton, who was big back then. They were terrified. They didn't understand the show.

Preston Beckman I think what really turned it around was the testing. We had cable systems throughout the country, and we would put any pilot on a channel on the cable system, and we would recruit people to view it. Then we would say, "We are going to call you and ask you a series of questions." *ER* was an extremely high-testing pilot. I also remember very vividly how the cable operators told us how people would stumble upon it. A lot of the operators said that people were calling, asking when it was going to be repeated. They said they'd never had that happen before.

Noah Wyle They screened it, and Don Ohlmeyer didn't like it and said, "I'm going to bury it." The projectionist of the theater that did the screening said, "You should test this with an audience." So they pulled the *Tonight Show* audience out and screened it for them, and it tested higher than any NBC pilot that year. Ohlmeyer said, "I don't believe it. I want to test it again." So they pulled a second *Tonight Show* audience out, and it went even higher. And that's pretty much how we got on the air. Because of those two random tests.

Kevin Reilly (NBC Vice President of Drama Development) One thing that came out of the research was how sorry everybody was to see Julianna go.

John Wells There was this wonderful chemistry between George and Julianna. She was very talented, and so the scenes that were meant to be kind of throwaway scenes, you couldn't kind of take your eyes off of her.

Julianna Margulies After the *ER* pilot filmed, I said goodbye to the cast, wishing them luck with the show, packed my bags, and flew back to New York. After one week home, I was offered a job as a series regular for a show I had guest starred on the year before called *Homicide: Life on the Street*. Tom Fontana called to say that they wanted me to join the cast. I would have to move to Baltimore if I took the job, but Tom Fontana and Barry Levinson were at the helm of this heralded show filled with great actors, and it would be a full-time job! I decided to go for a run in the park to clear my head before calling back. When I got back to my apartment, there was a message on my answering machine. It was George Clooney: "I heard through the grapevine that your character tested really well. I can't say for sure, but if you are thinking about taking another job you might want to hold off. I think they are going to offer you something on *ER*."

Neal Baer If you watch the pilot, Sherry is looped to say that Carol is not dead. We just felt like we couldn't tell the story as richly as we wanted to without another woman. We talked about it a lot in the writers' room, because there was George and Eriq and Tony and Noah and Sherry. There were four men and one lead woman, and nurses whose names were "Nurse" in the pilot. So, we thought it would be interesting to have Carol attempt suicide, not see her for several episodes, and then bring her back. It didn't make Michael Crichton happy.

Julianna Margulies When I get brought in on the gurney, [Susan Lewis] for some reason [put] her clipboard to her mouth when she said, "She's brain-dead." So you don't see [her saying it]. They just looped different lines saying, "She's gonna be okay," or whatever, and they brought me back to life.

Ellen Crawford When the Emergency Nurses Association saw the pilot, they were really concerned that the takeaway would be that nurses are taking drugs.

Lydia Woodward We spent more time discussing the fact that if you watch the pilot and knew anything about medicine, she was very clearly dead at the end. So, there was a little bit more conversation about the fact that we resurrected her from the dead than the fact that we were saying, "Oh, mental health, mental health."

Noah Wyle As [Carol] lay on her deathbed, the looks and energy that everybody else conveyed about their feelings towards her was so powerful, that when they tested the pilot, her character tested way through the roof, way higher than it [probably should have] based on the scenes that she had to play. I think Rod Holcomb is instrumentally responsible for her character lasting the run of the show like it did.

John Wells To Don Ohlmeyer's credit, as soon as the testing showed something else, he gave us the best time slot in television. He literally said to me at one point, "What the hell do I know?"

The two-hour pilot premiered on September 19, 1994. The second episode that aired on September 22, 1994, marked the drama's time slot debut on Thursdays at 10:00.

Preston Beckman The reason we premiered *ER* on a Monday was because it was premiere week and we needed *Seinfeld* to be on the schedule. We wanted our Thursday night to be intact because we made a lot of money during premiere week with our shows. So, we had to figure out what to do with the two-hour pilot. I said, "Hey, our Monday movie is pretty much our women's movie, and if this is going to work, women are going to drive the ratings for the show. So as far as the viewer is concerned, this is a Monday movie." We can preview it on Monday and run the second episode that Thursday. We felt good that we were going to get an audience for the show. We had no idea how big it was going to be, but we didn't think it was going to be rejected based on the evidence we had.

Leslie Moonves I remember CBS ran the two-hour pilot of *Chicago Hope* the Sunday before NBC ran *ER*. I remember I was in a hotel room in New York scared to death. It was like, "We've put in all this work. We've spent all this money. What if *Chicago Hope* beats us up badly?" The irony was that a couple years later, I went to CBS and *Chicago Hope* became *my* medical show.

Kevin Reilly The conventional wisdom was that *ER* was interesting, but *Chicago Hope* was the more commercial show.

Preston Beckman CBS announced *Chicago Hope* as their Thursday at 10:00 show before we announced *ER*.

Leslie Moonves CBS played dirty with the advertising campaign over the summer. They said, "We've got David Kelley, and NBC has a bunch of people who haven't done that much television."

Jeff Sagansky (CBS Entertainment President) We had another David Kelley show called *Picket Fences*, which had won the

Emmy for best drama two years in a row. Plus, we had an incredible cast. *ER* had an incredible cast, too, but nobody knew it then.

"We would go to do exterior work in Chicago. I remember thinking, *Oh my God, [our] lives have changed.* We decided to go and have dinner. When I walked with Tony and George and Noah and Eriq . . . it was [like] walking with The Beatles. I think women were throwing their panties at them. I remember just sort of standing back because the crowds came in and they were screaming for the guys. I was like, oh my God, this is crazy. No one threw their panties at me. But they were like rock stars, these guys."

—JULIANNA MARGULIES

Peter Roth I was at Twentieth Century Fox at the time, and we were bursting with pride because we had *Chicago Hope*. I was staying at the Hotel St. Moritz in New York for the upfronts in 1994, and I got a call from Warren Littlefield saying, "Would you mind if I got a look at *Chicago Hope*? We've got this show called *ER*. I'll trade shows with you." So, I agreed, and I remember I was watching an NBA game in my room. The NBA was on NBC then, and I started seeing these promos, "For twenty years the home of the greatest drama on television is NBC Thursday night at 10:00. First *Hill Street Blues*, then *L.A. Law*, and now the next great drama series, *ER*." Once I saw those clips, I thought, *We're cooked*.

Warren Littlefield It didn't take that long for CBS to move *Hope*.

Jeff Sagansky *Chicago Hope* was a successful show, but it was in the shadow of a *super* show. So it never got its due.

Preston Beckman I had a feeling CBS would move *Hope* to Monday night at 10:00 the day after New Year's. So, we announced we'd repeat the *ER* pilot on that day. In early December, Don Ohlmeyer got a call from *Chicago Hope* star Mandy Patinkin, who wanted to know what NBC had against his show. Don said to him, in so many words, "You're talking to the wrong person. You should talk to your bosses over at CBS. Because we had announced it."

Tommy Schlamme (Director) I hadn't heard that story. But you could tell me any story that starts with, "I heard that Mandy did this," and I'll believe that story. I've known Mandy even before [he starred on] *Chicago Hope*. We both have places in upstate New York, and Mandy and [his wife] Kathryn are not very far from us. There's a great Christopher Guest joke. Do you remember the play *Love Letters*? It was two people reading. Christopher once said, "Mandy's taking *Love Letters* on the road as a one-man show."

Ohlmeyer would later tell Entertainment Weekly *that "I always had a great deal of respect for Mandy for doing that. But my job was to kick the shit out of CBS." NBC ended up doing that to CBS and ABC, too: The first, twenty-five-episode season of* ER *averaged 19.08 million viewers. It became the second most-watched show on prime time behind* Seinfeld.

Julianna Margulies Who knows why some shows are hits and others fail even when they are brilliant? Sometimes it's how the stars align. I had no idea what ratings meant at the time.

John Wells [The actors] made it someplace you want to show up every week. You [wanted] to spend time with these people.

Anthony Edwards We were so lost at the time. Everything was so foreign—all the medicine was hard to learn. I had no idea what the layout was. We were lost, but we knew that we were trying to make it real. It wasn't until we saw it cut together that we realized it was something superspecial.

Rick Rossovich (John "Tag" Taglieri) At this point, no one knew it would explode. No one knew the show in the soundstage next door, which was *Friends*, would be the monster it became. No one knew anything.

John Wells We were trying to say that there was an artifice in a lot of what was on the air and that the audience knew there was an artifice to it. And that we were going to do something that looked different from that and was different from that.

Preston Beckman I remember the summer press tour before it came on, and Warren and I went to the *ER* presentation. That's when press tours were big deals. We were sitting in the front row and listening to the panel. I remember being so fucking impressed by John Wells, what he was saying, and what his vision was for the show. I remember I turned to Warren and said, "I have never had a showrunner impress me like that." I felt we were in such good hands with him, because he had a vision and he could articulate it, and it wasn't bullshit.

Noah Wyle Steven's camp was really not sure about whether they wanted to embrace it. Up until that point, to be fair, he hadn't had the most success in television. Most recently, at that time, he had *SeaQuest* and *Earth 2*. There were a lot of big swings that almost happened but didn't. So, we sort of cemented his reputation at Amblin Television for him.

George Clooney I remember when we were at the upfronts. People who don't know what the upfronts are, it's when they sort of present the new series for the year, and we hadn't seen anything of our show yet. We were standing backstage. Julianna wasn't allowed to be there, because she was supposed to be dead, and we were standing backstage and they showed it and the place went apeshit, all the affiliates. We were a bunch of actors who struggled, quite honestly; we were all sort of fighting for careers, and suddenly, it was like, oh, we're going to be working for a while.

2

Medical Records

Subject: ANTHONY EDWARDS

Presents as: MARK GREENE

Character Family History: Greene was briefly married to Jennifer, and together, they had a daughter, Rachel. Greene married Elizabeth in season 7, and together, they had a daughter, Ella.

Other Hospitalizations: Edwards played the son of a doctor in the short-lived ABC comedy in 1982 called *It Takes Two*.

Diagnosis: An experienced Hollywood veteran. Of all the actors, Edwards began *ER* with the flashiest résumé, having appeared in *Revenge of the Nerds* and *Top Gun*. "I couldn't imagine anyone else playing Dr. Greene," Edwards said. "I didn't know who else was up for the role. I didn't ask. I'd been in and out of NBC a lot for TV and network movies. I'd been acting since I was sixteen, so I didn't have anxiety. I just knew it was right."

What Got His Heart Pumping: "Fear really drove a lot of it," Edwards said about those early years. "I remember in the pilot going, I had no idea where that door went, what the thing was. The first day . . . they're giving us a pig's foot and here's a laryngoscope and all this stuff that ultimately became second nature."

Advance Directive: Edwards was fully supportive of his character dying of a brain tumor in 2002. Eight seasons was more than enough. "The number of angry, older women in my neighborhood who told me, 'How dare you leave the show!'" Edwards recalled. "'But I wanted to be with my kids.' 'We don't care about your kids. We want our Thursday night at ten o'clock, and we want you in it.'"

Subject: GEORGE CLOONEY

Presents as: DOUG ROSS

Character Family History: Ross was a playboy with several gal pals, but his heart always belonged to Carol, who is the mother of his twins.

Other Hospitalizations: Clooney played a character named Ace in a short-lived comedy for CBS in 1984 called *E/R*. The Elliott Gould starrer took place in Chicago and even featured actors who would go on to guest star on *ER*, including Mary McDonnell (who played Carter's ice queen mother, Eleanor) and the late Conchata Ferrell (who once guest starred as a mom who goes on a *Jerry Springer*–like show and reveals that her daughter is dating her half brother).

Diagnosis: A Tinseltown old soul. "The one time that George really cracked me up is when we were in Chicago and Red Buttons was with us," remembers Lydia Woodward. "Red

Buttons is like old Hollywood. He was talking about when he was shooting *Sayonara* with Marlon Brando, while George and I and a couple of other people were sitting around at the Ritz and having drinks. George was telling stories, too. I just remember looking at Red and George and listening to them go back and forth with these stories. At some point, I couldn't decide who was older, George or Red Buttons, because George had equally funny stories."

What Got His Heart Pumping: Advocating for the extras. "In the early days, George was someone who was famous for being really kind to background actors," recalled Yvonne Zima. "The background actors always had a very chintzy craft services table. Clooney went to a cabinet that was locked up with food—I think he got a crowbar—and he opened it up and started throwing chips, snacks, and fruit to the background actors. He was always an advocate for background actors on sets. If they weren't warmly dressed, he'd be trying to get them blankets and coats."

Advance Directive: Clooney let it be known early on that he didn't want to renew his contract, so he left in season 5—but reprised his character for the season 6 departure of Julianna Margulies and for an episode in the final season.

Subject: ERIQ LA SALLE

Presents as: PETER BENTON

Character Family History: Benton fathered a deaf son named Reese but later discovered he wasn't the biological father. It's implied in the series finale that he married girlfriend Cleo Finch.

Other Hospitalizations: He played a doctor in the 1992

series *The Human Factor* and played a terrifying character named Dr. Peoples in the 2005 thriller *Inside Out.*

Diagnosis: A thoughtful and unappreciated trailblazer. "When you talk about representation on television, the relationship I'm most proud of on the show is the one that [La Salle] and I had, because he played an unapologetically talented Black man who didn't cater to anybody's opinion or didn't care to be liked," said Noah Wyle. "It was an unpopular character to play and an unpopular stance to take. I didn't understand it at the time. I don't think a lot of us understood what he was doing at the time, but in retrospect, he was standing for something that was extremely significant. He was on the vanguard of something way ahead of his time."

What Got His Heart Pumping: Early in the show's run, *TV Guide* refused to feature La Salle on the cover—despite having given the real estate to the other leads. "A lot of us had been on the cover of *TV Guide*, and they promised Eriq a cover but kept pulling the cover back for some reason. Then they decided that they were going to drop it altogether," remembered Noah Wyle. "Eriq wanted to complain publicly, because he felt that he was getting short shrift. George came to him and said, 'You can't fight this fight.' He said, 'Well, why not?' And he said, 'Because it just won't look right if you are crying for something that you're not getting. It looks like an actor whining because he doesn't get his due. We'll fight the fight for you. It looks better if we spearhead it.' So George created this campaign and he wrote a hell of a letter to the editors of *TV Guide*, and he went back into the archives and found that they had put more cartoon characters on their covers than African Americans, and that the only time they ever put African Americans on the cover was for February, the shortest month and Black History month. Eriq got his cover."

Advance Directive: La Salle jogged off into the sunset in season 8 but returned for Greene's funeral and a couple of episodes in the final season.

Subject: JULIANNA MARGULIES

Presents as: CAROL HATHAWAY

Character Family History: She was briefly engaged to Dr. John Taglieri but ultimately paired up—and had girl twins with—Dr. Doug Ross.

Other Hospitalizations: She played pathologist Dr. Nancy Jaax in the 2019 limited series *The Hot Zone*.

What Got Her Heart Pumping: Going to work at the Warner Bros. lot. "On any given day, you would see famous actors driving in their golf carts, eating at the commissary, or walking to their bungalows where their offices were. Clint Eastwood and Kevin Costner had offices right near Stage 11, where we filmed *ER*; the cast of *Friends* was right next door to us; *Lois & Clark* filmed two stages down. Our first Christmas on the show, George Clooney gave the whole cast bicycles with our names engraved on them. It was so fun riding around the lot, swerving around these huge airplane-hangar-like buildings. I couldn't believe I belonged here."

Allergies: The way she was treated when she walked away from *ER* in 2000. "I received a lot of flak when my six-year contract was over, and I chose not to stay on the show . . .

the first time I spoke about it publicly was during the commencement speech I gave at Sarah Lawrence College in 2010. The reason I brought this up in my speech was that I wanted to impress upon the students that life decisions should be made for only yourself. I wanted them to understand how important it is to make choices based on your own needs and beliefs, not someone else's."

Advance Directive: Her character fled Chicago to reunite with her soulmate, Doug, in season 6. She reprised her character in the final season for one episode.

"There was this young man who came up to me in a drugstore once, and this was about 1997. I was looking at a wall of toothpaste. Literally, three hundred fifty choices of the same thing. I'm standing there trying to decide what to buy, and this young man comes up to me, in his late twenties, and he said, 'Excuse me, I don't mean to bother you.' I turned to him and said, 'Hello.' And he said, 'I just wanted to let you know that I'm HIV positive and I saw the show last night. I'm going to start getting treatment today because of what I saw on the show.' I don't know his name, but I remember his face. I've been thinking about this a lot lately, and one wonders sometimes what the purpose is. Why are we here, really? What are we here to do, and what are we going to leave behind? And so [when] I remember this young man, maybe I'm leaving something behind that really made an impact. I hope that's the case."

—GLORIA REUBEN

Subject: NOAH WYLE

Presents as: JOHN CARTER

Character Family History: After several failed relationships at the hospital, Carter married Kem (Thandiwe Newton) in season 12. He was still wearing his wedding ring in the finale.

Other Hospitalizations: He played a doctor on two episodes of *Sesame Street* in 1996. In 2025, he reunited with John Wells, R. Scott Gemmill, and technical advisor Joe Sachs to executive produce and star as Dr. Michael "Robby" Robinavitch in *The Pitt* for HBO Max.

Diagnosis: A doctor in disguise. "Noah Wyle was very interested in the medicine, and he really wanted to be completely accurate," remembers director/producer Jonathan Kaplan. "He was constantly questioning the doctors. They had this big autopsy book, I remember, which was quite gross. But Noah would sit there with the doctors, looking over the autopsy book."

What Got His Heart Pumping: Anyone who doesn't recognize and appreciate the "unassailable profession" that is medicine. "I can honestly say that anytime I've ever been around a physician or nurse while they're plying their trade, I've always been really gratified by how little it means to them that I'm there in the face of what they must do. That's a sensibility we've tried to employ when we play these people. Doctors are beset often by bureaucratic pressures and personal problems. But you check all that baggage at the door and just take care of the person in front of you."

Advance Directive: Wyle's last shift as Carter was in season 12, but he returned for the final season.

Subject: SHERRY STRINGFIELD
Presents as: SUSAN LEWIS
Character Family History: A divorcée (her ex, Chuck Martin, was played by Donal Logue), Susan dated a Chicago Memorial psychiatrist named Dr. Div Cvetic in season 1 and enjoyed a brief fling with John Carter. She watched over her niece Little Susie after her older sister Chloe fled Chicago, but begrudgingly gave her up when Chloe returned and pledged to start a new life in Arizona.
Other Hospitalizations: She and a few of her fellow castmates, like Noah Wyle and Mekhi Phifer, reprised their roles for *ER: The Game* in 2005.
Diagnosis: A restless spirit. Stringfield raised eyebrows when she left *NYPD Blue* after only one season in 1994, only to leave *ER* two years later. "Everyone has to deal with this work-obsessed environment," former *NYPD Blue* producer David Milch once said. "If you don't, people don't like it. Sherry's situation reminds me of the tulip craze in Holland in the seventeenth century. There was this collective decision that tulips were the greatest thing in the world. Sherry is like someone who says, 'They're just tulips,' and it pisses people off."
What Got Her Heart Pumping: The constraints of series television. "There's a big price you have to pay, and I think it's the real big sacrifices that will be required of you," she said.

Advance Directive: After leaving the show twice, she reprised her character a third time in the series finale.

Subject: LAURA INNES
Presents as: KERRY WEAVER
Character Family History: Weaver entered the ER as a divorcée. She was adopted and met her birth mother, Helen Kingsley, in season 11.
Other hospitalizations: She voiced the character of Dr. Brander in a 1997 episode of *Rugrats*.
Diagnosis: A groundbreaker for depicting a lesbian who comes out later in life. "I thought it was fantastic and very interesting, because there was a lot of story there. I started learning more about people who come out later in life and why that would happen. It seemed to very much track with her personality, which was extremely compartmentalized. So I thought there were a lot of reasons that it makes sense that somebody like Kerry would be expressing this later on."
What Got Her Heart Pumping: The idea that her character, who had a limp, suffered from degenerative hip dysplasia "which is something that is more commonly known among German shepherds."
Advance Directive: She left the ER in season 13 to take a job as a medical talking head for a station in Miami. She returned for two episodes in the final season.

Subject: GLORIA REUBEN
Presents as: JEANIE BOULET
Character Family History: A widow who later married Reggie Moore and adopted an HIV-positive boy named Carlos.

Other Hospitalizations: Reuben played Dr. Selma Orchard in a pair of episodes for *The Blacklist* in 2015–2017.

Diagnosis: Reuben changed the narrative around HIV with her compassionate characterization of a heterosexual woman who contracts the virus from her husband, who had been unfaithful during their marriage. "Up until that time, there hadn't been an HIV-positive, regular character on network television," she once said. "Jeanie Boulet was ahead of her time. She was a heterosexual, married, professional woman, and she got HIV from her husband. That whole storyline was ahead of its time."

What Got Her Heart Pumping: Reuben took issue with the writing when the scripts had Jeanie "suffering from anything . . . it kind of defeats what we're doing with the character." It was important to her that Jeanie persevere, despite her HIV status. "For her to get sick and die, I would really fight against that." And whether or not she wanted it, Reuben suddenly became the poster girl for HIV in the female population. "She was getting these requests to talk in front of Congress," remembered John Wells. "She was getting requests to appear at all these fundraisers. She became that person and that was a heavy burden for her that I didn't ask her if she wanted to take on. It just seemed like a good story. And it became, I don't want to say debilitating, but it became a huge burden that she had to carry, where she had to come to us sometimes and say, 'Are you sure about what I'm saying? Because there are a lot of people who I'm going to hear from, like, tomorrow.' "

Advance Directive: Reuben got her wish in the end; Jeanie leaves the hospital to spend more time with her family. "A joyful finale for my character, believe it or not," she said.

Subject: MICHAEL MICHELE
Presents as: CLEO FINCH
Other Hospitalizations: She played Dr. Samira Terzi on two episodes of *House* in 2007.
Diagnosis: Joining the NBC drama in season 6 as a pediatrician was a game changer for the actress, who previously starred in *Homicide: Life on the Street.* "It meant everything. *ER* bought me a beautiful home. The home I still live in today. It not only gave me an extraordinary opportunity, but it opened other doors. And when those other doors opened, I was able to have other experiences, and because of *ER*, I could step away for a little while when I had my son. Well, for a long while. It was a gift to me. I don't know what I would have done, because after *ER* came *How to Lose a Guy in 10 Days* and *Ali* and *Dark Blue.* All of these have been wonderful opportunities and quite frankly, *ER* still helps me today in my career. I'm no longer playing Dr. Finch, but it's a role that will be with me throughout my entire career. I'm very, very grateful for that job."
Advance Directive: Michele quit the show after three seasons because the commute from New York City to Los Angeles for work "just about killed me."

Subject: GORAN VISNJIC
Presents as: LUKA KOVAČ
Character Family History: He's a widower who ended up marrying Abby Lockhart. Together, they had a son.

Diagnosis: A Croatia-born transplant to the US who got to participate in the development of his own character. "We agreed upon a backstory that Luka's wife died during the Vukovar siege and bombing," Visnjic said. "We talked about how comfortable I would be going that route, and we set up certain boundaries. They were very, very respectful. I had a say in anything that was regarding Croatia or the war or Luka's backstory, even with the name. The first day, they came with some names. They were not even Croatian, but they sounded Croatian to them. And then I was like, 'Guys, why don't we just go with a simple name like *Luka*?' They were like, 'Luka? That's Italian.' Well, my God, there are many Lukas in Croatia. It's an international name. My grandfather's name was Luka. So, they were like, 'Okay.' And *Kovač* was actually my best buddy's last name from Croatia."

What Got His Heart Pumping: The notion that he was a replacement for George Clooney and how there may have been a lot of pressure because of it. "I remember my first day coming to work. All the actors had the same parking lot, so I just parked my car, and I saw George and he was like, 'Oh my God, you're the new guy. Congratulations. You're going to love it so much. Everybody's so nice on the show.' He was really uplifting and trying to make me comfortable, and it was like that from the rest of the cast, really. They teased me a lot when I was like, *People*'s sexiest import or something like that. They were . . . sorry I have to say it . . . fucking with me. But it wasn't like, 'Oh, George is leaving. You were arriving.' Nobody was talking about that."

Advance Directive: Kovač and Abby move to Boston in season 15 to start a new life.

Subject: ALEX KINGSTON
Presents as: ELIZABETH CORDAY
Character Family History: She married Dr. Mark Greene in season 7, and together they had a daughter named Ella.
Other Hospitalizations: She played Dr. Marla Thomkins in a pair of episodes for *Private Practice* in 2011.
Diagnosis: A gifted and malleable actor. "She's just brilliance personified," said Lydia Woodward. "She could do anything. It didn't matter what you wrote; she would just send it through the roof for you. And of course, she was British, so it just added a kind of different little twist on things. You could play around with her being dumbfounded by American stuff, which is, of course, not hard to do."
What Got Her Heart Pumping: Kingston was "horrified" when a *Radio Times* article took a quote of hers out of context about her leaving *ER* because she was "part of the old fogeys who are no longer interesting." "I [was] for *ER* because they had no right to be tarnished with the ageism brush because they [were] absolutely not that at all," the actress said later. "We mutually felt that my character's storylines had run their course, all of the characters that Corday had been involved with have left the show, and we agreed that maybe it was time to move on."
Advance Directive: Her character left in season 11 and returned to England, but she came back for the series finale.

Subject: MING-NA WEN

Presents as: JING-MEI "DEB" CHEN

Character Family History: She gave up the son she had with Frank Bacon for adoption.

Other hospitalizations: Dr. Sara Kwan in 1999 on the series *Outreach*, Dr. Aki Ross in the 2001 *Final Fantasy: The Spirits Within* animated film, Dr. Lee on a 2022 episode of *Young Sheldon*, and Dr. Fong on *Karate Kid: Legends* in 2025.

Diagnosis: Wen wouldn't let the unconscious bias of the Hollywood casting process impact her quest to snag a part on *ER*. "This particular role was definitely not written ethnically," said Wen. "I don't think they were thinking that, *Okay, this particular part is definitely for a white actor.* I think they were writing a character, and it's sort of like a general image. But at that time, most of the people that got called in were Caucasian actors. We always had to fight for the bits and pieces, let's say, back in the day. So as always, it was me plus ten Caucasian actors waiting to audition for this part. So, I always try to figure out a way where, aside from being the only Asian in the room, how I could also stand out and make them change their mind about, well, this character could go Asian. I remember the audition scene was me having to perform a rectal exam, a definite highlight in my career after four years of Carnegie Mellon studying Shakespeare and the various masters of theater. So, I thought it would be kind of a good, fun visual if I brought along my own pair of latex gloves. There was a chuckle. Many of them laughed. I think that was one of those elements that sort of makes an actor stand out in a room, like they've creatively thought about how to present the scene. So yes, being the serious actor that I was, I took it to its full theatricality with the insertion."

What Got Her Heart Pumping: Wen had a say when her character's first name was changed when she returned to the show in 1999. "They wanted to sort of surprise Carter, because if he saw my name on the board or whatever, he would recognize that as, 'Oh wait, So-and-So is coming back.' So, they wanted to create a different name, and they were thinking like Colette or some other Anglo name. And I was like, 'Well, that doesn't make sense. Why would she have another English name?' I said, 'If anything, and I know a lot of my friends have done it, they reintroduce their Chinese name into their life instead of taking on an Anglo name. Maybe she has this epiphany of wanting to be closer to her culture, or closer to her other birth name?' I also said I could put in a little Easter egg and have her name be Jing-Mei, because that was my Chinese name for June in *The Joy Luck Club.* And I just love how Carter still refuses to call her Jing-Mei and still calls her Deb. It's kind of a brotherly thing to do."

Advance Directive: Jing-Mei returned to China to bury her father in season 11.

Subject: MAURA TIERNEY

Presents as: ABBY LOCKHART

Diagnosis: Tierney's addition to the show—along with her affair with Luka Kovač—helped to take the sting off losing Clooney and Margulies. "Writers write to people who can really act, and Maura's an extraordinarily talented actress," said John Wells. "You know that whatever you bring to the character, she's going to give you something that's unexpected and moving and wonderful. Maura has sort of created that for Abby's character by being so terrific. Maura proved, right from the beginning, that she was never going to take the easiest choice in the scene. [She] always was working hard to try to find something interesting to do with the character, which is no small feat over the number of episodes that we do."

What Got Her Heart Pumping: Getting used to the fame that came with working on *ER*. "It's different being a TV actor, especially in a hit show," she said. "You're in people's homes; they know you in a way that's more intimate and familiar. People would just come up to me and say hi. When my character was cheating on [Luka], people were angry with me. And when my character fell off the wagon, we were in Chicago shooting on location, and some of us went out to a bar afterwards. I was having a glass of wine, and people came up to me and said, 'You shouldn't be having that wine.'"

Advance Directive: Abby left the ER in season 15 to move to Boston with Luka and her son.

Subject: ERIK PALLADINO

Presents as: DAVE MALUCCI

Diagnosis: Palladino drew upon his early work in sitcoms and his dramatic experience in the 2000 movie *U-571* to help flesh out his *ER* character. "People loved Dave and hated

Dave, which was exactly the intention," said Palladino. "He was abrasive, emotionally guarded, and not a fully developed person yet. He was trying to figure out what kind of guy he was going to be. But that was the fun part about playing him. What I liked is that he was probably the funniest character on that show, and people really liked the stupid, goofy stuff he did. And I attribute a lot of that to [the writing of] R. Scott Gemmill, who went on to do *NCIS: LA* and *The Pitt*."

What Got His Heart Pumping: He was uncomfortable at first with his overnight star status after debuting on *ER*. "I think it was the third episode I was on, and I remember Noah Wyle telling me at the time, 'This show, it's not going to change you. But it could change everyone around you.' And I was like, 'What do you mean?' He goes, 'Friends who have known you your whole life might start acting differently. Even your family might act a little differently.' No one acted differently when I was on some low-rated sitcom, you know? But there was something about *ER*. I went to a deli in New York City to get a sandwich, and it was the day after an episode aired. A woman turns to me and goes, 'Oh my God, are you that new actor on *ER*?' She said it loud enough for the room to hear. I had not experienced fame like that in any real capacity. I sat down to eat my sandwich by myself, and everyone was staring at me. I got nervous and had a cotton mouth. I remember it was the worst-tasting sandwich I ever had."

Advance Directive: He was fired by Kerry Weaver in season 8.

Subject: PARMINDER NAGRA

Presents as: NEELA RASGOTRA

Character Family History: She married Michael Gallant before he went off to Iraq.

Other Hospitalizations: Dr. Lucy Banerjee on the 2012 TV series *Alcatraz*; Dr. Lapham in the 2018 movie *Bird Box*; Dr. Sarinda Khatri in 2017 series *Fortitude*; Dr. Smith in a 2020 episode of *Black-ish*; and Dr. Maryam Afridi in the 2023 series *Maternal*.

Diagnosis: Art felt like it imitated life for Nagra, who was a TV novice when she first joined the show. "That first episode when I come in, things are falling off the ceiling," Nagra recalled. "Kerry Weaver is shouting at somebody and getting mad, and I'm looking around this hospital, thinking, *What am I doing here?* And it was sort of perfect because I genuinely was nervous, so I was allowed just to be nervous as opposed to coming in and knowing everything as some characters do."

What Got Her Heart Pumping: After attempting one on *ER*, stunts give her the heebie-jeebies now. "The writers went, 'We are going to have Neela play ice hockey.' I was like, 'What?'" Nagra recalled. "It was me and Scott Grimes, who is already a fantastic ice hockey player. I didn't know anything about ice. I could barely skate. So in between my work, we went to training. It was like I was training for the Olympics, but I was in good shape by the end of it. But I got a little bit obnoxious about my skating, and I was trying to do these crossovers as you're going 'round a circle before we were about to film, and this was just an awful moment.

One leg went one way, the other went another way, and I literally tore my medial collateral ligament. I just felt completely winded. We had to use these girls to basically stunt double. So now if I do a job and I have to run a lot, which I had for my last cop show, where I needed to jump out in front of a car, I was like, 'Yes, please, please have the stunt double do that, because I've learned that I don't need to be doing that.'"

Advance Directive: Neela reunited with Ray Barnett in Louisiana in episode 20 of season 15. She appeared briefly in the final season via a webcam, talking about her new life.

Subject: MEKHI PHIFER

Presents as: GREGORY PRATT

What Got His Heart Pumping: "The only pressure I felt is that I had never played a character like that before, played a doctor. So that was one of the things that was like, wow, man, I hope I can pull off this doctor thing. I knew [about] the accolades of the show and how impactful it was and how great it was for television and the entertainment industry, but I just wanted to do a good job as a doctor. I just wanted to go in there and be able to use a scalpel and my stethoscope and everything else that was at my disposal to the best of my ability. That was my main thing."

Allergies: Any other medical show. "I feel like *ER* was the premier show when it came to being a doctor and the medical procedures. I mean, we had real doctors there every day as creative consultants. We were always able to defer to them to make sure that everything was authentic. Also, they were able to marry the mix of the drama with the procedures like I've never seen anybody else do before in any other show. So, I wouldn't say it ruined me from watching any other doctor shows. But I was there, and I know the impact that *ER* had on television. So, when it comes to the medical shows, I haven't really watched a medical show consistently since *ER*."

Advance Directive: Pratt died after entering a booby-trapped ambulance that exploded at the end of season 14.

Subject: SHARIF ATKINS

Presents as: MICHAEL GALLANT

Diagnosis: Getting into the orbit of John Wells can pay off big-time. After casting Atkins as a jazz singer in the 2002 movie–cum–backdoor pilot *The Big Time* for TNT, Wells offered him the new role of Gallant for the 2001/02 season of *ER*. "*Big Time* was more than just a film," Gallant said. "It catapulted me into the big time. . . . [*ER*] was one of those shows that for the longest time was the show to watch, the show to try to be on, you know what I mean? And for me personally, for that to be my proverbial coming-out party here in Hollywood and just with my career, I couldn't have dreamt up a better start."

What Got His Heart Pumping: Advice from Maura Tierney when he was struggling with a scene in *ER*. "She said, 'Sharif, just make a choice. Make a choice.' And it's interesting because one of the things that I keep with me, and anytime anyone, if I'm talking to an acting class or what have you, sometimes I just say, 'You know what? Sometimes you just have to simply make a choice. You gotta make a choice and go with your gut.' Those are some good memories. Good memories."

Advance Directive: Gallant was a member of the US Army Reserve and was called to serve in Iraq. He was killed off in the penultimate episode of season 12.

Subject: PAUL MCCRANE

Presents as: ROBERT ROMANO

What Got His Heart Pumping: The opportunity to break away from the typecasting he had been facing in Hollywood. "I played a lot of fragile characters, for lack of a better way of saying it, or highly sensitive characters. I got tired of it in the theater. But in film and television, that's what people remembered. So, I said to my reps at a certain point that I was no longer interested in playing those types, and I wanted to branch out and play some bad guys. They thought I was out of my mind. But then I got *RoboCop* back in the eighties, and then I was sort of a bad guy."

Allergies: McCrane worried he was being launched as a one-dimensional pain in the ass. "For a brief period, I longed for a bit more. But very quickly I enjoyed it because the truth is, there were extraordinarily few scenes where, if my character was there, I wasn't pushing the pot. My character was there to cause trouble. There was always some juice there. A little bit of Romano went a long way. You don't want a meal of jalapeño peppers, but if he comes in, he makes an impact, and then he's gone."

Advance Directive: Romano died when a helicopter crashed on top of his pitiful, one-armed body.

Subject: SHANE WEST

Presents as: RAY BARNETT

Diagnosis: Joining *ER* felt like a significant rite of passage for West. "With *ER*, I was twenty-seven, twenty-eight, growing into an adult," he said. "I did *Once and Again* when I was twenty years old. It was my first series, and I was being taught by some of the greats, Ed Zwick, Marshall Herskovitz, and working with Billy Campbell and Sela Ward every day. I was being thrown into the fire, for sure. I didn't know what I was doing. *ER* was the transition. Now you're an adult! You may not feel like it yet, and you look young, especially in season 11, but you're joining a show created by phenomenal writers and producers with an outstanding cast and an amazing history. The goal was to fit in and not screw up."

What Got His Heart Pumping: Visiting other teaching hospitals after doing *ER* and realizing he knew everything that was going on. "I was doing the series *Salem* in Shreveport, Louisiana. It was a very physical show, so we were at the Shreveport hospital a lot. It was fun to feel like I knew what they were doing. Everyone's usually kind of scared and worried; people have those preconceived ideas of a hospital. But I felt like I always had a smile on my face when we were in the hospital because I knew what was going on."

Advance Directive: Barnett ends up losing his legs in a freak accident. During his third season on the show, Shane knew his contract was set to expire. He said, "I was a little low on the totem pole. So, I had the opportunity to find another television show. I was cast in a show that ended up being about lawyers. I heard that I got the new TV show on my way to a read-through for an *ER* episode. The producers were all 'congratulations on the new show,' but they knew they had to write something in. Because I had such a good relationship with everyone on the show, they could have killed me. They could have killed Ray. But they decided to make it more powerful by taking his legs. I was like, 'Can it be one leg?' And they're like, 'No, it's got to be two. It's more effective.' And then I was like, 'Can it please be below the knee for future life and family?' And they're like, 'Okay, we'll make it below the knee.' So, I got one win there." West left in season 13 but returned in the final season to surprise his former gal pal Neela in a Frankenstein costume during Halloween.

Subject: JOHN STAMOS
Presents as: TONY GATES
Diagnosis: Stamos appreciated how Gates was everything he wasn't. "He comes in hot, where I tend to be more relaxed. He's an impulsive maverick, where I usually weigh pros and cons before leaping. He's a take-charge kind of guy who's been through the Persian Gulf War and braved the streets as an emergency paramedic. He has a troubled past, where I've been loved and nurtured since the day I was born."
What Got His Heart Pumping: He was credited with giving the show "the additional boost it needed" in season 13. "*ER* doesn't feel like a vestige of the show like it once was," NBC Entertainment president Kevin Reilly told *Entertainment Weekly* in 2006. "John is definitely a draw. After Noah [Wyle] left, we were down a man, so there was room for another male character. John has the right amount of chemistry and charisma."

"After five years of playing Dr. Doug Ross on *ER*, George Clooney thinks he can make a go of it in the movies. Can you believe the balls on this kid? When he leaves *ER*, producers are looking for a replacement and I'm thinking, who better than me? Right? A no-brainer. I'd taken meetings with John Wells, the show's cocreator and showrunner in the past. He's a titan of television and someone I've always wanted to work with. This is my shot. Enough time has passed from *Full House*. I have Broadway cred under my belt, and I'm beginning to be taken somewhat seriously. I am so ready when interest heats up in my playing a new doctor on the upcoming season of the still-very-hot medical drama."

—JOHN STAMOS

Advance Directive: He helps to refurbish a car for Samantha Taggart in the series finale.

Subject: LINDA CARDELLINI

Presents as: SAMANTHA TAGGART

Character Family History: A divorced mom with a son, Alex, and an adopted stepdaughter, Sarah.

Other Hospitalizations: She played Dr. Megan Tillman in a 2011 episode of *Person of Interest*.

What Got Her Heart Pumping: *ER* helped Cardellini break out of a long run of playing teenagers "even though I wasn't a teenager anymore. I thought, *Well, I'll play young until I can't do it anymore.* I was in no rush to make that happen. But I was wondering what I was going to do next. I had a lot of stuff happen in my real life and I'd been traveling a lot. I had lost some people, and I just wanted to be near my family and friends. I really wanted to stay committed to film, but I got this phone call, and they said, 'John Wells would like to meet with you, if you're interested.' They said there's this role of this woman who comes on *ER*, which I hadn't really watched ever. She was a woman who had a child when she was young . . . she's running from something, she's always in motion, and she's going to get involved with the doctor. Then they sent me home with episodes to watch. I hadn't seen anything like that on television. The acting was so fantastic, and [she] was somebody I feel like I knew growing up, who was a nurse and had a job, was trying to make ends meet. That was something I hadn't played yet."

Allergies: Her character's rejection of Luka Kovač. "It didn't make sense to me, because he's the nicest guy in the world."

Advance Directive: In the series finale, she and Tony Gates hold hands, suggesting they may have a future together.

Subject: SCOTT GRIMES

Presents as: ARCHIE MORRIS

Character Family History: Archie, who was a sperm donor, ended up having four children. "There were probably more who didn't want to get a hold of me," said Grimes.

Other Hospitalizations: He played Dr. Zabel—a callback to *ER* writer David Zabel—in a 2014 episode of *Shameless*, which was from John Wells.

Diagnosis: Comic relief at first, Morris ended up taking on great responsibility in the ER. "They made me chief resident at the end of a season when I was a guest star. I was like, 'Oh, maybe I'm going to become a regular.' Then it was just because nobody else wanted the job. So my greatness came from circumstances that I should not have been in. Nobody else wanted to be chief resident! Then I started to get better and started to care more, so by the end, I was running the ER. It was a strange, strange but wonderful, kind of arc."

What Got His Heart Pumping: The adrenaline rush that came with being on such a behemoth show. "It was like the Olympics of television. It was a trial by fire. If you didn't stick it, you were gone. It wasn't like they were jerks about it. They just didn't write to you anymore if you couldn't figure out that dance. I remember the first scene that I did with Noah Wyle when he came back. It was this kind of emergency surgery thing with wires and tubes everywhere and I'm ducking. It wasn't really choreographed except for with some props. We messed up a couple things, but we kept going until they said cut. I just hugged Noah and went, 'That was the most exhilarating moment of my acting life.' He was just so good at that. And if you can be good at it, you'll stay on that show. But you have to really concentrate. You have to really fit in, and there's no class you could take to get ready for that. The class was the show itself."

Advance Directive: Morris appears in the series finale.

3

ER Entrance

One of the more indelible aspects of *ER* is its forty-one-second, Emmy-winning title sequence—a fever dream of flashing blue images, floating X-rays, and harried doctors. To achieve the perfect opener for his vision, John Wells called upon the agency Pittard Sullivan—one of the industry leaders in title production that had created memorable sequences for films like *The Client* and *Grumpy Old Men* and TV shows like *Falcon Crest* and *Picket Fences*. Cofounder Billy Pittard assigned the job to creative director Suzanne Kiley while James Newton Howard—already a GOAT for creating music for such films as *Major League, Pretty Woman, Grand Canyon*, and *The Fugitive*—composed the underlying tune.

Billy Pittard (Senior Title Designer) Suzanne and I went in to talk with them to learn what the show was about, just the nature of it, the setting of it. At that point in history, my company was doing a lot of main titles. We already had one Emmy for titles and a lot of nominations. We had a very talented group of designers working in the company doing a lot of different things. We were branding television networks, but we had a sweet spot for doing main titles, because winning an Emmy was the highest honor that you could get. We did bigger projects, but you couldn't get an Emmy for them. We were just a bunch of designers, so the idea that we could work on a show that might become a big hit and impress our friends back home was always there. Anyway, we were a hot shop for doing main titles.

Suzanne Kiley (Principal Title Designer) *ER* was presented to me as fast-paced and gritty, not what a polished hospital environment would feel like. I had already worked on the visuals for the storyboards, but I didn't know what the music was going to be yet. They gave us the pilot so we knew we would want to highlight the main characters. I had already shot all the images that you see that are very filmic and bursting with light. It was all shot on film in slow motion. I used the inspiration of X-rays. All those bursts are totally organic, and they weren't created in post. It was all blues and greens. I didn't have the music beforehand. I knew I wanted the font to be simple and kind of iconic, something that would be easily recognizable, but not over the top. There's the word *emergency* in lowercase that is Typewriter [along with the actors' names]. The *ER* is blocky, all caps in Bank Gothic.

Billy Pittard We were very excited to hear that James Newton Howard was going to do the music. There were parts of the music that sounded like an abstraction of a siren. It just resonated with this whole concept of the emergency room. You are kind of floating and there are the hospital colors and the lights and everything. It was almost like you were on a gurney being rolled down the hall while disoriented.

James Newton Howard (Composer, *ER* theme music) I feel like what John Wells talked about was strength. That's what I tried to portray, how these people are under intense pressure. I wrote it in, like, forty-five minutes on synthesizers. A lot of times that happens. I hear it with songwriters all the time. Suddenly, they get an idea and the lyric kind of falls into place. Anyway, it was a very short piece. I think the only addition that I made over the dub was by a guitar player named Marc Bonilla. The rest is me. In those kinds of pieces of music, I am often the only player there, but that's not that unusual these days. I use a lot of electronics in my work, and most of the guys out there do that in their sleep just like I do. It should sound good if you know what you're doing. If it doesn't sound good, then you don't know what you're doing.

Suzanne Kiley I remember getting it and going, "Oh my God, this is perfect."

Julianna Margulies You can't really sing it. It doesn't have a melody.

John Wells I put the Eriq La Salle air punch into the title.

Eriq La Salle They originally had me coming out and jumping for joy. It didn't feel right for his character. I had studied martial arts for several years at that point, so I improvised the punch.

James Newton Howard I thought it was the centerpiece of the titles. That really communicated power to me, and it was shot so beautifully. I mean, you can only be that effective if you're getting it from the screen. In other words, if the images aren't good, nobody looks good. I'm not taking away from what I did. I think I wrote a good theme, but I wouldn't have written that good of a theme if the show hadn't been as good as it was.

Suzanne Kiley The punch was so iconic.

Eriq La Salle There are memes. I get a kick out of it.

Billy Pittard Now I'm going to tell you a story that you may have not heard at all. At the same time, CBS was also coming up with a medical drama called *Chicago Hope* with David E. Kelley, another genius. We had worked with David on *Picket Fences*, so he called us to ask us if we would do the main title for his new show for CBS.

Suzanne Kiley *ER* came in first, and Billy assigned it to me. I started working on it, but then for some reason, it was put on hold for a little bit, and then I got assigned to *Chicago Hope*. *Chicago Hope* was a little bit more skewed toward a high-end hospital feel, but not as gritty. That's what I tried to achieve, and obviously, you didn't want either title to look anything like the other one.

"Even though *Chicago Hope* was a medical drama, it just seemed so different from *ER*. We didn't even think there was any conflict. Even though we had a bunch of designers working at the company at the time, Suzanne got that job, as well. They had a nice piece of music by Mark Isham. It was high quality, but much more traditional. The *ER* music is not traditional."

—BILLY PITTARD

Suzanne Kiley It was kind of a hard assignment because then *ER* came back, and I ended up working on both. I did feel bad, but I was like, well, they're not telling me to stop working. I guess Billy felt that it was what it was. But I was aware that it was not going to be taken well by somebody.

In 1995, Pittard's wish for adoration came true: He and Kiley received an Emmy nomination for Outstanding Individual Achievement in Graphic Design and Title Sequences, while Howard received a nod for Outstanding Individual Achievement in Main Title Theme Music. Chicago Hope *didn't earn a nomination for its titles, but Isham received one for the music.*

Billy Pittard David Kelley saw how the *ER* main title was nominated and *Chicago Hope* was not. He was pissed. I completely understood. I tried to explain, but he didn't want to hear it, and I don't blame him. In retrospect, it's like, yeah, I wish I had told him, but what do you do? I mean, it was such a weird coincidence that it happened that way. Everything we set out to do, we were going to do the absolute best that could be done.

The ER *title would go on to win the Emmy in 1995, beating out shows like* Star Trek Voyager *and* The Promised Land. *Howard lost to composer Jerry Goldsmith, who won for* Star Trek Voyager, *but would end up winning his first Emmy in 2001 for writing the main title music for* Gideon's Crossing.

James Newton Howard Jerry was one of my big supporters in my early days, so I was never upset to lose to Jerry Goldsmith or

John Williams, ever. Obviously, it's more fun to win, but I was not upset by it at all.

Suzanne Kiley People loved the title. At that time, it was a new type of look, not as digital and more filmic. No one was really doing the longer titles. They were shortening the titles and doing a cold open to try to bring the viewers into the show quickly. It was probably one of my most favorite projects I ever worked on.

Billy Pittard The style was fresh, and it was highly imitated. Kyle Cooper is one of the great main title designers, for sure. His first megahit was doing the titles for the movie *Seven*. If you look at it, it's kind of influenced by Suzanne's *ER* title. It's got that multilayered, choppy kind of abstraction to it. Suzanne's title and the style she developed was definitely seminal to the industry.

The drama's titles were continually updated over the years with images of the new actors before ER *eventually abandoned them in season 13 and went with a blink-and-you'll-miss-it opener featuring music from Martin Davich.*

Scott Grimes (Archie Morris) I grew up hearing the theme to *ER* and pretending to physically do my opening thing. I was in my second year as a regular when *ER* stopped doing the opening credits. So I was like, wow, I just made it. I loved my shot so much. I think I had the best one, because it came when the music swelled. When every actor ended their run, John Wells would frame our first call sheet and the picture from our opening credits. I still have it. It was a very sweet gesture.

4

Doctor Speak

Banana bag. CBC. Chem nineteen. Coag panel. These aren't the kinds of terms typically uttered in your average American film school. To continue the example set by Michael Crichton, John Wells recruited real-life physicians like Lance Gentile, Fred Einesman, and Joe Sachs to do the heavy lifting when it came time to create medical mysteries for his County General staff. In at least one instance, Wells didn't have to go far to find a helping hand: Neal Baer, a writer-producer on *ER* from 1996 to 2000, had known Wells since the fourth grade. As Baer likes to joke, "How do you get into show business? You go to Holly Hills Elementary School outside of Denver, Colorado."

All the writers, former medical students or not, were given a crash course on hospital life; as writer-producer Carol Flint remembers, new staffers spent time in Los

Angeles–area emergency rooms to get a feel for the madness. But it was up to Gentile, Baer, and the other doctors-turned-writers to not only make the drama feel authentic but ensure the actors looked and sounded like real physicians.

Neal Baer Michael Crichton didn't make up the medical stories on *ER*, post-pilot. I did. And Lance. Lance and I were the first doctor-writers as far as I know. Usually, doctors sprinkled the medicine on post-scripts being written. I became a pediatrician, and Lance was an emergency physician. That became Doug for me versus Mark and Kerry Weaver for Lance.

Lance Gentile I was on the StairMaster, and I read about *ER* in *The Hollywood Reporter* or something. I saw the names *Spielberg, Crichton,* and *Wells,* so obviously, it seemed like a pretty good project. And I just did this movie about an ER doctor, so I was trying to get started in Hollywood. I thought I ought to call this guy and see if I can get involved. I was an ER doctor for decades, I really knew the world, and I thought I could contribute to it because I had the doctor's point of view that most people didn't. John's extremely smart, and he totally got that.

Neal Baer All the stories were inspired by things I read or experienced myself, which is what really changed the medical show. When Noah goes to the OR the first time, and he knows the answer to the capital of what was then called Zaire is Kinshasa. That happened to a friend of mine. I call it the *cultural minutiae* that made the show so special. It could only be known by doctors, unless you were an ethnographer and had lived with doctors. In other words, when we did an episode where Carter does his first spinal tap and is nervous, Greene takes him through it, and Nurse Connie says, "Oh, a champagne tap." And Carter's like, "What's that?" Greene says, "If there are no red blood cells, I have to give you a bottle of champagne." So, Carter does it, he gets no red blood cells, and he shares the bottle of champagne on the roof with Susan. You could only know about a champagne tap if you had lived it. If you ask doctors to tell us cool things, they're not going to think of a champagne tap.

Lydia Woodward We would go through the broad strokes of the character arcs, and we'd say, "Well, we kind of want Dr. Greene and his wife to be having marital problems, so we need to have 'em have some kind of fight." And then on another board, the doctors wrote up a bunch of medical stuff that could happen, so we looked over there and said, "Well, okay, I'll do the appendectomy. That sounds good." It was kind of thrown together loosely, but we had the doctors there to help us every step of the way.

Jack Orman (Executive Producer) A little information is a dangerous thing, because when you end up doing so many episodes, you start understanding at a surface level how these things work. So, I would find myself arguing, "Wait a minute, they need the head CT!" This exasperated the doctors.

Lance Gentile I was the one who created "one, two, three" when they moved people from one gurney to another. We used to do a lot of riding on gurneys. It was very dramatic. I used real nurses from my practice. I figured they'd be much better than background artists who had no medical experience. I hired them all, a lot of my friends and nurses who I worked with. They loved it. I mean, if somebody's hanging an IV, they know how to hang IVs. They totally knew how to do it right in front of the camera.

Neal Baer Our show was very different from *Grey's Anatomy,* obviously. We had that richness. *Grey's* is like an expensive

General Hospital. It's just buffed up to shine more. They would do social issues, but I hated their abortion episode, where Katherine Heigl says, "This is between you and your maker," or whatever horseshit that she said. It was preachy.

CCH Pounder (Angela Hicks) The thing that I remember most about *ER* was the giant leap that it made from *Dr. Kildare*, where people with strange things were healed in thirty minutes.

George Clooney All the doctor shows we watched, [they] would do eye surgery and heart surgery, remember? That's what the shows were.

CCH Pounder Our doctors, technical doctors on the set, were very particular about what instruments were used and how we must have gloves on and masks. I mean, they were sticklers for that. I really appreciated that because the one thing that *ER* taught people was the feeling of what it might be like if you ended up in hospital. That was a first.

Carol Flint (Executive Producer) We were dedicated and committed to being realistic. Sometimes, yeah, it was fiction. There would be a flood on the fifth floor, so a person had to give birth in the emergency room because for some reason the OB was not accessible. But we didn't have preposterous kinds of things happening for the sake of it being preposterous or showy.

"Ron Howard once came up to me and said, when he did *Apollo 13*, he used what we did on *ER*. He had actors rattle off technical stuff even though nobody really understood what it was. It really set the tone. He said *ER* was his model for a lot of the dialogue, doctors rattling off shit to each other while the audience goes, 'I don't really know what they're talking about, but I feel like I'm a doctor! Yeah, get me a CBC! I think I need a chem seven and maybe a chest X-ray, too.' That's something *ER* invented; they chattered to set the vibe and to not explain what was going on. In the past with medical dramas, something would be happening, and they would make sure the audience was following along. We abandoned that. That led to a sense of urgency and tension."

—LANCE GENTILE

Noah Wyle If there's anything that the original ensemble in particular felt proud of, it's that we hit the ground running. We felt very strongly about earning credibility within the medical community. First and foremost, we wanted these guys to feel and look and sound like real emergency room physicians. So we spent a lot of time shadowing people around their hospitals, reading a lot of books, reading a lot of diaries being kept by medical students, asking a lot of questions, taking various procedures and equipment home so we could practice on our own.

Jack Orman Other writers would just make up the medicine, which would drive some of the doctors crazy because they're like, "Wait, hold on. Who gave you this?"

Lance Gentile We tried not to have convenient comas.

Neal Baer We did an episode with Carter because it happened to me. It started with Carter examining a kid who he thought had Bell's palsy, like a paralysis of his facial muscle. He doesn't see anything else that could be causing it. He presents it to Dr. Ross, who goes, "Did you check the kid's ear?" And Noah's like, "His ear? It's facial paralysis," and Ross goes, "Ramsay Hunt syndrome. That's a syndrome which causes paralysis, not Bell's palsy, because you have a herpetic lesion in your ear." Carter did it. Ross goes, "Pretty bad thing to miss." So, Carter freaks out and must call the family and can't get hold of them. He ends up going to the house because he's so freaked out that he may have missed something bad, and the kid is fine, and the family's like, "What are you doing here?" Then because he's so afraid of making a mistake, which we can all identify with, so then a woman comes in with vague symptoms. She hasn't felt well for a long time, so he shotguns her and orders like $10,000 worth of tests because we can order tests as medical students. He's afraid he's going to miss something. He uncovers a rare problem with antiphospholipid antibodies. And everybody's like, "Oh my God, Carter, this is brilliant." That happened to me. When I started *ER*, during hiatus I detected antiphospholipid antibodies doing a rheumatology rotation at UCLA. Then I would get letters saying, "Oh, I saw your show. And I told my doctor to do a test for that, and I have it, too."

John Wells We used to do a postmortem on Fridays to discuss the episode from the night before. Since there was no social media, it was more anecdotal and talking about what our friends and families were saying.

Lance Gentile John used to give me all the bad letters from all the doctors who were complaining. He would just say, "Here's another one." So, I would say to them, "It's not supposed to be a documentary." And a person could ride on a gurney. It's possible. That would be my answer. That was the test. Could this possibly happen? And a lot of our stories would be like, "Could this possibly happen?" Yes, maybe. Okay, good. We can do it.

Lydia Woodward *ER* was wall-to-wall medicine, which is what made it unique. That terrified everybody at the get-go. In the first season of the show, I was a supervising producer, and I was the person who got on the phone with the network and the studio and took their notes on any script. It wasn't something that every writer did; it was one person. And I was the person that year. I remember it was on the second episode, I was on with someone at the studio, and they were reading the second episode, and they sort of had this kind of exasperated tone in their voice and they literally said to me, "But does there have to be so much medicine?" I just kind of took a breath and said, "Well, yeah."

Jack Orman The interesting thing is that medicine has evolved. While I was on the show, there were doctors who were routinely doing spinal taps for meningitis. Now, as I understand it, that's a specialty because there are different ways to screen for this and medicine has evolved such that they don't have to do spinal taps. A lot of ER doctors are not trained on how to do spinal taps now, and we did it all the time.

Lance Gentile They were all real conditions. Maybe that's why in the early days *ER* was so revolutionary. We did a lot of real stories. Obviously as time went on, you ran out of cool stories. It got less and less unique and more of a generic medical show. That's inevitable.

Hand-holding was a given when it came time to prep the actors. There were presentations on the basics of ER life, while Lance Gentile tried to make it easy for the ensemble by recording the medical terminology on cassettes to help the major players learn their dialogue.

Lance Gentile This was in the cassette days. So, George would get a cassette with all his lines, et cetera. Everybody would get one so they could come on set and know how to pronounce stuff.

Ellen Crawford Lance ran the meetings, and I remember one of the things he told us is if you make a mistake, you don't say *oops*. You say *there*. We learned basic terms. We learned how to fake an IV, how to fake compressions, that sort of thing.

Yvette Freeman That's the one thing that gave me the willies was saying the words right and memorizing them. They were like nonsensical words.

Noah Wyle It was daunting. I mean, I used to say it's like learning Latin, and someone said, "No, it *is* Latin." Oh, right. Well, that would explain why that sounds so Latin-esque.

Emily Wagner (Doris Pickman) You were speaking words that are not normal sentences.

Maura Tierney (Abby Lockhart) There was one thing I had to say. . . . It was a medicine that I could not say. Ceftriaxone. And for some reason, *ceftriaxone* is not a hard thing to say. I had to say, like, "Five grams of ceftriaxone," and I couldn't say it, and John Wells was directing, and I was terrified.

Erik Palladino (Dave Malucci) I think what happens on *ER* or in any medical show is in the beginning, all the medical dialogue is a foreign language, right? "CBC, chem twenty, type and cross for four, cross-table C-spine, chest, and pelvis. All right, everyone, pick up the pace in ten minutes, this patient will have a chest tube, Foley, NG, and plain films. In fifteen minutes, he'll either be in the OR or dead. I'm in Thora-Seal!" That was literally my audition scene, by the way.

Alex Kingston (Elizabeth Corday) I always knew exactly what I was doing in the ER. You had to be seen to be doing everything exactly right. So, learning the lines, it made complete sense to me why I was saying what I was saying.

Laura Innes (Kerry Weaver) If you didn't know your lines cold, you were screwed. At least I would've been. My poor husband would just drill them, and he'd go, "You know them." And I'd go, "No, let's go again." It was a lot of homework. I just think it was honoring how doctors would really say that stuff, they wouldn't hesitate. It would just be something that rolls off the tongue.

Mekhi Phifer (Gregory Pratt) I would go over the lines while I was doing other things. So, if I was working out, if I was at a club, if I was in my kitchen by myself, I would just walk and talk the lines. It was very much a 'pat your head, chew bubble gum at the same time' type of scenario. I never really learned the lines just sitting still.

Anthony Edwards You had to know your words.

Jonathan Kaplan (Co-Executive Producer) They all had to have shortcuts. I mean, the surgery scenes were the easiest because they were wearing masks, and if they screwed up, the rule was just keep going because you can always dub it in later.

Parminder Nagra (Neela Rasgotra) I just started rapping [the dialogue]. Literally rapping it because it was kind of like music. Those were my techniques. And then of course, you look across at Noah Wyle, who's got a photographic memory, and he'd learn it within five seconds. I'd be like, "You're so annoying. It's taken me three days to learn this!"

Yvette Freeman There was a thing that George Clooney did in the beginning by writing the words on stickies and putting them on one of the actors' foreheads to remind him of the line. That's why his head kept moving, kind of like he had a thing with it.

Everybody used that. Everybody would also write on the side of the bed, maybe on the sheets until someone said, "Stop it. You're messing up the sheets!" You got one of them long words or whatever you got to say. You better put it phonetically somewhere.

Lyn Paolo (Costume Designer) George would be leaning in intently, staring into the poor victim's eyes, saying, "How can I help you?" But in fact, he was reading his lines off the pillowcase to the right of [the patient's] head. There were lots of pillowcases with lines on them.

John Wells I found it more effective to embarrass and humiliate than scold [them for writing on the props].

Jonathan Kaplan George had all these ways of hiding his lines. When we'd do a trauma scene and he was involved, he'd come in and the first question he'd asked me was, "So are you going to be above the patient for this first stuff? How are you going to shoot this?" I realized that's how he preferred it. So, I'd say, "Yeah, yeah, we'll be above the patient." He would chat up the patient who was getting paid to lie on a gurney for a half day, and he would pin his lines to the patient.

One time I laid out a scene for George. Basically, he comes down the stairs and goes over to the nurses' station and then crosses into the room. I left the set, which was the last time I ever did that. I came back, and it was changed. George is walking down the hall now instead of coming down the stairs. I said to the assistant director, "What changed?" He said, "Don't say anything. I'll show you." So, the AD and I walked the path that George would take, and his lines were on a cue card that was attached to a rack of equipment. The camera couldn't see it because it was driving away, but George could see it as he's walking. He had all these tricks. He was a master at it. You'd never know he was reading his lines. Then somebody comes up and hands him some phone messages and he'd be thumbing through the phone messages, which were his actual lines.

Noah Wyle George was so shameless. He wouldn't just write them on Post-it notes. He'd write them on the clipboards. He was reading off them while he was doing the exam. The more brazen one was—even after he left the show for several years—I'd look at the pillowcase underneath the patient's head, and I'd see the faint outline of some of his old lines that he'd written so he could look at the patient and read them. I did have Mickey Rooney put a big-ass cue card on my chest for the scene we played together on *ER*.

Yvette Freeman I wasn't a star, so I couldn't write on the sheets. So, there you go.

Goran Visnjic (Luka Kovač) Sometimes it would be a specifically difficult word or something. I would just try to stick it someplace, but rarely. You would try not to lean on that. That would be a last resort. But I mean, Jesus, I'm still going to do it for some other shows if there is a problem. If you get something last second or something changes on a set. You know what they like to say, "We just need one good take." That's all it needs. As long as it looks good on the screen, who cares?

Erik Palladino If I was holding a clipboard, I would always sneak the dialogue on there, the medical stuff.

Troy Evans (Frank Martin) In the early first season, Noah Wyle was on one side of the gurney and George Clooney was on the other side. Noah has a clipboard with a page of medical gibberish. He's trying to give this report to George, but he's stammering. He looks up and down from the clipboard. The director yells cut. George said, "Noah, when I turn the TV on Thursday night, I don't want to see you looking back and forth to me and the clipboard and the patient. For Christ's sake, be a man. Put your head down and read it!"

Scott Grimes I think Noah taught everybody right away that even doctors are looking down at charts. Why not write some of your dialogue on that chart? Because it ended up being one of those tricks that looked more real than if you didn't do it. Noah also taught me when you're walking down a hallway in the ER, you're not just looking forward or looking at the other person. There's a cart coming over here. You've got to take advantage of the situation. Why not write your stuff down there?

Sharif Atkins (Michael Gallant) A lot of the medical jargon, no matter how much you're around it, no matter how much you're steeped in it, you ingest it, you know what the heck you're saying and what you're talking about, but three, four, five episodes [later], a good 75, 80 percent of it just flies away.

Shane West (Ray Barnett) At the end of the year when they do the little wrap parties and show the blooper reels, I was usually in the background laughing. I was proud of myself. I was told one year that I was counted on for not messing up often. That made me grin ear to ear because I was a baby when I joined that show. So that was all that I needed to know. Go in there, learn your stuff, and everyone's going to mess up. Except maybe Noah Wyle, who would never mess up.

Scott Grimes There's a line that one of the writers came up for me to say two weeks before I had to say it, so [medical expert] Joe Sachs came up and told me because he knew the word was going to be difficult. I can say it perfectly now—it was *oligoanalgesia*. No joke, when we filmed it, it didn't come out of my mouth correctly. That was the only word I struggled with the whole time.

Neal Baer I did the first experimental study in 2000 to really look at what people learn from TV. It was based on two episodes with Julianna Margulies, one on the morning-after pill, which, believe it or not, twenty-four years later, we're still dealing with that, and cervical cancer and human papilloma virus. We surveyed, and it was a journal called *Health Affairs*. It's shocking how much they learned. There's a lot that *ER* gave birth to, along with the fact that there are real doctors on every show medical series now.

John Wells The Kaiser Foundation did a survey of where people get their health information, and they called us up and said, "We want to come and present it." I'm making these numbers up, because I don't remember what the exact numbers were. But it was like 15 percent of people get their information about medicine from their doctor, 16 or 17 percent got it from what they read in the newspaper, and 84 percent got it from watching *ER*. I mean, it was that crazy. This is when we realized we had a public responsibility to be telling the truth all the time, and to not simplify things simply for dramatic purposes.

5

Medical Minute

A Look Back at "Love's Labor Lost"

Season 1, Episode 19 | March 9, 1995
Written by Lance Gentile
Directed by Mimi Leder

One of the winningest episodes in *ER*'s fifteen-year history was this disturbing installment about a thirty-year-old pregnant woman whose condition deteriorates under the care of Dr. Mark Greene. When the good doctor discovers that an attending obstetrician was unavailable to help, Greene decides to deliver the baby in the ER, with tragic results. Starring Colleen Flynn as the expectant mom, Jodi, and Bradley Whitford as her distraught husband, Sean, the plotline involved ensemble members Noah Wyle, Julianna Margulies, Sherry Stringfield, Ming-Na Wen, and Ellen Crawford. It won multiple Emmy Awards for writing, directing, sound mixing, editing, and sound editing.

Neal Baer It was inspired by something I heard about. I won't say which hospital. It wasn't exactly how it happened. I mean, we had every bad unforeseen problem in the book coming at Greene, like he couldn't get her airway and stuff like that. I pitched it in the room. It was fun because we often tried to make episodes a little heavier for one person or another. Like, this one would be Eriq La Salle's episode, or this would be George's episode, or this would be Tony's or Sherry's. And then maybe once a year, one of them would get a big episode like Tony got "Love's Labor Lost."

Lance Gentile My job was to mess Greene up a little because he'd been too successful and he was doing too well. It's a drama about emergency medicine. How can I make this realistic in the context of what the drama needs? We were trying to be real. We wanted the medical community to think we were doing well in terms of accuracy. Obviously, it's a bunch of interns and residents that are running the world, so you must set some fig leaves in place. Where is the obstetrics person? Why aren't they there? Why does this have to happen now? In my case, I said they were delivering twins, and everybody was tied up with it. I had to get a reason why there was no OB around to help.

Anthony Edwards All I knew before the script came in was that he was going to have the worst day a doctor could have.

Mimi Leder (Co-Executive Producer) We knew it was going to be a great one. I had my choice of what to direct. The point of view of that episode changed dramatically halfway through. It shifted to Dr. Greene and things falling through his fingers and him trying to save this woman's life and this baby's life. I felt up for the challenge and lucky to be directing a story of that magnitude and of that intimacy.

Anthony Edwards That [scene] was kind of reflective of what our job is as actors and what the reality is. Even when you have all the information, it's always an imaginative place you're in. Whether you've seen the scene before or after, when you're in that moment, it has to be filled with emotional and intellectual imagination that will keep that illusion alive. I think good acting is a lot about trust. You trust them and you go to that place, and they go, "That seems like it works well!" Luckily, two months later, it did. The script was a powerful read.

John Wells I knew Colleen from *China Beach* and I knew Bradley's work, so when their names were mentioned, I responded, along with Mimi, to the idea of how wonderful they would be in the roles.

Colleen Flynn (Jodi O'Brien) I think they told me that she died. They said it was important to fall in love with her and feel a connection to her. That I remember very distinctly—that it was very important people fall in love with her right away. I was incredibly scared and flattered that that was something they thought I could do.

Bradley Whitford (Sean O'Brien) It was nice because Tony and I had worked on *The Client* and we had shared an apartment in Memphis when we were shooting there, and we had been friends before that. I remember Tony was frustrated in terms of work. Back then, [actors] would often do a TV movie, which may or may not be a pilot depending on how that went. That was what

Tony was going off to do right after *The Client*, and I remember thinking, *Oh, God, I hope it works out for him.* Then it became the biggest TV show. [*ER*] just leapt right out of the gate.

Colleen Flynn I went straight to the props people. They had so much to do with my fake belly and all the intravenous stuff.

Rick Ladomade (Special Effects) That was a good example of props used in a more emotional, narrative type of thing. We had fake babies made and belly pieces. We had a place where we had prosthetics made. It was called Creative Character Engineering, and we would send actors there. They would mold the body so they can get the right size, the right skin tone, everything to make it feel just right. We also had a special kind of emergency medicine gurney that we would hollow out. We would make it so it dipped down like a foot and a half so that we can sink somebody in there. Their head would lie flat where the pillow is, and then their legs would come back out flat. We would lay the prosthetic piece right over the top. Once we draped it and everything, you could not tell that it was a fake piece. It looked like it was seamless all the way across. We built two different bellies. One was a pregnancy belly that looked like a normal pregnancy. When they pulled up her gown, she looked great. And then the other one was a special prosthetic piece that we could use to cut for the C-section. Blood would come out because it was all rigged with tubes. We would pull out a prosthetic that looked like a real baby in distress.

Colleen Flynn I was on the table a lot. People were working hard to rig me up for continuity. I didn't take a lot of breaks. I just stayed there. People would break, and I would just lie there by myself.

Anthony Edwards The takes were long. They were like mini plays. They would take like two minutes or whatever the length they were in the scene, because doctors don't stop. It was the ballet of it. I mean, the truth is it'd be very difficult in modern hospitals for that situation to go that far down. There'd be a little more backup. The actual order and what happens is very real. It was early in the show. We weren't as comfortable or familiar with every aspect of our medical stuff. I remember being really challenged and really frustrated trying to get it right and having to be coached by one of the DPs who was calming me down in between takes. We really wanted to get it right.

The action gets so intense in the moments leading up to Greene performing the emergency C-section that Deb Chen knocks over a surgical tray. "Everybody, just take a deep breath," responds Greene, who then performs the surgery with vital assistance by Susan. The falling tray would later become a well-worn trope in medical dramas, much like the sight of a doctor riding on a gurney with a patient. In fact, "Love's Labor Lost" featured Sherry Stringfield enjoying a little ride-along with Flynn's Jodi on the way to the OR.

Lance Gentile The falling tray happened in a real OR. I followed the chief resident at County–USC, and they were doing a C-section. I thought, *Wow, that's cool.* I made that mental note to put that in there.

Mimi Leder I remember that it worked so well with her knocking it over. I wanted it to feel like we were whirling into a chaotic moment and then *bang*—suddenly everything stands still. For a second, no one is breathing and then everyone catches their breath, and you've got to keep going.

Ming-Na Wen (Jing-Mei "Deb" Chen) I can see Colleen's face vividly. It was such a traumatic episode to do.

To help inject a little levity in an otherwise grim situation, the props people came up with a bright idea to scare the bejesus out of the actors.

Bradley Whitford I remember during the horrible surgical scene, Tony's reaching in and he pulls out an alien baby.

Rick Ladomade It got so intense that some of the cast was almost in tears because it was so real. We were notorious for joking around to keep up morale. I mean, we loved realism, but morale was so important, too. So in between scenes, we put the alien baby in the belly for the C-section. Only Anthony Edwards and I knew about it. I was dying. And then they pulled out the baby thinking they were pulling out the real baby, and we scared the crap out of everybody. It was an alien-looking monster baby with teeth and everything. They went running out the door screaming. Everybody came up to the windows. What the fuck is going on?

Ming-Na Wen Oh, I screamed. I screamed because he pulled out this green, bloody, goopy, ugly baby that was alien with teeth and gnarly claws.

Anthony Edwards We really lost it then. The show was so intense that we probably laughed more than most comedies.

After some initial worries, the baby survived Greene's emergency C-section. The mother's life, however, was in immediate peril: The OB specialist arrives and takes one look at the mother's incision before shouting, "What did you use, a chainsaw?" Despite multiple zaps from the defibrillator and a very sweaty Greene performing nonstop CPR, Jodi ends up dying on the table. Greene then has to deliver the sad news to Sean, who's in the nursery rocking his new baby.

Lance Gentile We weren't allowed to kill any babies early on.

John Wells The story itself was so emotionally moving that the shooting of it was not difficult, but very traumatic, because so many of us had or were having children at the time.

Anthony Edwards We used to watch the episodes together at lunch on the Thursdays they aired. That was fun. So, I saw it. That night, I had worked until 9:30 or 10:00, so I came home like three-quarters of the way through the show, and my wife was watching the show. I didn't have my key or something, and I was like, "Can you let me in?" And she was like, "I'm not letting you in! You killed her! You are not allowed in this house! You just killed a *mother*!" She was half joking. I think she finally let me in halfway through the 11:00 news. It was a nice compliment to get.

"I was doing a rotation in Boston, and I told my attending that a woman was coming who's pregnant and she has high blood pressure. Everybody's freaking out because we did the episode 'Love's Labor Lost' and they don't want this woman to die. They all think she has preeclampsia. But the attending sees some other little things and does some tests, and it turns out she didn't have preeclampsia, in which case you must deliver the baby, or the mother can stroke out and the baby will die. You really must know, so the attending was stalling. And it turned out the pregnant woman had a pheochromocytoma, which is a tumor of the

adrenal gland, which can cause you to have high blood pressure. So instead of delivering the baby, they operate on the woman and take out her tumor, and she's okay. And the baby wasn't delivered prematurely."

—NEAL BAER

Bradley Whitford Tony was extraordinary. It was one of the few times I've seen something I was in that I was just as caught up as the audience was. It surprised me that a television show can make you feel that deeply, especially one that I was in! When you're in something, the art is kind of taken out of it and I remember seeing it when it aired, and it was just upsetting. My sister was a nurse at a birthing center at that time, and she was very upset about that episode. It really did traumatize everyone.

Lance Gentile Every ob-gyn I ever knew called me the next day said, "What the hell?" Because every one of their patients called them and thought they had eclampsia. So, we certainly raised awareness of that disorder, that's for sure. I scared all the people to death who were pregnant, which I wasn't really trying to do.

Rick Ladomade That episode really scared the crap out of people. It was very unsettling. And it was not only to the viewers but to the cast. It was shockingly authentic.

In a strange twist, the episode's writer, Lance Gentile, would end up competing with Michael Crichton for an Emmy in the writing category. Crichton was nominated for writing the ER *pilot.*

Lance Gentile This was my first TV show. I said to Michael, "You created the show, man. There's no way I'm going to win." He said, "No, you're going to win." I reminded him that he was

Michael Crichton. I was, like, Dr. Joe Nobody. I said, "Why don't we have a bet?" We bet a hundred dollars. I bet on him. He bet on me. I lost. So, I bought him a really nice pen, like a Cross pen, and put the hundred dollars in the box with the pen, and then I wrapped it up in the pilot episode. I won an Emmy for the second television script I ever wrote in my life. Still to this day, it amazes me that I won that Emmy and he didn't.

6

Preoperative Work

To achieve that unparalleled level of authenticity, John Wells assembled a team of producers, directors, costume designers, and props people to help make his ER feel like a real place that viewers could visit should they ever, say, find themselves injured in a car accident or stabbed in the Windy City's Washington Park. Much of the credit for the frenetic pacing goes to director Rod Holcomb, who set the tone in the pilot by creating what's commonly referred to as a *oner*—a continuous shot that can go on for several minutes without a cutaway. Sorry, fans, of those addictive walks and talks on *The West Wing*: Though the oners were a hallmark of Aaron Sorkin's political drama on NBC, that's not where they got their start. Once associated with movies, oners became the norm on *ER* because they ramped up the drama. But they began out of sheer necessity.

Christopher Chulack If you look at Rod Holcomb's pilot, he used the Steadicam for oners, but not to the extent they evolved [over] the series. When we started shooting the episodes, the cuts would come in and they would be short because everybody talked so fast and they weren't standing around and explaining the medicine. And the procedures were short. Production was like, "You guys have got to fix this. You can't keep doing that." So, the scripts got longer. But now instead of a sixty-page script, we're shooting a seventy-page script. How do you do that in seven days? People say necessity is the mother of invention. I just say necessity is a mother, and we just had to learn how to shoot these long takes. That, in a very unromantic way, is how the oners happened. Then of course we fine-tuned it, and it became a style. I hired Guy Bee, who was the Steadicam operator and who was a big part of that style.

Tommy Schlamme I was given an enormous amount of credit for the oners because it was such a part of the design of *The West Wing*, and I had been shooting that way for quite a bit. I mean, I was shooting long oners on *The Larry Sanders Show*. But in *ER*, they had this space and Rod Holcomb kind of went, "Maybe if I used the Steadicam . . ." I mean, the visceral nature of it, feeling like you're really in that place.

John Wells We used one-shots because we were filming in a real location with low ceilings, so we had limited ability to light. We had to use lighting from the ceilings, so we used a Steadicam to move quickly so we could do the one-shots. The best way to move around was with the Steadicam, since there was no room for the dolly and the place was small. We didn't have time to build the set for the pilot because of the pickup date, so we were on an accelerated timeline. When we got picked up, we built the set to match the location but widened the halls by two feet. We didn't want it to seem like a different place, so we kept those same ceilings.

Jack Orman A lot of shows had open ceilings for lighting and stuff, but the way the show was designed, everything had to be anything that the camera could possibly see that was made to look real, so you'd forget after a while that you're not at a hospital.

John Wells We warned all the actors. I said, "We're just going to turn on overheads. You're not going to see a lot of bounce cards. We're not going to try and make this pretty. All of you are very pretty to begin with."

Guy Norman Bee (Steadicam operator) We would design these scenes where they would walk through hallways and doors. We kept pushing ourselves. They would look at me and go, "You think you could do this where you change direction here and go back through this hallway and into curtain area one and then into trauma room two?" I was up for any challenge because a lot of [producers] of the traditional television were trying to fight their way out of it. The camerawork is a little flashy, if you know what you're looking at, but it sucks the audience in instead of calling attention to itself in a way that takes the audience out of the story.

Christopher Chulack Guy was like a ballerina running around with a Steadicam, this little skinny guy with long hair. It was amazing to see.

Neal Baer Suddenly, you could be on the fly with these doctors running down the hallways.

Noah Wyle When Guy Bee came in—and he's only about 140 pounds—he could work this camera like I've never seen anybody ever before work it, or since. He just was honest. He brought a pace and a vitality to the show through the lens of the Steadicam. We shot everything on the Steadicam after that, because we could. So, the look and feel that I think you're referring to has a lot to do with technology that we began to be able to use because of the talents of the operator.

CCH Pounder Here you are, you've got gurneys barreling down the corridor, things are happening left and right, and it's almost cowboy action in the medical field. It was and still is, I think, a very exciting show to watch.

Guy Norman Bee I used what was called a quote-unquote *lightweight* Panaflex camera, but it was still around 75 pounds at the time. I weighed about 150, so I was carrying half my weight around. It was very physically demanding. I used to bring a bag of T-shirts with me every day, and I would go through like six or seven of them. Once I took the Steadicam off to take a break, I would have a soaking-wet T-shirt.

Christopher Chulack And remember, it was filmed, and that was heavy. A thousand feet of negative in the magazine is not light.

Jonathan Kaplan For a trauma scene, the doctors would set it up, and the camera operator and I would watch as they were setting it up and start to figure out how we were going to shoot it. I never knew this before, but where the head nurse stands is like the head of the bed. It's important, so if someone is walking by and looking in the trauma room, they know who everyone is by where they stood.

Guy Norman Bee Everybody had a real interest in nailing these shots and doing them well. Of course, it was a fate worse than death when we would do these long three-minute shots and if we landed on a doctor and he or she flubbed the line, they were like, "God, Guy, I'm so sorry." It was like a funeral.

Abraham Benrubi I'll tell you, man, you didn't want to be the person who had the last line in those oners, because if you screwed up in any way, we had to shoot the whole thing again, and everybody would give you grief. That was a favorite thing of Clooney's, placing bets on how many takes we were going to have to do and who was going to screw it up. He would often sabotage takes so that he could win the money back.

Yvette Freeman It was scary as crap. How would you like to be the last one in one of those Steadicam shots? We would do, like, twenty-some takes of one scene to make sure everybody was right. So, if you're the last one in that scene speaking and you mess up and it's about the twentieth time, everybody's like, "Oh, shit, we got to do this again."

Ellen Crawford We always had a much larger page count than any normal show, because it moved so fast most of the time. We had twelve-page oners on a regular basis, but just because you do one shot of twelve pages doesn't mean it doesn't take a long time. It had to be perfect. So if you had the last line of a twelve-page oner, it was terrifying. If it's all right up to that point and if you mess up, that's it. You had to do it again.

John Wells Poor extras would come in and get slammed. You know, people who had one line. I would warn them in casting, "You think it's going to be cool, and you think it's no big deal because you have just one line. But I promise you, we'll probably be at the end of a four-minute single take, and then it'll come to you and you've got to say that line and you're going to freak out." And it happened a lot. People would get right to the end and go, "There's the camera."

"I think one of the things that I remember that I'm a little embarrassed to tell is that we had a patient in the ER who was all hooked up to all this stuff. We worked very, very quickly. So we'd get in, shoot, shoot, shoot, shoot, and the minute lunch was called, everybody would dash off for their half hour or whatever, and we left this guy hooked up to the curtain, I forgot about it. I think he had an intubation tube, not down his throat, but in his mouth. Everyone ran off and then the crew would play *Call of Duty* or something on the computers on the set. They were always chomping at the bit to go play *Call of Duty*. We just left this guy who made muffled calls for help. That was not our finest hour as physicians."

—LAURA INNES

Lily Mariye (Lily Jarvik) We were a real ensemble, and it was evident every time we were in a trauma scene. When someone forgets a line, you must start the whole thing over. It could be George Clooney; it could be me. It could be somebody who walks in who we have never seen before, and he has one line. There was a real feeling of equality at a certain point when you're doing those scenes because nobody's more important than anyone else, and everybody has to depend on each other.

Parminder Nagra There was nothing like it on TV. Before the director would even come in, we would choreograph the scene with the medical technician or consultants who were real doctors who worked in ERs, and then they would break down what was going on and we would choreograph the scene, and then the director would come in and maybe tweak a few things for camera.

Guy Norman Bee We tried to put things in our way like moving carts and trays and gurneys and stuff to make it look a lot more treacherous than it really needed to be. We were trying to create that chaos and feeling of insanity.

Jonathan Kaplan I remember I did this oner with something like six pages, and it was nicely choreographed, if I do say so myself. And they all worked it out. It ended up with a close-up of Alex Kingston, and she is telling someone, "Give him sixty of whatever the medication was." I yelled, "Cut!" We got it. Everyone cheered. People really get into it. It was exhilarating.

Laura Innes I never did get hit by a moving camera. I think I probably did more bumping into things myself without help from anybody, because the oners were elaborate and walking backwards with a gurney and stuff like that.

Ellen Crawford I got clocked in the head during one Halloween episode where I was dressed as Florence Nightingale. There was somebody in training with the Steadicam, and there were all these moving pieces.

John Wells If you go back and watch the beginning of the show, for the first two years, we were constantly banging through those doors with the overhead camera, up from the ground, you know. Then we really just got sick of it. In the third or fourth season, we said we're not going to do it anymore.

Yvette Freeman It was like a dance. We were the ones that danced more than the leads, because they stood there and spoke their lines. We came flying in there to hand them something and they turned around and told us what to do. So, you had to know your camera, you had to know how and when to duck. You learned and the show taught.

Pam Morrison (NBC Publicity) The action was so much fun to be around, but it was just hard to not be in the way when you were on that set. They were always spinning the cameras around, and you were like, "Oh, shit, I've got to duck down behind the nurses' station right now."

Ellen Crawford Almost all of the nurses were also musical comedy performers or musical theater performers, which came in handy when you're trying to make your way around a gurney.

Lily Mariye I started [performing with] a ballet company at a very young age. My first job in Los Angeles was as a dancer and a singer and an actor in the movie *The Best Little Whorehouse in Texas.*

George Clooney We were proud of the fact that we weren't milking a scene for emotion. Some kid would die, and we'd be like, "Well, that's too bad." And you would walk away and you'd get a tap from Eriq La Salle, or you'd look over at Julianna and she'd wink because we'd go, *Oh, we didn't ham-bone it up*, which was the danger of a show like this.

Troy Evans There was this scene where something horrible happened at a high school football game. I think a riot took place. The ER was flooded with middle-aged people with broken limbs, cheerleaders, beaten and bloody football players. Jonathan Kaplan is directing. We do the first take and it doesn't work quite right. Jonathan gives a couple of notes, and this football player who's there on this gurney has his arm up and asks Jonathan, "I just wondered, do you have any notes for me, sir?" And Jonathan said, "Do you have any idea what it is that we're doing here? This is the crap that goes in between the commercials. Do your job." He was in the kid's face. And I'll tell you, it worked because when you saw that episode on television, that kid on the gurney looked traumatized.

Lily Mariye There were days where it became normal for us to be there for sixteen to eighteen hours. I remember being in one trauma room with George and Julianna and it was probably midnight. In a real ER, when you use gloves or gauze or whatever packaging you use, you just throw it on the ground. You don't have time to look for a trash can in an emergency. At the end of an emergency, the cleaning people come in and sweep up all the debris on the floor. That night, we'd been there so long, they were just piles of stuff on the ground. In between takes, the three of us just laid on top of the stuff to close our eyes because we were so exhausted.

Guy Norman Bee We used to say we'd go down in the submarine at 7:00 AM and come back up when we broke for lunch. We had what they called a *walk-away lunch,* meaning we would go to the commissary or sometimes we'd all jump in Noah's Jeep and go to In-N-Out Burger, Smoke House in Burbank, or something quick. Then we would come back, and we would go under in the submarine for another six hours.

Once the Steadicam swooped into a trauma room, viewers would get a too-close-for-comfort view of the mayhem that was transpiring on the critical care beds. Wounds gushing. Limbs akimbo. Patient monitors, suction devices, and anesthesia machines filling up space where the doctors and nurses weren't. This was the prop team's Symphony No. 3—a cacophony of gurgling sounds and ominous beeps to make viewers feel like they were actually standing at the foot of the gurney.

Rick Ladomade We always felt if a real surgeon or real doctor was watching the show on TV, they could reach through the television and really pick up the instruments that they would use for that scene or that procedure and be satisfied with it. That's kind of how we were back in the day. We are showing a lot of detail. If you're going to portray what really happens in an ER where you're showing that darker, grittier side of what medicine really is, you want it to feel raw. You can't stay away from what's real, and that means that the audience, whether they want to see it or not, we want them to see that as well. So if you're doing a thoracotomy, you're opening somebody's chest and their heart is beating, you want to see that, right? I mean, that's part of the psychological layer of what that's all about.

Christopher Chulack We always just kept it real, and we didn't exploit it for exploitation's sake. In other words, if it was real and a little gross, that's how we shot it. As writer Lydia Woodward would say, we wouldn't over-egg the pudding. The budget felt tight, at least in the beginning. I mean, we were going through latex gloves, and we were picking them up off the floor to reuse them. Don't use so much blood, everyone!

Anthony Edwards All the good stuff came out of trying to do it for real.

John Wells We had a lot of mistakes. We didn't try to make anything perfect. That added to the chaos of the moment. So you felt there was a certain amount of danger. And some of that danger was the fact that it was all dangerous.

Rick Ladomade We went through gallons and gallons of fake blood on every episode. And there were different kinds of fake blood. There was blood that's kind of watery so we could pump it through IV lines and through machines. Then there's thicker, more coagulated blood that you put on somebody, so it looks like it's real and oozing. And then there's blood that's not going to hurt an actor if you put it into their mouths. And the number of prosthetics! We had about twenty-five giant locker boxes that held our prosthetics. We probably had at one time 120, 150 prosthetic pieces that were just in there for storage. And most of them we could never reuse because they were specifically designed to fit a character. And because they were made of silicone, they would start to slowly dissolve after time. When we would make a prosthetic piece or a chest piece, it would be $8,000 back then. We would spend thousands of dollars, and after a year, they'd disintegrate.

Christopher Chulack Once the show got legs, then we could do whatever we wanted to do, and we became very good at it. Although I got to say, we were always responsible. We never wasted money just because we got a thirty-five share. I mean, we were good producers.

Rick Ladomade Back then, there was a lot of medical equipment. It was a new show at the time, and obviously before Covid, medical companies were a lot more relaxed and willing to work with us. We could really experiment. We didn't just want it to look real. We wanted it to feel real. We would reach out to every medical company. It didn't matter if it was an IV or X-rays, we went after every kind of equipment for every kind of procedure. We were able to use amazing medical props that were key in telling stories, because if you were trying to write a script about something and it was about a certain procedure, you needed to have that procedure. You needed to make sure the actors felt like they were really doing it. We had thousands of props, but it's the little medical equipment, like a scalpel, that sometimes carried the biggest emotional weight at the time that the audience really believed that you were doing something. I always felt like what the audience doesn't see, they don't know.

Jack Orman It wasn't product placement because it wasn't like people watching *ER* were going to go and buy an ultrasound machine. Rick was able to get equipment at little to no cost because it was featured on the show.

Goran Visnjic We would use a thoracotomy to crack open a person's chest for open-heart surgery in trauma. There would be lungs underneath, and those lungs were working. You would see them filling with air. Rick, our prop guy, was underneath the gurney with the pipe in his mouth, and he would be blowing up the lungs. They were so low-tech. There were no artificial intelligence computers, remote controls. No, there was a guy underneath the gurney making those lungs work with his own lungs.

Rick Ladomade It had to be timed perfectly. And we couldn't, obviously, put a real tube down someone's throat. So, what we would do is kind of fake putting them in. Some of the tubes were able to retract a teeny bit.

Maura Tierney The real way we [cheated] on our show is time, because there are things that we'd do in trauma—and there's always a doctor there, and it's all about making it look real, and we're all informed as to what the procedure [was]—but we [did] it really fast. And so when you see it really done, it just doesn't happen in thirty seconds—it happens in three minutes.

John Wells Truthfully, there aren't that many things that happen in any given ER. [The writers] were desperately giving us new medical stuff all the time that we could try, even though they've never been done outside of, like, a neurological suite. But the circumstances change, and I think what works is that we all have a dread of being in these situations with our family members, with ourselves. By changing the circumstances . . . all the context changes.

Scott Grimes John Wells once said, "Hey, man, I'm just opening the newspaper and seeing these things." And reality was far more exaggerated and cheesier than what you could write, like an airplane crashes in the middle of a city. I mean, he read about it and then decided to do it. I think there was an episode where a bunch of people came in after participating in cheese rolling, you know, like what they do in Europe by throwing a block of cheese down a hill? We had a bunch of people come in who were injured in the cheese-rolling thing. I think Laura Innes was directing that episode and she was like, "Okay, we've gone a little too far now." But I think as long as the acting is good and people are selling it, then anything is possible.

George Clooney If you're going to have a baby that's a week old, you can only have 'em on the set for what, thirty seconds or something. And they would cover 'em in strawberry jam, literally.

Julianna Margulies And cream cheese.

John Wells There was a reluctance at the beginning of the show to have certain characters, including babies, die. But that didn't last for long.

Ming-Na Wen Many, many times, I was not able to put the X-ray into the slot to make it stick, or the X-ray would be backwards nine times out of ten. Then our experts would come in and be like, "No, no, no, no, no. That's not how the X-ray's supposed to look. It's supposed to be the other way." We wouldn't know!

Lance Gentile Some people were more interested than others. Noah Wyle took it very seriously. He would also practice suturing. He could sew up your face, let's put it that way.

George Clooney I would see Noah stitching a pig's foot off camera, just practicing.

Jonathan Kaplan There was an informal poll of all the writers. They felt like Noah in real life could pull off a surgery, because he was that much more prepared than everybody else. Noah was more interested in medicine. He would want to know, for example, if you're giving someone medicine, if there was another medicine you could give if it wasn't part of the scene.

Neal Baer I was doing a rotation in the ER at UCLA, and I was sewing up some kid's leg who had cut it open while playing baseball. And the father said, "I bet Noah Wyle could do this better." And I was like, "I bet he could."

John Wells He takes his craft seriously. I mean, if I needed to be intubated and nobody else was around, I'd say grab a knife.

Jonathan Kaplan Others, like Clooney, couldn't care less about the medicine.

Noah Wyle I remember in the first season, George, Tony, and I went across the street from the Warner Bros. lot to the Smoke House restaurant to have lunch one day, and Tony brought his then-infant son, Bailey, to lunch. We were all in costume wearing our lab coats and having our lunch, and Bailey ate a french fry and started to choke on it. The three of us began to panic, and a busboy ended up coming around and clearing the boy's throat. We laughed afterwards at how silly that must've looked for three guys that looked like doctors to be totally losing their cool and having the busboy come in and save the day.

Shane West We were always trying to hide our hands from the camera just in case it looked like we were failing miserably at what we were supposed to be doing. I had a good trick that I developed on my own because we had to put on the rubber gloves so fast in scenes. Your hands start to get sweaty. So the natural trick that was taught to me was to put baking powder or some sort of powder into the gloves that dried it off, and then you could put the gloves on easier. That absolutely worked, but sometimes it still was difficult to do that under the duress of how everything was being filmed. So, what I would do is I sneak off camera, and I would put the glove on the tips of my fingers, sometimes even just the tip of my thumb. So, you'd have five fingers rolled a little bit, just the tips. When the camera got to me, I would pop the glove on. Man, you just wanted to kind of fit in and just not slow the machine down.

Parminder Nagra I do remember Mekhi once putting a tube down the throat of a young actor, and he was like, "Dude, you've got to just bite down on the plastic tube." Then Mekhi had to swap it out for a shorter one to make it look like it had gone in. But then Mekhi pulled out the wire, and he was like, "Oh, shit, it's the wrong way." It wasn't in correctly, but the fact that he even knew that it wasn't in the correct way showed how much we had done it.

George Clooney We all felt like, literally, we were like Doug Hennings. We were like magicians. When you're going to intubate somebody, you've got this big giant tongue depressor that would kill the extra if you had to slam it down their throat . . . the minute the camera gets behind your back, you switch it out, you jam half a tube down somebody.

Noah Wyle I had this trick where I'd hide the short ET tube underneath my sleeve, and when [it came time for] the switch, I'd take it out of my wrist basically and into the guy's mouth. And I thought to myself the other day, *That's so unsanitary.*

Maura Tierney They all make jokes about how many times they were vomited on. I once had to step *over* vomit in one of the episodes, and one of my patients vomited *blood,* but I never got vomited *on.*

Rick Ladomade We always were able to make retractable syringes. They were different sizes, anywhere from a 1 cc to a 10 cc to a 60 cc syringe, depending on what the scene called for. And they were spring-loaded, so the needle would retract back into the housing of the syringe. We got better at making syringes where we could put fluid into the syringe. So, if we were delivering medication and you pumped it, it didn't hurt the patient; the liquid would push into another chamber. But no matter how much research or how much work you put into something, you always feel like something could go wrong. Especially when you're dealing with medical equipment, because it's real stuff. So, we would have to dull the scalpels. We had to make sure the machines are safe. We had to make sure the defibrillators were not real. Our machines didn't have radiation in them for X-rays. There were so many things that we had to make sure was safe to use. Fortunately, we never really had anything major happen with props. Sure, sometimes when you're trying to create a scene, the hose comes off or breaks and the blood doesn't squirt. But we never stopped, and we were always driven by wanting more. We never settled for what was just good enough.

"One time I was on a plane and somebody got sick. Literally, this is not a joke. I mean, I'm not embellishing, I'm not lying in any shape or form. They asked for a doctor. I saw a few people look at me, and I'm like, 'Look, I don't know what you're looking at me for. If it's not in the script, I can't help you.'"

—MEKHI PHIFER

In the beginning, most people assumed Lyn Paolo's job as ER*'s costume designer was relatively easy; after all, everyone just wears scrubs in a hospital, right? She quickly set them straight.*

Lyn Paolo Back then, most shows featured three people in a room. There wasn't a 360 shot of a hospital with two hundred extras and forty people in the cast. Every person who came through that door, we had to tell their story in thirty seconds. Is this a gang member? Is this a Midwestern housewife? Is this a kid from a hockey team? So, to me, it was unbelievably daunting. Back then, most ER doctors wore green, and most surgical residents wore blue. If you're a medical professional, you know exactly who everyone is by the color of their scrubs or what's in their pockets. That was a note Michael Crichton had given early on, and I do think we achieved that on *ER*.

Ellen Crawford We wore peach scrubs for the longest time.

Lyn Paolo Peach was chosen early on, and I think it was more about availability than anything else. But it was never a great color for Julianna Margulies.

Lily Mariye The company stopped making that color. So, the wardrobe people said, "Okay, we must find a new color." They got this deep, beautiful maroon color. So, Lyn changed us all into that.

Lyn Paolo We did tests on Julianna, and she looked great in the burgundy. Then Steven Spielberg, God bless him, said, "The blood is the story. We want to see the blood. The burgundy scrubs would never show that." That's why we went to the pink.

Lily Mariye We were all like, "Oh, you're right."

Lyn Paolo Another part of *ER* that was difficult is that every time someone came through the door and you saw who they were, we had five, six, seven copies [of their costumes] that had to be prepared so if they were cut and if their injury continued to bleed, we had enough multiples to reset.

Abraham Benrubi I was always amazed, because I couldn't even stand on the stage of *ER* without sweating, and George would be playing basketball for an hour straight in his white lab coat and not sweat at all. He had this weird immaculate thing where he just wasn't dirty.

Lyn Paolo It wasn't just George, by the way. All the lads would be out there playing. The hoop was right outside of Stage 11. But look, they were all supposed to be untidy and working long hours. It never bothered me, and we always had multiples. My concern was always more about there were always cars zooming down the road and one of them would get run over. But I never had a problem with them playing basketball. My God, they deserved it. They were working so hard.

7

Medical Minute

A Look Back at "Motherhood"

Season 1, Episode 24 | May 11, 1995
Written by Lydia Woodward
Directed by Quentin Tarantino

Huge ratings weren't the only way to gauge *ER*'s success in its first season. The show was so hot that Quentin Tarantino—who had just turned Hollywood on its ear with *Pulp Fiction*—rang up John Wells and expressed interest in directing. He was assigned a Mother's Day–themed episode that juxtaposed the birth of Susan Lewis's niece with the death of Peter Benton's mom. Valerie Perrine guest stars as Susan's flighty mother, while Kathy Griffin shows up briefly as a Little Rangers scout leader named Delores. There's even a beat involving Doug Ross, who changes his mind about moving in with his latest gal pal, Diane (played by Lisa Zane), before Carol Hathaway is set to marry John Taglieri in the finale.

Warren Littlefield John calls me and he goes, "Hey, Tarantino wants to direct an episode." And I was like, "You're kidding me. Fantastic. Do it." We were kind of the shit back then. The show was reaching a crazy level of popularity, and artists were eager to work on it. I mean, it was [on] the cover of *Newsweek*. And the first season, it was this phenomenon. And you had a cast that was brilliant and fun to work with, and so the word kind of got out. It had a little Tarantino flair, and it was a great episode of *ER*.

Julianna Margulies He was such a big fan of the show.

Lydia Woodward Quentin wasn't lined up to direct ages in advance the way you pretty much have directors set for the next four or five episodes. That episode was already in the works. We knew what it was going to be. It was not at all designed with Quentin in mind. It was completely independent of Quentin. This was episode 24 of the first season. Normally, you stop at 22, but the network asked us to do two additional. We were so exhausted that year. It was a very, very grueling year. But John Wells and I laughed because he and I have worked together on shows, and we're so used to people cutting us short on episodes and canceling us after *x* number of episodes. So, when they asked for two more, we were like, "Well, yeah, of course we're going to do two more."

Sherry Stringfield With everyone that season, the [producers] were kind of like, "We're going to dive in [to the characters' lives] a little bit." And that episode was one of the earliest examples of those conversations coming to be. They wanted to tease out a little bit of [the characters'] personal lives, so audiences would be like, "Oh, they're not just doctors. They're people, too, like you and me." And Susan's relationship with Chloe, they succeeded there. Especially with Tarantino directing.

Julianna Margulies It was a thrill to work with him, because oftentimes it was a hard show to direct. And George used to say that the worst thing was when you'd see the new director for the episode come and open the script—this huge, gigantic script—and they would go [*sighs*]. You just knew you weren't in good hands when someone sighed so heavily like that. But with Quentin Tarantino, he had everything planned, and he wanted to be so in control of his work that he only did one take. He only did one take, so they didn't have a choice to edit.

Abraham Benrubi Alexis Arquette was a [bystander] in that episode, because I remember there was a scene where she was supposed to come bursting through the doors and she wasn't quite getting it. So, Tarantino threw down his headset and said, "I want you to do this." He went out and came running and slid across the floor through the ambulance doors. He just got super physical with it. Quentin got the take he wanted.

Lydia Woodward He changed nothing. He was quite possibly the easiest director I have ever worked with in my entire career—not that other directors were difficult or anything like that. He literally only added one thing. When Susan is trying to get her sister to the hospital because she's going to give birth, she's rummaging around her apartment looking for her car keys. It was Quentin's idea to use this thing called the Clapper. There was this weird thing called the Clapper that was advertised on TV all the time where you clapped and your keys made a noise. It was this electronic deal. Anyway, Quentin said, "Let's have her clap to find her keys." And I said, "Sure, that sounds good." Quentin only wanted that funny little tidbit of a thing.

"I'll never forget this. We were eating pizza at the big nurses' station, at the front desk. And it was very important to Quentin that the pizza was pepperoni pizza. And at the time, I was a vegetarian. So, I went to take a bite of the pizza, and I picked the pepperoni off. And he said, 'Cut.' And I said, 'What did I do?' And he goes, 'You have to eat the pepperoni.' And I said, 'Well, I'm a vegetarian.' And he goes, 'Uh-uh. Well, Uma ate a burger.' He was referring to the scene in *Pulp Fiction* where [her character] eats a burger. And I looked at him, he just stared at me, and I went, 'I got you. I got you.' Because, it was like he was saying, 'Don't be precious.' There's a reason he wanted pepperoni pizza."

—JULIANNA MARGULIES

Rick Rossovich I got to watch him work his way around a bit. He was red hot at that moment so that was a tell, but I don't know that he brought it any more forward than where the runaway train was headed.

Christopher Chulack He was like a kid. He just loved it. He showed up on the first or second day wearing scrubs.

The episode began with a decent helping of gore: A man was brought into the ER after he was impaled with a rebar; Peter Benton let John Carter pull it out of the man's gut during the delicate surgery. Susan Lewis also got to deliver her niece—with a special request by Chloe to either play or, ultimately, recite the lyrics from The Beatles' "Blackbird." Then Susan Lewis joined Carol Hathaway for a special retreat to the hospital's roof for some much-needed rest and relaxation.

Lydia Woodward I have no idea how that rebar idea came about, except we had a million stories from ERs all over the place, and we'd all been down to [Los Angeles County+USC Medical Center] and done a lot of observation there. Basically, there's almost nothing you could do in an ER setting that hasn't happened. I'm quite sure many people have been impaled on rebar over history. [With "Blackbird,"] I don't know about it being a personal favorite so much as an album I was very familiar with from way, way back in the day. Chloe was such a quirky offbeat, deadbeat character and I wanted something retro for her to be into, something very much not from the '90s. I specifically wanted Lewis to sing "Blackbird" at the end for its resonance vis-à-vis Chloe—"broken wings"—and the baby—"you were only waiting for this moment to arrive." Oddly, I was kind of into French rap at the time, so that's why I threw that into the birthing scene. Sometimes it's fun to be a writer!

Sherry Stringfield That sunglasses scene [on the roof] was very fun to shoot.

Lydia Woodward I wrote all of that.

Julianna Margulies [Sherri and I] put on the sunglasses, and we were both like, "Okay, we—our characters—would never wear sunglasses like this, indoors, at work." But it's Quentin Tarantino. Anything's possible. He had us take off the sunglasses, and then when we saw [the walk] in slow motion, I just thought, *Oh my God, this is the coolest thing ever.*

The rooftop scene was captured in an unforgettable photograph by NBC's Chris Haston that you can still find on the internet today.

Chris Haston (NBC Photographer) In between shots, I said, "Let's get a picture of the ladies up on the roof with the buildings in the background." They were drinking Cokes on lawn chairs. I started taking a picture of them with their Coke bottles and one of 'em was smoking, but there wasn't going to be smoking in the scene. Quentin goes, "Hey, can I get in on this?" Then I think they might've all lit up and had cigarettes, and they rolled up their sleeves. And Quentin put his arms around them like, *We're badass.*

I took this picture, and I got a call from [NBC's head of photo] Paul McGuire a little while later [because John Wells was concerned] it wasn't the image of the show. But to me, it truly was. The rawness of *ER* is sort of behind the scenes. This is what these nurses would do. They're hanging on the rooftop, drinking Cokes and smoking cigarettes. [He was afraid] it was one of those "I never want this photographer back on set, and I'm going to get in trouble for this." But the next week, I ran into John Wells on the set and said, "Hi, John, how's it going?" He goes, "Hey, great, man. Good to see you." He didn't know it was me. The important thing is that photos created currency. Having a half page in *Time* magazine would've been worth half a million dollars to get that picture there. But this ran for free, and it probably brought up the viewership. I think that was very iconic and a nice feather in my cap.

Even though the episode was considered a success—it would end up averaging 33.1 million people—it did have at least one major detractor.

Lydia Woodward I can tell you that Michael Crichton considered it, and bless his heart, Michael Crichton considered it the worst-directed *ER* episode to date.

Neal Baer The only time I know that we heard from Michael was when Quentin Tarantino directed the fantastic episode, and Michael got all bent out of shape about that for reasons I don't know why. I thought it was great. And I love the variety. I love the different voices of writers. John didn't change voices. There was a real freshness in those years.

8

Pain Management

The last place you want to find an ill-natured caregiver is in a hospital, but John Wells and his writers figured out a way to introduce doctors who were both brilliant yet occasionally dislikable at the same time. Their first such irritant was Laura Innes as Dr. Kerry Weaver, a by-the-book chief resident with a real knack for getting under everyone's skin. She was followed two years later by Paul McCrane's Dr. Robert Romano, an egotistical surgeon who made life absolute hell for characters like Peter Benton and Dave Malucci. But Robert Romano, like Kerry Weaver, also had the ability to show tremendous compassion, like when he secretly signed to Benton's son, Reese, to "take care of your father," or when Weaver tried to protect Jeanie Boulet, whose job as a physician's assistant was briefly in jeopardy after she tested positive for HIV.

Jack Orman I saw them as conflict characters, not villains.

John Wells Michael Ironside and many others played additional antagonists. We never perceived them as villains, just characters with different POVs.

Laura Innes I remember one of the producers, Lydia Woodward, came up to me outside of the soundstage and started talking about the testing they would do. The audience literally has dials they turn when they are more interested or less interested. She said when my character comes on, there's a spike. The interest can come from maybe being enraged or maybe curious, I don't know. And then lucky for me, there was an article in *Entertainment Weekly*. It was a review of the season, and it had a caricature of me. It said, "This is what this show needs, some more conflict." Those things conspired to help me a lot.

Paul McCrane I think what they intended was that Romano was a highly competitive guy. His MO was that he had to be sort of top dog, so he would mess with or jokingly put down anybody he felt even the slightest bit of competition with or threatened by. At least that's the way I saw it. That's the way I played him. So yes, he would sort of be insulting to maintain his fragile, insecure sense of dominance.

John Levey Paul embraced that that was his role, and he became this snarling little bastard of a dog. He loved twirling his mustache in the ER. The best actors get to do something that is outside of themselves. They love the idea of accessing a little part of them that isn't really in their life. Who would ever play Medea if they didn't think it was going to be juicy and fun?

Paul McCrane It's funny because after the first season and when they asked me to come back, there was a very, very brief period where I kind of lamented that they seemed to be writing the character as one flavor.

Laura Innes I was in an old department store buying a quilt on a Friday morning [after *ER* aired] and I heard these two women talking and looking at me. I had no idea what was going on, because I had never been on a high-profile show like that. And I heard one of them say, "I just want to slap her across the face." And I was like, *Oh my God. I guess they're talking about my character.* So, I brought my quilt to the counter and was *super* nice to the cashier.

Paul McCrane There were also times, obviously, where Romano clearly did respect people who were good at their jobs. It was a dual thing. I don't mean to make a whole thesis about this, but I think there was a duality to it in that he personally had to consistently, even conceivably, engage in dominance dynamics, but also understand and respect when people were good at their jobs.

Lily Mariye I think we as characters thought Kerry was tough and sometimes not fair. But I always would give her the benefit of the doubt because she was a woman in a male-dominated profession, and God knows, my character understood what that was like. I felt like she could be irritating, but she overcame a lot to get there. And if that's what she had to do to do it, God bless her.

Paul McCrane I enjoyed the fact that the way they wrote the character allowed me to have an outsized impact for a minimal amount of time on-screen. I thought they used the character smartly that way, as sort of a dramaturge. That's smart. You don't want to soften him up and make him too humanized, make him less reprehensible too often, because then he loses his impact.

Then the few times they do crack his humanity open a little bit, it ends up having more impact.

Jack Orman One of my favorite scenes from Mark Greene's exit arc was after Greene's cancer came back and Corday was having a moment by herself in the lounge. Romano came in, and she just sort of ranted about it and said, "What am I supposed to do? Go home and watch him die?" Romano said, "Yes, you're supposed to take care of him until he dies." He definitely had that human side to him, and I think he cared for her. I think we saw it on occasion, but we were also very careful not to go treacly every single episode, because we don't want to give the audience a toothache.

One of the characteristics that helped to humanize Weaver was the fact that she used a cane to walk. But it took some time before viewers learned why.

Laura Innes The writers said to me, "You know what? We don't really know, and we don't want to have to decide right now." They liked that it was a bit of a mystery. People didn't know what her deal was. I ended up going to observe a physician who had gone through polio, so she used a cuff crutch. I also have an older sister who had polio. So, I had a little bit of knowledge that sometimes you're stronger and some days you're weaker. So, it didn't necessarily have to be wickedly consistent.

Noah Wyle [Her] commitment to that cane and the way that [she] embodied the physical performance took a toll over the course of the season. I remember [her] telling me [she] had to do extensive bodywork just because of the way [she] was spending so many hours a day in a difficult body position.

Laura Innes I had a little bit of stuff. The bottom of my spine has a little curve. I mean, it doesn't really bother me, but yeah, they said there's a little hook there. I was like, *Shoot.* But you know who helped me a lot was [technical advisor] Jon Fong, who worked with us. He said, "When you're not in the scene, switch arms and just use the other arm, so you'll balance." I was like, *I never thought of that.*

Innes had some trepidation about speaking publicly about her character's hip dysplasia.

Laura Innes I got a publicist who's still a dear friend, and I remember saying to him, "Well, I don't know if I want to do stuff out in public, because then it will sort of dissolve the mystery of this character's disability." Of course, my publicist was like, "What the hell are you talking about? You're going on a talk show and you're going to talk about this." But the other interesting aspect was that during this period, it was considered fine for somebody who didn't have a particular disability to play that role. I have a friend who is a comic, and she is in a wheelchair. After I got the part, I started getting scuttlebutt that this was not cool. So, I called my friend Nancy and was like, "What's this about?" She very passionately and thoughtfully articulated to me the problem. At that point in time, she was kind of like, "Well, this is the nature of the world that we're in. What you can do is from the inside try to create more opportunities for differently abled people." If I were casting this show now, I would not cast me, unfortunately. Selfishly, the timing worked for me, but gosh, it's been an enormously interesting and important thing to keep learning about, to understand the most effective and common-sense way to deal with this challenge.

Weaver's condition was eventually repaired in surgery, and she would remain in the ER until season 13, when her character left to take a TV job in Florida. But she wouldn't be the last doctor in the ER to work with a disability. In the first episode of season 9, a helicopter rotor severed Romano's arm as he was trying to evacuate a patient during a monkeypox outbreak.

Paul McCrane John Wells and Chris Chulack asked me to come in for a meeting and described how they intended to have my character lose his arm. And I said, "Okay, so how much longer will I be on the show?" Because I couldn't fathom a one-arm surgeon staying on the show. And John was like, "No, no, we're not getting rid of the character. We're just doing this." And honestly, in my mind, I thought, *That's very sweet, but I can't fathom I'll be on for too long.* It's not like I arm-wrestled them, so to speak. I got what they were planning for the character. I just said, "Okay, you're the writers, I'm the actor. I'll do what I can."

Little did he know that his character lost his arm to divert attention away from a medical snafu the writers made in the previous episode. In the initial script for the season 8 finale, dubbed "Lockdown," two kids are diagnosed with monkeypox after coming into the ER covered in white pustules. Their father had just taken his family to South Africa for work, where it is likely they contracted the virus.

Jack Orman One of our director-producers, Jonathan Kaplan, who is a very talented guy with a lot of passion, rightly pointed out, "This just sounds like a letdown. You just kind of laugh when you hear monkeypox, even though it's a serious disease." I told him he had a good point. So, I turned to Joe Sachs, and said, "Could it be smallpox?" And Joe says, "Yeah, it could be smallpox." So, I'm like, hey, problem solved. Just keep it smallpox. We have our great cliffhanger.

"Both of my kids were born at Cedars-Sinai in Los Angeles, and both times were during the run of *ER*. I remember this experience of walking down a hallway and I saw some exhausted residents who had been there on their twenty-fifth hour or whatever coming toward me. They looked up and knew me, didn't know from where, but their eyes quickly averted because they knew I was trouble. It was both fun and disturbing because I also can't tell you how many times people who worked in medicine and particularly who worked with surgeons said, 'Oh my God, you're exactly like all the surgeons I work with.' I was both shocked, a little amused, and disturbed."

—PAUL McCRANE

The episode ends without the ER receiving an official diagnosis, but the doctors continue to suspect it's smallpox.

Jack Orman We finish everything up and go on hiatus. We go to our retreat in late May or early June to start to brainstorm the next season. *Okay, where did we leave off? Smallpox in the ER.* And then Joe says something like, "Yeah, well, this is going to be interesting because now we're now living in two medical realities." I said, "What?" He said, "Well, in the real world, smallpox is eradicated. And now in our fictional world, smallpox exists." I said, "You told me it could be smallpox!" So now we're in a situation where we must make it monkeypox, which was kind of a letdown. It's going to feel *really* lame when people come back to the show after three months and find out the cliffhanger was monkeypox.

So, I said, "We can deal with this for an act. But then we must have something *really* big happen as a misdirect." I remember we were sitting there on a lawn in a circle like middle schoolers, waiting for the bell to ring. *What are we going to do? What are we going to do?* And I remember R. Scott Gemmill to my left saying, "Well, we could cut somebody's arm off." I looked up and I said, "That's it. But who?" We spent the next twenty minutes landing on Romano.

Season 9 opens in the Democratic Republic of the Congo. A missionary doctor is seen taking a sample from a sick child who is covered in pustules. A monkeypox outbreak is confirmed.

Jack Orman We come back in [episode 1 of season 9], and there's still a handful of patients in the ER. Most of the episode is spent with them in quarantine. But we still need to get a few out. At the end of the first act, they start arguing about who's taking which helicopter. Romano's out there with Kovač, and Romano commandeers the helicopter. Then his clipboard goes flying, and he goes to pick up the clipboard and his arm is cut off. Everybody's like, "Where did that come from? Oh my God." As soon as we cut off his arm, the drama follows Romano's arm. Nobody's going to care that they waited all summer to find out it was monkeypox.

Writers' retreat on Orcas Island, Washington, in 1995. L to R: Chris Chulack, Paul Manning, Mimi Leder, Lydia Woodward, Carol Flint, and John Wells. (*Courtesy Lydia Woodward*)

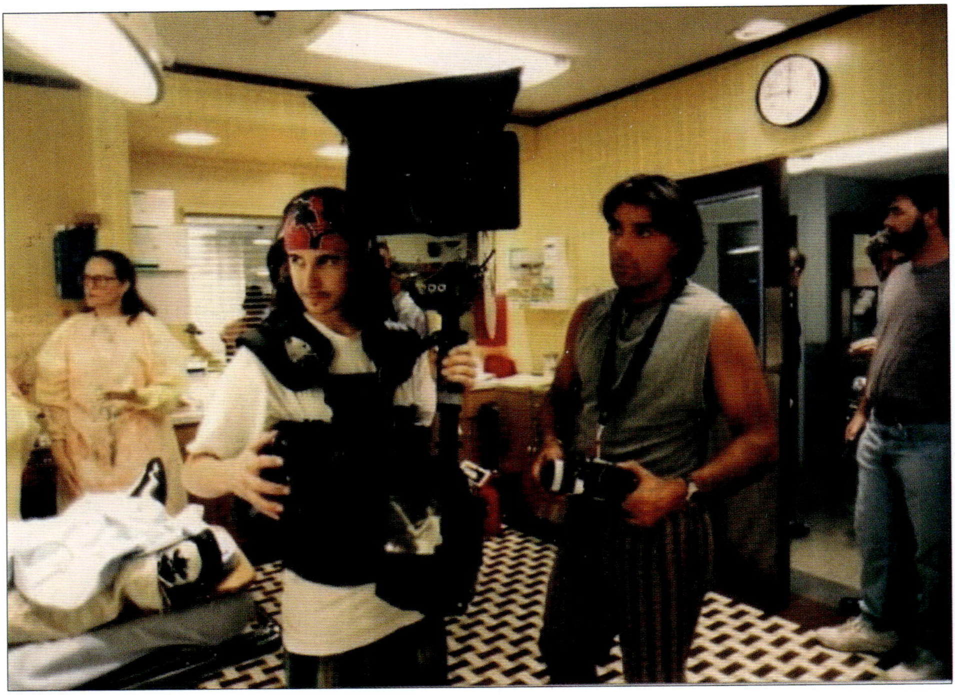

L to R: Steadicam operator Guy Norman Bee, first assistant cameraman Terence Nightingall, and first assistant director Tommy Burns on the *ER* set (*Courtesy Guy Norman Bee*)

(ABOVE) L to R: Anthony Edwards, Lydia Woodward, and George Clooney on the *ER* set
(*Courtesy Lydia Woodward*)

Ellen Crawford with director Quentin Tarantino
(*Courtesy Ellen Crawford*)

Carol Flint and Tommy Schlamme while shooting the live episode of *ER* (*Courtesy Carol Flint*)

Lily Mariye, Conni Marie Brazelton, Deezer D, Ellen Crawford, and Laura Cerón (*Courtesy Ellen Crawford*)

On location at Union Station in Chicago, shooting the episode "Union Station" for season 3. L to R: Anthony Edwards, John Wells, Carol Flint, cinematographer Richard Thorpe, Lydia Woodward, Sherry Stringfeld, and Chris Chulack. (*Courtesy Lydia Woodward*)

Ellen Crawford, Abraham Benrubi, Laura Innes, and John Aylward taking a break from filming a Halloween episode (*Courtesy Ellen Crawford*)

L to R: Ewan McGregor and Julianna Margulies in Chicago shooting "The Long Way Around" from season 3 (*Courtesy Lydia Woodward*)

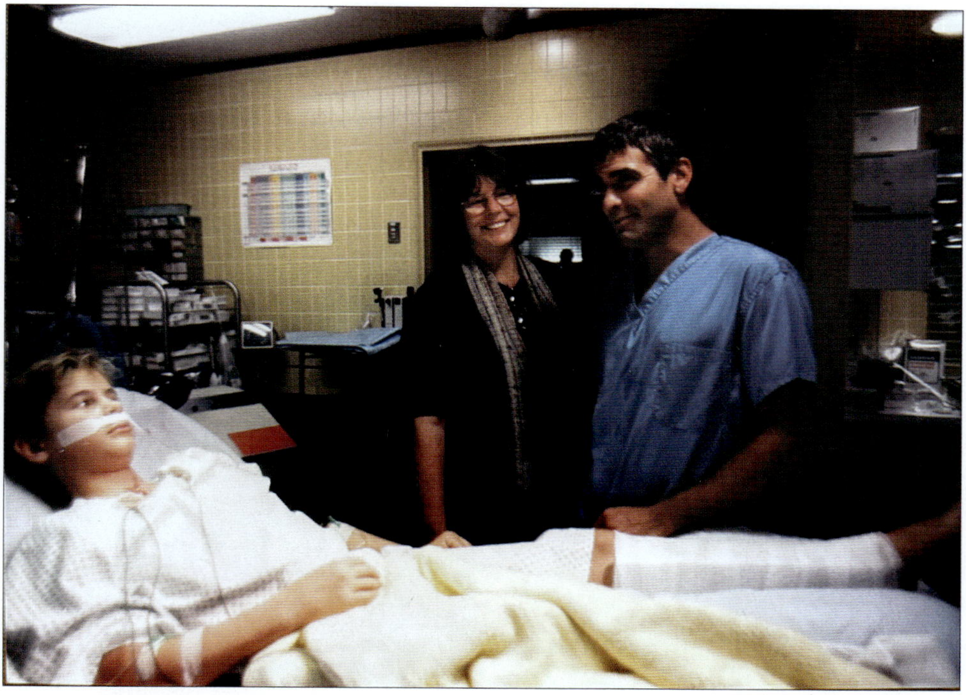

Lydia Woodward and George Clooney on the *ER* set (*Courtesy Lydia Woodward*)

ER's soundstage on the Warner Bros. lot (*Courtesy Lynette Rice*)

Paul McCrane There were a lot of interesting opportunities, including doing a mock robotic movement of a robotic arm and all that kind of stuff. It did offer a brutal way to humanize the character, to not only give Romano some schadenfreude or comeuppance but also to see his character suddenly put in such a disabled condition and to watch how he responds to that position.

Ultimately, McCrane was right; there's only so much you can do with a one-armed doctor in the ER. In season 10, the actor was told by the writers that Romano's story had come to an end. The question, however, was how.

Paul McCrane I absolutely would've stayed on that show until the bitter end had it been my choice, no question. There are different types of contracts for actors. You either sign for a certain number of episodes, or you are in what's called an *all-shows-produced contract,* meaning you get paid for every episode no matter how much you're in it or not. And at that point, I had an all-shows-produced contract for my character, and John Wells immediately said, "But don't worry, we're going to pay you off through the rest of the season." It was a nice severance package, so to speak. And for the briefest moment, I think John said something like, "Look, I'm sure you're interested in some other opportunities and things like that." I checked in to say, "Have I given anybody the impression that I'm unhappy here?" They said, "No, no." So honestly, I did a quick calculation in my mind, and I realized this was not a conversation about a decision to be made. This was me being informed in a very professional and kind way.

Right around the same time, Scott Grimes joined the show as Dr. Archie Morris, but in a very limited capacity—or so he thought.

Scott Grimes I was supposed to do only two episodes. I was supposed to kind of kill somebody or be responsible for them dying on the table, and I quit. I remember when we were filming the scene where I quit, and one of the crew members walked up to me and said, "Hey, I just read episode 6 and you're in it." And I'm like, "I'm quitting. Literally, we're doing the scene right now." They brought me back to kill me in the helicopter crash that Romano ended up dying in.

In episode 8 of season 10, Romano catches Morris smoking weed outside of the ER and threatens to expose him. But what ends up happening is a helicopter transporting patients off the roof malfunctioned and tumbled into the courtyard, crushing Romano to death.

Scott Grimes The original scene was, I'm the one that died in the helicopter crash. Here's my guess, not to be controversial or anything. That was at a time when *ER* was being shaken up and there was a lot of money being spent on the show, as it should have been. I just think they were trying to get rid of big money and keep the little money. Paul McCrane just made way more money than me. He was awesome. He ended up directing a bunch of episodes. They just switched it up and said, "This other redhead is a little cheaper, so let's keep him."

Paul McCrane The rumor I heard after the fact was that they wanted to have a spectacular ending for a character, and they had decided on this helicopter drop as the way to do it. There was a horse race going on over which character they were going to take out. I don't know who else was on that list, but Romano was one of them. I don't know how the final decision was made. So, my understanding was that they were planning on a spectacular demise, and somehow, I won. This could be entirely bullshit.

John Wells I can't speak to what Paul McCrane thought!

David Zabel It did end up being Romano, but I don't remember starting off from the place of like, "Oh, we've got to kill somebody. Who are we going to kill?" I just remember thinking like, well, this is such an epic event that's happening in the hospital that it should feel like we don't get out unscathed. Our little world in this ER doesn't get out unscathed, so someone's going to pay a price. Maybe that's a different way of saying the same thing. It wasn't quite as bloodlusty as like, *We've got to kill somebody!*

Paul McCrane What I recall saying was, "You're very kind to say you're sorry about the timing" and "I can't say that I'm not surprised, and I can't say that I'm not disappointed, but you have nothing to apologize to me for. I came on this show seven years prior as a guest that became a recurring, then a cast regular, which also started my directing career." I have nothing but gratitude, and that's honestly how I felt. So that was that. My Moby Dick came back and took out the rest of me.

Scott Grimes If you think about it, nobody ever found out that I was smoking weed, because Romano was the only witness.

9

Medical Minute

A Look Back at "Hell and High Water"

Season 2, Episode 7 | November 9, 1995
Written by Neal Baer
Directed by Christopher Chulack

Fans of George Clooney in a tuxedo have writer Neal Baer to thank for this high-octane episode following Doug Ross as he saves a boy stuck in a drain during a hellacious storm. Casual viewers no doubt marveled at the episode's high production value, when, in reality, a movie light attached to a crane doubled as a helicopter while *The Waltons'* pond on the Warner Bros. lot served as a waterway that threatened to take out a young boy. And the rain? That came courtesy of a porous hose that was strung across the scene. But at least the water was heated.

Neal Baer A few years back, I ran into George's wife, Amal, and I said, "I put your husband in a tuxedo." She was like, "Oh, *ER*." Because when I did "The Gift" in year one, the Christmas show, I put George in a tuxedo for a Christmas party, and he got in a fight with Carol's boyfriend, played by Rick Rossovich. People were like, "Oh my gosh, you put George in a tux. He's so handsome!" When I got the luck of the draw to do George's episode in year two, "Hell and High Water," the storyline was that he was not getting picked up at the ER because he was too reckless in terms of doing stuff for kids and in his character's private life. So, I thought, I'm going to put him in a tuxedo and make him a reluctant hero and then put him on the helicopter.

Lyn Paolo We got ten tuxedos for that episode, and they were all Armani.

Christopher Chulack He starts off in the ER working, and then he goes to a job interview in his suit or whatever, and then next time you pick him up, he's driving his car to go on a date to some function and he's in a tuxedo. It was the first time we really went outside. The story took you outside of the ER, and it was a little bit of a stretch for us. And I remember trying to figure out how to shoot it and whatnot. *The Today Show* was following our production. I went to ask John about something. I was standing in front of his desk, and I said, "I think I want to use the pond back here." I said, "I just hope it turns out."

Lyn Paolo Every episode got bigger as the studio realized that they had a hit on their hands. I mean, sometimes it felt like we were doing an action movie.

Neal Baer George is the hero, and he ends up staying in the ER because we can't obviously get rid of George in season 2. We shot in a tunnel that we made on the lot and in [the pond].

Christopher Chulack We shot Clooney's car getting a flat tire and a little boy coming up to him asking him to save his brother near Lake Shore Drive.

Neal Baer The grate [over the tunnel] breaks, and they are flooded in this lake. Doug can't find the kid. And he's screaming, "Ben, Ben!" He dives in, and he comes up. We always do the series of three. He lifts the kid up, and the helicopter above is putting light down on George as this Christlike savior. I wrote that the light is shining on him.

Christopher Chulack We figured out how to make it look like it was a helicopter light. I just visualized the whole sequence where he pulls the kid out of the water and lays him down and does the tracheotomy, and then we hit him with a light. It wasn't all that complicated. There were a couple of angles on it, and George was a little pissed at me, because before he gets the kid on land, there are three cuts where George pops in and out of the water. Then he comes up with the kid, the helicopter light hits him, and then he has to walk out of the water and walk out of the lake and come up on shore, right? George was having trouble because the kid wasn't light. He was thirteen or fourteen years old. He had to walk up the bank of this lake, and he really had trouble getting out. And he says, "Couldn't you have cast a lighter kid?" I said, "George, you want a light kid or the best actor?"

George Clooney This kid, the actor, was like thirteen years old, and he's like, "I don't rehearse." And I was like, "Well, I'll tell you what, when I'm on your show, we won't rehearse."

"George gave everything to it. They were in water all night long for days. It was an amazing feat. It wasn't a fake night; it was a real night. I remember the props people. One person was at one end of the tunnel and the other was at the other end, throwing in leaves and branches. They were feeding the debris into the tunnel, and then it was coming out, and they would gather it and do it again."

—NEAL BAER

Christopher Chulack The water was warmed. We had a big tank. It was a big deal to make the water warm, to keep it flowing and blow it out of the pipe. Even in the tunnel and in the tube, the water was heated, and it was clean, obviously. That was quite an undertaking by our special effects guy, Scotty Forbes. It was a big deal.

Neal Baer I remember Cameron Diaz came for a visit. She was a friend of George's, and she came to the set one night when we were shooting, just hanging out. I was like, "Oh my God, Cameron Diaz is standing right here!" I've run into her several times since, and she's like, "You're the one who shot the episode with George in the tunnel in the rain."

Lyn Paolo We had so much fun on that episode, even though everyone was soaking and it was miserably cold.

Christopher Chulack won a Directors Guild of America award for helming the episode and was nominated for an Emmy, but he lost out to Chicago Hope*'s Jeremy Kagan.*

Christopher Chulack I was disappointed about the Emmy, but that's the way it goes. At the end of the Emmys, they told everybody who has an Emmy to come on up onstage. We won for the show that year, so all the producers went up, including me. I felt a tap on my shoulder, and I turn around and it's John Frankenheimer, who won an Emmy. He's a big, tall dude, six foot four. He looks at me with his blue eyes and says, "You should have fucking won tonight. I voted for you. I was on the blue-ribbon panel. I don't know what those other people were thinking. You're a hell of a director, man." We became pretty good buddies.

10

Funny Bone Specialist

Before George Clooney ever set foot on Stage 11, he used to refer to himself as "the world's richest unknown actor." Having spent a decade either accepting unforgettable roles or starring in failed TV pilots, Clooney admitted to *Entertainment Weekly* back in 1996 that "I was lucky enough never to get really famous from any earlier show." So, when the time came to don the green scrubs for a drama that finally looked to have some legs, Clooney was not about to take anything for granted.

"In the pilot episode, George pulled us all into his trailer. He said, 'Okay, guys, this is going to be different this time around. I've done a lot of shows, and what's killed all of them in one way or another is a lack of cohesion,'" Noah Wyle said in Warren Littlefield's *Top of the Rock: Inside the Rise and Fall of Must See TV.* "'This is the show that's going to do it differently. We're going to be nice to everybody. We're going to know our lines. We're going to be on time. We're not going to have any division between cast and crew. This is going to be family.' He just laid it all out there, and we were young enough and green enough to fall in lockstep behind him."

From there, the tone was set. Anthony Edwards might have been the ship's captain—he came in with the biggest street cred, having starred in *Top Gun* and *Revenge of the Nerds*—but Clooney was its cruise director. He made it his job to keep the set humming and happy.

Christopher Chulack He and Anthony were a very good team. They didn't get things out of hand. They were like referees. George was just easygoing. He was very smart, and savvy about the business on all levels. John Wells said the cast and the rest of the crew took the lead from Tony and George. John would say, "We have a self-cleaning oven for a cast." There were no petulant people. I mean, the show was getting forty shares. This thing was a rocket, this show. And it could have turned bad, but everybody stayed in line, and it was quite something. It was quite a family.

John Levey I think he recognized that this was a role that could take him where he wants to go. George had done so many pilots, so much work. Anthony was another kind of leader, but he had basically come from features, so television was a little new to him. George organized screenings for all the actors on Wednesday nights in advance of the premieres, and he taught Noah about the ratings. That first year, I think they rented some kind of bus to go to the Emmys together. They really became the first four guys and two gals. That six became quite a unit.

Jonathan Kaplan It was wonderful working with George. He's too good to be true. Everyone would always say, "What's he *really* like?" They want to hear dirt, and there's no dirt.

Ellen Crawford It's hard to come in for one day or more into a company that you don't know. It's not an easy gig.

Guy Norman Bee I remember we had a two-hour lunch one day to hear the Warner Bros. lawyers talking about watching our mouths around these [extras]. It was mainly to cover themselves, but George was like, "This is my family. I came to work. You guys are protecting yourself. What are you doing to protect us? One of the grips had a wallet taken out of one of his carts. How are you protecting us? These people who get these jobs, these background artists, there are no background checks." It was a little testy for a bit.

Rick Rossovich There was one director on a couple of episodes, but thankfully, I didn't have to work under him. I recall hearing secondhand that he lost his cool on set when a guest actor couldn't remember his lines. The director chastised him, I guess, and George stepped in and came to his defense as it devolved.

Lance Gentile By the time I directed, it was like the end of season 1, and things had gone George's way. We used to do a lot of Steadicam shots, and I would say, "The camera comes around here, and you'll be there and say whatever." But George would totally ignore me and do whatever he wanted. And so often, if you look at that episode, and probably a lot of episodes, he would be off camera when he felt like it was fine. That was part of his charm. The camera wasn't always on the actor who was talking.

It made it feel real. George did it on purpose. I don't know if he did it to make me crazy. But it was helpful.

Emily Wagner George was incredible. I went to Chicago quite a few times when we would shoot there, and I remember being in my hotel room so tired and George was like, "Get down here. We're going out." I'm like, *Fine. I guess I should go out with the leads of the show.* But at that time, they were not at all who they are now, so it didn't feel weird. He was just Georgie. Georgie the actor. I mean, you could yell *cut,* and George could make a joke and then go right back into it. I remember watching and being like, *How does he do that? How does he go from that to that in two seconds?* Even though he was a young actor, he was quite sophisticated in terms of his craft.

Laura Cerón (Chuny Marquez) My first day on the job, I remember meeting George Clooney, because of his eyes. I remember him looking at me straight in the eyes, and he had his big, luscious lashes. Everything that everybody says about George Clooney is what he was, just a gracious guy, super friendly, and cool. But I know I got flushed.

Abraham Benrubi He used to do the greatest impression of Billy Bob Thornton's character from *Sling Blade,* just spot-on.

Carol Flint My son, who was in middle school at the time, would come to the set, and George would play basketball with him. To this day, I find it very sweet that my son was included in those ad hoc basketball games.

Gloria Reuben Women love him. Guys want to be his friend.

Yvonne Zima (Rachel Greene) I remember one time playing football with George Clooney on the back lot. He didn't know, but the football hit me square in the face. I just remember hiding it and pretending it didn't hurt. I was pretty sure that day my nose was broken. I always joke that I think George Clooney broke my nose, but he doesn't know it, and that's okay.

Parminder Nagra I met George on my thirtieth birthday. I was taking the cast out for dinner for my birthday, and he just happened to be at the same restaurant. He knows Maura and Goran and all those guys from before. So, next thing you know, he's coming to sit on our table, and I'm just looking across going, "Oh my God, this is George Clooney." Anyway, he told all these stories and then toward the end just disappeared. I went to go get the check, and the waiter went, "It's already been taken care of. He took care of it." I was like, *Wonderful!*

Jonathan Kaplan George played a pediatrician, but he always said, "I'm not going to get married. I'm not going to have kids." We all said, "Yeah, right." He had two basset hounds and a Vietnamese potbellied pig. Those were his pets. I just remember going to George's house to see the pig and the basset hounds, who were named Abbott and Costello.

Pam Morrison So there was one day I had a reporter there. She was doing a story about the live episode. We were on set for a while, talking to a few other actors and producers, so we were waiting for George. She said to me, "I don't get him. I just don't get all the buzz around him. He's okay. He's not that gorgeous." And I was like, "Oh, have you ever seen him, met him, or talked to him?" She was like, "No." I was like, "Okay, well, I'm going to check with you after this interview and see if your opinion has changed."

So, he came on set, and I introduced them. When George talks to you, he gives you his full attention, and his eyes are incredibly beautiful. You just find yourself kind of going, *What?* It's hard to keep your train of thought sometimes. Seriously. So, I introduced them, and she started talking to him, and he did this thing where he crouched down a little bit. He is more eye level with somebody who's a little shorter than him. He's got his arms folded and looking at her intently and answering her questions. He is a good interview. He wants to give you the answers that are going to help you. I walked away a few feet to give them a little space, and I was just watching her thinking, oh my God, she was just melting. After twenty minutes . . . it was a long interview for being on set . . . he gave her a hug and walked away. She just looked at me and went, "Oh my God." I was like, *Yeah, I know. That's our George.*

Abraham Benrubi He's super charming. It's not hard to believe. You kind of just let him do whatever he wants and hope he'll rub some of it on you.

Rick Rossovich George kept it light and the energy good. He was the obvious alpha without trying. He's deserved all the success he's enjoyed, and the fact he came back to the show briefly [for the final season] is a testament to what a family feel it had.

Clooney was also about having a good time. Mindful of how dreadfully long and tiresome those seventeen-hour days could be, Clooney always found a way to keep the mood light.

Anthony Edwards We laughed nonstop. The image I always have is we were on Stage 11 and were just laughing. Next door at *Friends,* you go onto that stage, and it was like a cemetery. There was nothing. I'm like, it was a total reversal.

Lyn Paolo They all were little rascals, and there was a lot of laughter. They had wheelchair races down the hallway. Who could tip the wheelchair onto two wheels and zoom around the fastest?

Maura Tierney That show was just as funny on set as *News-Radio.* I mean, you would think not, because we were all so serious. But I mean, sometimes you couldn't pull us all in a scene together because it would take too long to shoot. You'd be laughing and there's like, someone dying on the table in front of us or whatever.

Guy Norman Bee I mean, it couldn't have been any better. Everybody honest to God enjoyed each other. We all really enjoyed each other's company, and there were a lot of practical jokes. Nobody was safe from the perpetual ball-busting. The worst part was that every day we'd have like fifty to seventy-five background artists almost fill the hallways up on gurneys or wheelchairs. We all told dirty jokes thirty years ago, so the PC world wasn't as PC as it is now. It was a lot of fun, but at the same time, we all got called to the carpet sometimes, like, "You guys gotta watch what you tell us, because somebody might get offended and sue us." I mean, it made sense.

John Wells There were practical jokes that sometimes slowed down production, and I would have to tell people to get refocused. But it was an extremely professional cast, so it wasn't a problem.

Noah Wyle Very early on, you don't leave the table first when George is at the table. Even if you have to use the bathroom, you sit there and hold it, because the first person leaves the table, George will go, "You know what we should do?"

Julianna Margulies You went to run to your trailer for a ten-minute break, and when you went to open the door, you couldn't because it would be lubed.

Ellen Crawford You always answered a phone knowing it might be full of lube. He would put it on the phones.

Abraham Benrubi If somebody was super diligent, they could probably go through and pick out every moment where my character answers the phone and you see me react to something on my ear.

"Eriq La Salle showed up late in the first season. He was doing something in Portland, and he goes, 'There's this woman, she's like a stalker. She's chasing me in Portland. Thank God I got away from her. This woman Melody, she's a nut. I'm just so glad to be away from her and be in LA.' He leaves. I looked at Noah Wyle, and I said, 'You understand the mistake he just made? He told you everything. He told us her name.' So, I called FTD, and I got a hundred-dollar bouquet of flowers sent to his trailer. We're watching him and he comes out and opens the door and sees the flowers. He goes, 'Hey, flowers!' And the card says, 'I'll see you on the set tomorrow. Love, Melody.' He comes running out and goes, 'I've got to get a restraining order! I've got to get a restraining order!' Noah and I are there in the emergency room doing something and Noah starts to smile and Eriq's like, 'Oh no, no, I get it. Oh, man, you guys.' And I'm like, *Goddammit.* So, I ran outside, and *Family Matters* was shooting next door. I run over and grab Urkel's nameplate off his door, and I switch it with Eriq La Salle's nameplate. I come running back in, and Eriq's like, 'Man, you guys, you scared the hell out of me, man.' I was like, 'When did you figure it out?' And he's like, 'Well, when Noah started smiling.' I go, 'Do you think Jaleel will be mad?' He's like, 'What are *you* talking about?' I go, 'What are you talking about?' He goes,

'I'm talking about the flowers.' I go, 'I don't know about any flowers. We're talking about switching the nameplate on your door.' And he goes running out and sees *Jaleel White* on his door. He goes, 'I've got to get a restraining order!' "

—GEORGE CLOONEY

Lily Mariye It was like having an annoying brother on the set with you who you loved, but . . . he's your brother.

Laura Cerón George could be in a room and have a garbage can, and he'll entertain himself with that garbage can the whole time. It's like, give him anything. I have tons of nieces and nephews who do something with nothing to entertain themselves. They remind me of George. Here's this guy who probably got encouraged to be creative or to allow himself to be creative. And that's why he is who he is.

Lyn Paolo For whatever reason, we all used to go to Las Vegas. One of the crew members had played a prank on George, so as retribution, George did that thing that he sometimes does by getting this guy very, very drunk. What our poor crew member didn't know is that there were sloppy pictures of him being taken. When we arrived at craft services Monday morning, there were giant, blown-up pictures of this crew member hanging down from the ceiling. We all looked and went, "Oh, George did that."

Pam Morrison I do remember this one day after the Emmy nominations or Golden Globes. There were a lot of nominations for the cast, but George was not nominated, and he was doing this fake outrage thing, like, "I'm the only one who didn't get nominated, and there's a reason. And the reason is I never get to cry. I never get to cry on this show. Everybody else has their big dramatic crying scene. Do I get to cry? No. And that's why I don't have a nomination." They were like, *Yeah, yeah, yeah. Okay, George.*

He was there for one scene, and he had to talk to a little kid who was in his hospital bed with his mother standing by. George's line was something simple like, "Timmy, we have to get your temperature now." George would turn to the kid and say, "Okay, Timmy, I'm going to have to take your temperature down," and just sob. The director would yell *cut* and say, "Okay, George. That was very funny. Let's do it again." George did that repeatedly, I mean, *repeatedly*. Finally, the director was like, "All right, George. It was funny seven times, not funny anymore. Stop it." One of the ADs came over to me and said, "I don't know if you've noticed, but you're the only one still laughing at him." And I said, "Oh, I'm sorry. I'm sorry. I should probably just wait outside until this is done." He was like, "That's a good idea." That's the only time I've ever been asked by an AD to walk off the set. But God, it was so funny. He just would not stop doing it.

Guy Norman Bee George played the pediatrician on the show, right? When he would act opposite a kid, like a seven-year-old, George would always come on the set, put his hand out, and say, "Hey, I'm George." The kid would say, "Hi, I'm Davey," or whatever. George would go, "How old are you, seven? Are you married?" Every time, we all knew as a crew it was coming, but the looks on these kids' faces!

Noah Wyle Steven Spielberg had done a movie called *Always,* about a year before *ER* launched, and we'd seen that he'd bought the cast Mazda Miata cars as a wrap gift. For Christmas, [Steven] got *us* all these little cell phones. So Mr. Clooney thought it'd be very funny if we all wrote thank-you notes saying, "Dear Steven, Thank you for the ~~Miata~~ cell phone." And he said, "You should do this. He'll think it's funny." I go, "Are you gonna do it?" He goes, "Oh yeah, I'm gonna do it." And so I wrote that letter, and it was the last Christmas present I ever got.

Abraham Benrubi He filled a trailer with synthetic ice. When you saw a patient's lung on ice, it was fake. It was plastic silicone ice. So when George first saw that, I could see the gears working, and at some point, he got like five hundred pounds of silicone ice and filled up Anthony's trailer. I think it was Anthony. All this ice just came tumbling out when he opened the door.

Ellen Crawford My character got married in the ER, me in my tennis shoes and dress. It was a sweet scene, but I had this dress that had a long train. It was an old-fashioned Cinderella kind of wedding dress with ruffles and a train. George decided that he would see how many objects he could place on my train before I would notice. I think by the end of the day, he got up to three cups, something else, and a phone—a whole desk phone—before I noticed. So yeah, he had fun.

Abraham Benrubi He tightly wrapped the toilet bowl in Noah Wyle's trailer in cellophane so you couldn't see that there was cellophane. When someone would go to urinate, the urine would bounce all over. And he loved to put a toilet seat on anything. That was a weird thing.

Yvonne Zima He used to go out of his way to make me laugh. One of the things he did was put Scotch tape on his nose and tape it up, like Lon Chaney in *The Phantom of the Opera*. He looked like a piggy, but he was still so handsome. A handsome guy must try a little harder to be funny. Then he'd put a hole in a water bottle and be like, "Hey, have you ever seen the hot-air balloon in the Crystal Geyser bottle?" He got me to lean in close, and then he'd squirt the water in my face. That really made the set life fun, because sets are inherently boring and agonizing. The days move very slowly sometimes. He taught me that water bottle trick, and then I would go on sets and carry on the legacy. I was the annoying little child to many costars on many different productions. I was like, "Want to see this hot-air balloon? It's inside." But I would screw it up.

Christopher Chulack Mark Tinker directed episode 2 or 3. Yeah. Was it 2 or 3? I forget. Really great guy. One day at lunch, he said to George, "Does this smell funny to you?" George leaned down to smell it, and Mark pushed the spaghetti in his nose a little bit. It was a joke. George smiled, and everybody was laughing. Well, George is a big prankster, right? So Mark finished directing his last day and we wrapped, and it was still light outside. George says, "Hey, hey, come on. Let's go outside and say goodbye to Mark. He's leaving." He made a group of us go outside. As Mark drove his white Mercedes past Stage 11, there was a frame around his license plate that said something like, well, I'm not going to tell you what it said. It started with HONK IF YOU'RE. I can't tell you the rest. It was a little more risqué than HONK IF YOU'RE HORNY.

Julianna Margulies His license plate said HONK IF YOU LOVE PUSSY.

Christopher Chulack Mark didn't know, of course, and he drove off the lot. Who knows how long he was getting honked at.

Rick Ladomade George had a fart machine, and during a serious scene with a new actress, right in the middle of the scene, he would press the button and just throw everything off.

Jonathan Kaplan I don't remember specifics of this, but somehow, [George's good friend] Richard Kind was out of town shooting something, and George got a hold of his keys and basically walled off a room in Richard's house. Clearly, money was no object for this prank. So Richard is bragging about the master bedroom and the little sitting room off the master that has a view of the backyard. George just walled it off. Those guys, that's what they did to each other. It was all affectionate.

Laura Innes It sort of makes you feel like you're included if you get pranked by George.

11

Medical Minute

A Look Back at "Union Station"

Season 3, Episode 8 | November 21, 1996
Written by Carol Flint
Directed by Tom Moore

In retrospect, the producers probably should have seen it coming. By the time Sherry Stringfield landed the role as Dr. Susan Lewis on *ER*, she had already scored—and subsequently walked away from—two impressive acting gigs in television, first on *Guiding Light* (a role she nabbed right out of college) in 1989, and then in 1993 on *NYPD Blue*. She lasted three years on the CBS sudser, but only one season on Steven Bochco's cop drama.

She made it to the beginning of season 3 on *ER* before deciding to call it quits. On November 20, 1996, *The New York Times'* Bill Carter broke the news that Stringfield was about to appear in her final episode as Susan Lewis—with no indication that she ever wanted to return. Warner Bros. didn't necessarily make it easy for the young actress to walk away from her $70,000-per-episode gig: Since she still had two and a half years left on her contract, she had to promise not to star in another series and to obtain permission to appear in a film. Stringfield later told *The New York Times* that it was the studio's way of sending the message to other actors that they should not "see this as a precedent."

Sherry Stringfield I wouldn't describe the situation as pleasant. [The producers] were in shock. They tried to talk me out of it. It took a long time to get out of my contract. At first the producers thought I was negotiating for more money or pulling David [Caruso] shit. It took them a while to realize it was about having a full-bodied life and getting out before I felt I'd sacrificed so much to get somewhere that I couldn't afford to leave. I'm from the theater. I never wanted to be a star.

John Wells Sherry Stringfield couldn't handle the lack of anonymity. She was coming apart at the seams. I tried to tell her it was a momentary thing. The moment could last three or four years, but it can't be recaptured. You may regret having stepped away, because it won't happen again. You only get to do it once, and you may not want to miss it.

Lily Mariye I knew that she was not happy, and that was evident for a while.

Noah Wyle That was hard. I had a big crush on Sherry. I was sorry to see her go.

Anthony Edwards I was sad when she left because I knew that those characters [Mark and Susan] were going to be spending a lot of time playing with each other, and I loved working with her.

Carol Flint I knew that the enormous success of the first season had not been easy for her. That was kind of not her trajectory. She was looking for something more subtle to happen, I think, in her career. I don't think she loved the endless publicity and all of that. So, I think it was a slow evolution.

John Wells The agents and the press agents and managers are the biggest problem. The desire to take this person and turn them into a commodity. Sometimes it works, but mostly, it's a disaster. It's the same thing that happens with professional athletes.

Pam Morrison In fact, we had just done a photo shoot that she was in, and it was just a few days later that they announced she was leaving. We were like, "Oh, all that art that she's in!" We were surprised. We would've made that photo shoot later in the week if we had known she was leaving. Most photo shoots were expensive, so I was like, *Shoot.*

"We loved beating up Mark Greene, literally and figuratively. He was such a good guy that we could give him a lot of problems because you knew your heart would go out to him. And I would say right up until

when he died, and in the show, he was just good at bringing the heart and then being able to break your heart. So, I think that probably guided us, knowing that we would want him to finally have the courage to declare his love, only to have it be too late."

—CAROL FLINT

Lori Openden I knew her agent at the time. He of course did not want her to leave the show. She just had it in her brain that it was the right time for her to leave and she had given everything to the character that she could. I believe she did it for the right reasons. In her own mind, I don't think it was a good decision career-wise, or for the show, or for her bank account. I believe the fame for Sherry was hard to tolerate.

John Levey When *ER* happened, forty million people were watching it at one time. That was probably 20 percent of the Americans who were awake at 10:00 on a Thursday night. I mean, it was huge. That level of success was thrilling to most of us, and life-changing for most of us. But I think Sherry was never comfortable with all that level of attention, the loss of anonymity and all of the negative things that come with all of the positive things that come with that level of success.

Sherry Stringfield It was a little scary. People I knew really well were taking my arm and looking deep in my eyes with the whole tilted-head thing, you know, saying, "We're worried about you." Puh-leeze. It's like when you walk away from a wonderful job like that, you start messing with everyone's priorities. It's like you're dissing them.

Carol Flint packed a whole lot of stories in "Union Station" before it came time for Susan Lewis to literally kiss off a now-divorced Mark Greene. Kirsten Dunst guest starred as a very young mom, John Carter was hooking up with a pediatric surgeon played by Glenne Headly, Jeanie Boulet was served divorce papers from her ex, and Nurse Lydia was about to marry her cop boyfriend [and real-life husband, Mike Genovese] by the vending machines. Susan even caught the bouquet.

Ellen Crawford It's funny. The entire episode of Hathaway's wedding was about the wedding. For my wedding, I wore a prop. It made me laugh. It was such a Cinderella kind of big floofy gown.

Mike Genovese (Officer Al Grabarsky) When they did the pilot, they wanted to do Ellen and I as a couple, and I was going to be the character who got accidentally shot by his wife. And as it turned out, I was in Hawaii doing a pilot for Don Bellisario, so I wasn't available. Ellen went in for the wife and they asked her if she wanted to read anything else, and she said one of the nurses. Then she got cast. So, I was already in their brain when they decided to do a cop-nurse romance.

Ellen Crawford We had become boyfriend and girlfriend. You didn't actually see [an engagement] happen because you didn't ever see us on a date or at home or anything. You only saw us at work. Then in "Union Station," [my character] brought in my wedding dress to return it because I'd had it with him. I think I said, "I'm taking this fake virgin outfit back and they better not give me store credit." His character came in and was saying, "Oh my God, I messed up. What do I do?" And they're like, "Well, there is a chaplain here today." So, we got married in the ER, me in my tennis shoes and my dress.

Here's the thing, though: We were secondary characters. We didn't know Sherry Stringfield was leaving, and that was supposed to be a big episode for Susan and Mark. The editor that cut that scene told me he refused to edit a wedding where there wasn't a close-up of the bride. But the focus [of the writers] was on the two leads.

The episode ends with Susan Lewis taking her name off her locker and heading to the station to catch a train to Phoenix to join her sister, Chloe—but not before Mark Greene is seen running across downtown Chicago in his green scrubs and flannel coat so he can finally bare his soul. "I want you to stay. I love you, and I'm stupid for not saying it before," he says. "We belong together. Tell me you don't feel the same." With one foot on the train, Susan says she's sorry, her life is headed in a new direction, and she doesn't belong in Chicago anymore. She then gives him a passionate kiss. As the train departs, she leans out the door to say, "I'll never forget you," and "I do love you. Bye!"

Lance Gentile There was never talk [about killing her off]. The show was trying to be normal. How can we do this in a normal fashion rather than she gets killed in a helicopter that crashes into the hospital? We weren't into that. They got around to doing stuff like that, but not at the beginning.

Ellen Crawford We had a different ending to that episode.

Carol Flint We put out a fake version of that script when he chases her to the train station and they fall into each other's arms. We all knew that was not going to happen, but we forgot to tell the director of that episode when we sent him the script. So, Tom Moore came on the first day of prep saying, "I just love the ending. Nobody ever does anything romantic like this anymore. This is so awesome." And my face fell. I realized that nobody had given him a heads-up. I had to break the news to him that that was a fake ending. We didn't put out those pages until the morning that we shot that scene, because it was so close to when it aired. Anyway, by then, Tom had reconciled with it, but his instinct was to have a happier ending.

Lydia Woodward I was happy for her. Everybody has things they need to do with their lives.

Carol Flint It's so funny because [the kiss] was the kind of thing that you kick around in a writers' room where you go, *Could we do that?* And then it would be, *Yeah, but then what does that mean? Does that mean she really does love him?* For Susan, she needed to reconcile with her sister and be in that environment. It's been a billion years, so I don't really know. I think there was something very real between Susan and Mark, but it was different for her.

Sherry Stringfield There's not one thing that prompted me to leave *ER*. It was the whole experience and looking down the road of knowing who I am. It was making me nervous. I was nervous all the time.

Abraham Benrubi I have a wonderful picture of Sherry Stringfield. I want to say it's like season 3, because the show was making money. She and I are at the craft service table and the only thing that was there, the only thing on the entire craft service table, was a single can of SpaghettiOs. I have this great Polaroid of her holding these SpaghettiOs at an empty craft service.

Anthony Edwards What's so great about Sherry is she has that inner strength to do what she believes in, what she thinks is right, and what's right for her at the time. She left because she needed to. And I was heartbroken, because she was such a fun actress to work with. And obviously Mark Greene was in love with her.

Neal Baer I love Sherry. And of course, I put her on my show *Under the Dome.*

Actors and executives have a favorite saying whenever a reporter asks them whether they would be up for a reboot of their old show or if they'd fancy the possibility of reprising an old character: "Never say never." Stringfield never said that when she talked about her 1996 exit, but she certainly started thinking about it a few years later. After appearing in 54, an episode of Touched by an Angel, *and the TV movie* Going Home, *in 2001, Stringfield returned to the series that made her a household name. By then, she was married with a young daughter. "Series television is either a nightmare or the best thing in the whole world. It really depends on, I think, where you are in your life," Stringfield said at the time. "It's a lot easier for me this time having a family, because with a kid, you're not going anywhere. So, I was really starting to crave a schedule and I'm actually really enjoying that now."*

By the time of Susan's return, a love match with Mark was simply not possible: He had already married Dr. Elizabeth Corday. And the series was about to undergo another big shake-up; Anthony Edwards and Eriq La Salle were preparing to leave at the end of season 8. She and Noah Wyle would be the only stars left from the first season.

Neal Baer I would say to John, "You've got to bring Sherry back." And he'd be like, "She wanted to leave." Of course, she did come back.

Sherry Stringfield I met with John Wells, and I was like, "I'd love to come back." And he said, "Okay, we'd love to have you back." That was it. I read the first script and showed up for work. It was really that easy. If it had been another show, I probably would have [been rusty]. But I did it for almost three years. It's like riding a bicycle. It felt like I had left mid-conversation, almost, and then I just walked back on and started up again.

Jack Orman I was running the show when she returned, and basically got a call from John [who] said, "Hey, Sherry reached out and she may be interested in joining the show again." And I always liked the character, and we were in the process of writing Anthony Edwards out and thought, wow, it's good to have another person with a long history with that character. Plus we also knew that Greene would be hard to replace.

David Zabel (Executive Producer) We never wanted to lose her in the first place, so it was great to bring her back because she was such a valuable character . . . a smart, strong attending physician. She was really the senior female doctor on the floor. She filled that void that we had for a while. And we were just trying to keep as much of the original mojo as we could while letting the show evolve. It wasn't like we were stuck in the past. We were trying to continually evolve the show, but we were also trying to always stay in touch with the past.

Sherry left again in 2005 and put out this statement: "I am extremely grateful for the time I spent on ER. *It is a wonderful show, and there are so many people I will miss. But I'm ready for new roles and new challenges."*

Sherry Stringfield You just kind of have to look at stuff and say, for some people, freedom, having their own schedule, and working on different characters, is much more important than having money. I didn't grow up in a mansion. And frankly, what the hell would I do with it?

12

Medical Minute

A Look Back at "Ambush"

Season 4, Episode 1 | September 27, 1997
Written by Carol Flint
Directed by Tommy Schlamme

ER didn't need stunts to attract a large viewership—the show was averaging more than thirty-three million viewers by the end of season 3—but George Clooney and Anthony Edwards still thought it would be fun to kick things up a notch by doing a live episode of the show. *ER* producer Carol Flint agreed to write the script—there weren't a lot of volunteers in the writers' room, and she had a background in theater—while past director Tommy Schlamme was brought back to helm the episode about a documentary film crew chronicling life in a big-city emergency department. As if that wasn't enough of a challenge, the episode also introduced Dr. Elizabeth Corday, a clever British doctor played by Alex Kingston.

John Wells I remember George and Anthony saying, "We ought to do this," and my looking at them like they were insane.

Anthony Edwards We were discovering that we were doing these long one-shots where we would go for three minutes without stopping in a trauma unit. It felt like we were doing it live because there was so much pressure not to mess it up. So, we felt it was kind of natural to do it live.

George Clooney [We'd] been a groundbreaking show, and we [liked] the idea of continuing that with a live show.

Lydia Woodward I thought it was fantastic and insane.

Carol Flint Season 4 seemed like a good time to have it. We were still doing something new. Yes, something that's such a big, instant success as *ER* could have easily gotten stale, but there was always something that the writers found to do to give it a fresh feeling.

Anthony Edwards The pressure to get it right was enormous.

John Wells We made a conscious decision before going into it that if we were going to do it, we were not going to compromise what we wanted the show to be.

Jack Orman In order to do it, Carol had to have the script ready early in July so that everybody else could understand episode 2, 3, 4, or 5.

Carol Flint It didn't take that long for me to think of the idea of a documentary crew. The only real story that had to be solved in advance, which nobody else had really thought about, because they weren't attracted to the craziness of the idea, was why it looked so different from what our show looked like. It was not going to be on film. It was going to be live. So I don't think it took me that long to think of the idea of a documentary crew.

Christopher Chulack I wanted John Frankenheimer [*Ronin, The Manchurian Candidate*] to do the live show, and I asked him one time at lunch, I said, "Why don't you come and direct one of these, man?" He says, "Nah. I don't know how you guys do it, and I need to know. I need to be smarter than everybody else." I said okay. He didn't want to direct it. So then when we decided to do the live show, I wanted to do it, but I couldn't. It would isolate me too much and I'd be lost for six weeks preparing the live show, just like a unit under itself. So I told John, I said, "I want to hire Frankenheimer." He said, "Yeah, whatever you want." So I called Frankenheimer and I said, "Hey, John, it's Chris. We're going to do a live show. I wondered if you would want to direct it." There was silence. I was like, "Hello?" He says, "Why the fuck would you guys want to do that? There's no way I want to get back into live television." He was an interesting cat, man. I really liked him.

Tommy Schlamme I remember George and Anthony talking about it during an episode that I was directing [two years prior], and I basically said it could be done. I had done a lot of variety shows early in my career, and I had even done one live. But I had no desire to be a live director. But there were no other directors who had done dramatic television *and* variety *and* a live show. So, I just had the short straw.

Carol Flint Instead of shooting for seven days or eight days, we rehearsed for seven days, and then we blocked it and everything. And then two days before it started, we said, "Wait, it's not going to be live on the West Coast. That's where our friends are." That was when we decided to do two episodes back-to-back to do it twice.

Tommy Schlamme We had done all this planning, and we all lived in LA, and I just thought, from a selfish point of view, that all my friends and family are going to see a tape-delay version of a live show. That's not very exciting. So, I said, "If there's not an economic reason not to, I think we should do it."

Lydia Woodward One for the East Coast and then a second one for the West Coast. Whose idea was that? I mean, oh my God. Once wasn't enough?

Warren Littlefield Don Ohlmeyer thought we were nuts. "You better not destroy the series." Once again, I put my faith in John Wells, but with Don's words ringing in my ears. I was also right there in the director's booth for both live shows.

Jack Orman Late in the game, there was a physical need for a tweak in the story. Carol realized that there needed to be an extra scene in an elevator, and it involved a long interview [with the documentary crew]. I would call it a monologue. Carol was like, "This actor is going to have a day to do this. Who's going to draw the short straw?" Carol identified Laura Innes as somebody that could come in and knock this out. She learned it and executed it live within a very short period of time.

Eventually, some 90 actors would participate in the live episodes, but a total of 120 people would be on set with eleven cameras capturing their every move.

Tommy Schlamme Everybody was always on set, except George, who would try to find the one place where the doors would close so he could not be on-camera. Everybody was onstage, including stage managers and people who on live shows must call, "We're coming to you in three, two, one." They were dressed as nurses or orderlies because there was nowhere to hide. That's why it had to be a documentary. We were going to see the cameramen. If you look at stills from the scenes, I could point out an orderly who's really a second assistant director.

Eriq La Salle It was such an ensemble thing, a team effort. Just like the theater. You're running around backstage, and then you come off nice and easy and say your last line, and then you bolt over here.

Lyn Paolo I would say 60 percent of the crew was on-camera.

John Wells I was very tempted to put on scrubs.

Lyn Paolo It was interesting, because some of the crew was like, "Well, I want to be a doctor." And I said, "No. We can't have every single person on the crew be dressed as a doctor, so I'm going to make you a nurse," or "I'm going to make you look like someone who lost blood" or "You're going to be going from this floor or that floor." People always ask that question about doctors, because that's where our head goes when we talk about the medical profession. But really, it's all run by nurses, isn't it? We would always be dressing our Steadicam operators because they were seen a lot. I could see their arms as they're helping! And we certainly dressed our real doctors who were there as tech advisors.

"I remember hearing we had rooms that were made to look like bathrooms. They had non-connected toilets. I guess we went away for lunch and somebody tried to use it for a major dump and left. There was no flushing."

—MIKE GENOVESE

Tommy Schlamme We didn't have a backup, because the night before, we shot it live ourselves as a rehearsal so that if something happened, they would be able to switch and just go to that. The rehearsal for both John and I was terrible. We had to make a lot of changes, but I wasn't okay that they would show it. I just went, "Look, John, we can't send this to New York. Just tell 'em to air 'Hell and High Water,' the great episode with George. People will be happy."

Lydia Woodward There was not an audience. The only audience were those of us who worked on the show and were in the stage next door that had been wired with a video feed, because obviously you couldn't be on the stage watching, because it was shooting around the entire stage.

Carol Flint Tommy and I sat in the truck. It was set up more like a sporting event where there was a truck outside of the stage. Tommy would be telling them what camera to go to. I just had to sit there and be nervous.

Tommy Schlamme There's an act where there's a gang fight. A gang shows up, and there's truly a fight in the ER. It was very well choreographed, but I wanted it to feel real. Some of the guys went a little farther than they should. At the very end, a guy sees the documentary camera guy, and he shoves him, which knocks the camera up. That was a way to go to commercial break. It was very dynamic, and apparently in the bleachers people erupted and started applauding. John got out of the bleachers, ran across, opened the truck, grabbed me by the shoulders, kissed me, and then ran out again. And I'm thinking, *Okay, that was a vote of confidence.*

The Cubs game that was airing in the break room during the live episode? That was real.

Jack Orman It was planned. When the decision was made to do the show twice, we were looking for opportunities to demonstrate it was live. At some point or another, either Carol or Tommy came up with the idea of piping the game in. So, if you look at the West Coast feed versus the East Coast feed, the game was further along. It was proof of concept.

Lydia Woodward There was about an hour break in between, and we were all out in between the stages during the hour intermission. All the actors were smoking. All these actors who don't smoke, we're all out there smoking. It was hysterical. They were so nervous, and everybody was just ramped up with anxiety. I mean, it was a high-wire act.

Carol Flint By then, everybody was running on adrenaline. I don't remember anybody freaking out.

Anthony Edwards Very little went wrong.

Lily Mariye After the East Coast performance, a bunch of us went to Maria Bello's trailer. Some other actors knocked on the door, so Maria turned on some really loud music, and suddenly, we were having a dance party to shake off the nerves. It really worked.

Tommy Schlamme I can tell you, after we finished the first episode, there was not a person who didn't want to do a second one. And then after the second one, it was like, "Bring on Hawaii!"

Carol Flint I remember during the second airing, Steven Spielberg came in to sit in the truck with us. I was nervous that everybody would be so nervous and nobody would be able to do their job. But he was wonderful and humble and put everybody at ease. I remember during the different scenes, he would lean over to me, and he would say, "Did you write that scene?" And I got to always say yes. It was a crazy night of high adrenaline, and so much fun.

The live episode also introduced Alex Kingston as Dr. Elizabeth Corday. The assumption was she was a replacement for Sherry Stringfield, who left in season 3.

Carol Flint I think that maybe that is how some people's brains work, but my brain didn't. We wanted to have another female presence. Obviously, she was designed to be a very different person. And the idea of her having surgical expertise was a good way to bridge her into Benton's world. It opened the possibilities with Dr. Benton in a way that obviously the Susan character did not.

Neal Baer Since Alex played a British doctor, I was doing all this research on how British surgeons are different. How are they trained differently? What do they say that's different?

Alex Kingston This character [was] bright, ballsy, and not terribly straight. To introduce someone into the show who's English and a little wacky allows Americans to see that the Brits aren't all Merchant Ivory characters.

George Clooney American actors have this funny thing about British actors, their sound. If you look back in the '30s and '40s, we even tried to sound British. *Oh, Dolly, I'm only doing it for your happiness.* So, we're always sort of intimidated somehow by an English accent. When Alex came on the set, we were in the emergency room and she's like, "CBC, blood typing across full units," and we're like, "She's good." We were immediately intimidated by Alex when she showed up.

Not everything went off without a hitch. In the second live episode, a syringe was supposed to be set for an actor playing an AIDS patient, who points it at the nurses and threatens to stick them with it. But the syringe wasn't returned for the scene, so the actor continued the scene without it. "I don't think the audience realized he was supposed to have it," remembers Schlamme. There were more moments like that.

Tommy Schlamme We had a baby that cried on cue in the first episode. It was unbelievable. He would cry and then George would start to talk, and then the baby would stop crying, and then the baby would cry again.

Pam Morrison The first time, the baby cried, and it was great. It worked perfectly. And then for the West Coast run, the baby—who was a twin, of course—was perfectly happy and had no intention of crying. They were sort of like, *Somebody make the baby cry.* You could see them all thinking, *Can we pinch the baby? What* *do we do?* Somebody kind of shook the baby a little bit, and the baby never did cry, so they just went on with it as if the baby were in distress.

Christopher Chulack The camera was late here, late there, but nothing that anybody would notice.

Tommy Schlamme I think Noah had a sequence where a man vomits on him, and it kind of looked fake to me. In the second episode, he had a tube and it came down, it came out much harder and splattered. Some of it went into Noah's mouth.

Lily Mariye It was Campbell's soup. [But] it was sitting in a tub, so it wasn't like delicious homemade soup.

Tommy Schlamme There was one incredible thing that the audience never knew about. We were very close to a catastrophe involving the Steadicam operator, who I still work with. He was young, and he was on *ER* that season for the first time. All a sudden, he's on a live television show, and he's running with this cable. A gurney comes through the door and [the camera is following it] all the way into the emergency room. At a certain point, Dave must pull away as he's going through the door, and then he follows them in. And what happened was, as the gurney turned, his cable got wrapped around the side of the gurney, which means as they're pushing it, it would've ripped the camera out of his hands and fallen to the ground. It was a single shot taking us all the way there. A real actor on the show playing an orderly saw the cable as Dave was turning around and was able to release it, right at the moment when the camera was already leaving Dave's hands. He pulled it back in and saved it, and then continued the shot.

Preston Beckman Throughout the history of *ER*, the most successful episodes were the ones where all of us would say, "Don't do this, don't do this." And they would. And John Wells, to his credit, would always [make it] work.

Tommy Schlamme Somebody did a behind-the-scenes film of "Ambush" that you can watch. I don't know who made it, but I just remember they sent it to me. What you see is the eruption at the end of the show. They had done it. It wasn't the explosion of the three actors who had to carry the show. It was everybody. For me, it's kind of carried on in the way that I work. It's not about one or two or three on the call sheet. Everybody is coming there and everybody's trying to make the best show possible. *ER* really didn't need the live episode to get more of an audience, but they might've needed it for each other. They needed to realize we're all in this together. It was an incredible experience.

13

The High Price of Healthcare

ER generated many headlines in its early years, but none were quite as astonishing as those that circulated in 1998 when NBC renegotiated the license fee that it paid to air the medical drama. After almost four years of stalled talks, the network finally agreed to fork over an unprecedented $13 million an episode for the drama, or $286 million per year for twenty-two episodes. According to estimates at the time, NBC was making roughly $500 million in profits from the show; the astronomical renegotiation gobbled up more than half of it.

NBC could have gotten away with paying far less for the series; after season 1, Warner Bros. TV had tried to renegotiate the roughly $3 million per episode the network was paying so it could plan for the future and start giving raises to the popular ensemble. But NBC wasn't ready to haggle over their standard four-year deal. Even though it was raking in big advertising dollars for its Thursday-night lineup that included the pricey *Seinfeld,* NBC had already renegotiated a new license fee for the Warner Bros.–produced *Friends* after its first season because comedies typically hold up better than dramas. *ER,* no matter how impressive its ratings were, would have to wait.

For a fleeting moment, NBC's lackadaisical attitude left open the possibility that the network was about to lose one of its biggest assets. And Leslie Moonves, who had left Warner Bros. TV soon after developing *ER* to head up programming at CBS, was eager to pounce.

Bob Daly (Warner Bros. Chairman and Co-CEO) They didn't really realize what they had. At least, I don't think Don Ohlmeyer did. Unlike when they reimbursed us for *Friends,* they didn't want to really reimburse us for what we had to give the talent for *ER*. So, I said, "Okay, we're going to take a chance on this one. We won't ask for more money. The hell with them. We will eat it, and they'll pay through the nose if it goes more than five years. They're going to really pay for it this time." So, I gambled on it.

Warren Littlefield We'd already made a billion dollars before the renegotiation began.

Leslie Moonves The studios would always come back and renegotiate with the networks, and the networks would give them more money. It happens all the time. When I heard that Don Ohlmeyer didn't want to step up at that point, I went to Bob Daly and made him a ridiculous offer to bring the show to CBS. I believe it was $12 million [an episode]. I'm not 100 percent sure, but it was up there. We figured out how much money *ER* was earning, and with the ratings it was getting, I think the number I offered was break even for the network. And I said, "Okay, if we get *ER* here to CBS, what's that going to do for the rest of the schedule?" Also, *ER* had a special place in my heart. *ER* was one of my babies back in the day.

Bob Daly When you have a hit show, the actors' agents always come in for more money after year two, or it depends on how big a hit it is right away. I never had a problem giving people more money. But if I gave more money, I asked for more time. So, let's say it was year two or three of the show. We would increase their salary for years four and five, which we had a contract on, and they would give us years six and seven. Obviously, it was to the advantage of the studio and the network to agree to do it because it's good to get the sixth and seventh year or whatever it might be, so you don't get held up.

Before negotiations officially opened at the start of 1998, ABC under Michael Eisner and Bob Iger had also been kicking the ER *tires. If the overtures from the competition weren't enough to pressure Ohlmeyer into finally making the deal, it was the call he received from Jerry Seinfeld that did. Over the holidays in 1997, the comedian reached Ohlmeyer in Aspen to say he wanted to end* Seinfeld *the following spring. At the time, Ohlmeyer told the Hollywood trades that Seinfeld's call wasn't necessarily impetus for the deal, but it "shifted the dynamics somewhat. You're never going to want to lose* ER*, but I think not having* Seinfeld *turned the Bunsen burner up even more."*

Bob Daly They were feeling a lot of pressure. They couldn't afford to lose *ER*. So, we made the deal, but I put two other conditions on it that's never been put on the television show. I said, one, we have Thursday night at 10:00 and you can't move the show. It's going to stay there. Two, was that after we closed this deal, NBC had no rights on the talent. They had no more creative control over the show as far as talent was concerned. George was going to leave after five years, and that's it. As for the rest of the talent, if somebody left for any reason, NBC couldn't renegotiate the deal. The talent stayed and there was never a problem, but I wanted insurance that it never was going to be a problem.

Leslie Moonves You want to know the truth? I rarely watched *ER* after I left Warner Bros. TV. It was too painful. Isn't that silly, though? I rarely watched *Friends* after I left, too.

Bob Daly To be honest, we originally wanted more than $13 million. My guys felt, and they probably were right, that we could have pushed them for another million or so. But we had a very good relationship with NBC. We had a lot of shows on NBC. So, there was a point where I didn't want to offend them more than I was doing. I basically said to our people, "We don't want to be pigs here." I did that because I wanted them to call me up to thank me, as opposed to calling me up to scream at me. Ohlmeyer was really stretched out at that point. That was a huge increase in licensing. I was a former network guy. I knew the pressure that they were receiving. Once you get a deal that you don't even expect to get, why push them more than that? It just didn't make sense.

Warren Littlefield We didn't own *ER*. We just rented it. After the first four years, we rented it for a lot more.

The cast and crew got to enjoy the sudden largesse, too. The five main cast members—George Clooney, Julianna Margulies, Noah Wyle, Eriq La Salle, and Anthony Edwards—were each *gifted $1 million checks while others like Laura Innes, Gloria Reuben, and Alex Kingston got $500,000. Meanwhile, executive producers John Wells, Michael Crichton, and Steven Spielberg pooled $6 million and distributed it to the crew.*

Christopher Chulack Spielberg and Crichton and John had profit participation, and they gave everybody a little stipend. It was very nice. They didn't have to. It wasn't a million dollars, but it was substantial.

Jack Orman It was one of the most amazing things that I've ever seen in Hollywood, because most people would not have done that. I remember seeing an editor crying right outside one of the buildings, and I walked up to him and said, "What's going on?" He was like, "I can buy a house now."

"We were always asking, 'What's happening in the future? What am I doing? What am I doing? I didn't have much, this last episode.' And then Jonathan Kaplan would come to me and say, 'Beware what you wish for. Enjoy the days when you don't have much work to do.' I'd be like, 'Okay, that's very ominous, Jonathan.' He's like, 'Yeah, believe me, you're going to hate me.' And then, I don't know, three episodes later, it would be Luka's storyline, with a Boeing 737 crashing in Chicago. We would be filming outside at night, and it would be horrible and cold, it would be crazy, and we would work sixteen hours. But it was exciting. People were going to say, 'Wow, *ER* did it again.'"

—GORAN VISNJIC

John Wells NBC was happy to have a low license fee through the first four years of the series, and I believe that was very financially beneficial to them. In my opinion, a renegotiation would've saved WB a great deal of money, but they more than made up for it after that four-year period.

Bob Daly Everybody was shocked. It was a huge deal. The only deal that was better than the amount of money we got for *ER* was when [Warner Bros.] released Jon Peters and Peter Guber to go to Sony. [*In 1989, the two studios settled a bitter contract dispute after the WB sued Sony for poaching the* Batman *producers.*] We got like $750 million.

14

Irregular Heartbeats

Even though *ER* will always be remembered for the realistic way it depicted life in a hospital, the love affairs will remain an indelible part of its legacy. (There's a reason why the clip of Doug and Carol's reunion has millions of views on YouTube.) No matter how hard the writers tried, however, not every coupling was as picture-perfect as Doug and Carol and Abby and Luka. Relationships were tried and abandoned as characters logged far too many notches on the bedpost. (John Carter, you insatiable tiger, you!) And oh, to be the poor sap who got dumped in the end! Case in point: Dr. John "Tag" Taglieri, Carol's perfectly good fiancé who was played by *Top Gun* hunk Rick Rossovich in the first season.

Rick Rossovich I had just finished *Navy SEALs* with Charlie Sheen. That was arduous at best and was no *Top Gun*, for sure.

I was kind of rudderless in a weird way. Jobs were coming, but what was I doing? The miniseries *The Gambler Returns: The Luck of the Draw* with Kenny Rogers and Reba McEntire. I really felt like a sellout. On top of that, the 1992 real estate market bust cost me all the assets I had built up from all the work I had amassed. I poured all my earnings into real estate deals in San Diego and had around $10 million that evaporated in the downturn. So, by 1994, my career was in a bit of a lull after being fired from a shit Universal cop show that partnered me with a thinking dog.

ER came in the nick of time, but at $2,500 for only a recurring role, it wasn't going to be my ticket. Nobody knew I was scraping bottom. I was on my third agent in fifteen years, so I needed to keep my current reps interested in me, too. I got to do some comedy, which was maybe one of my favorite moments. For the Thanksgiving show, I had a scene where I was plucking a big turkey in one of the operating suites. The feathers were just flying up into the air as fast as I could pull them!

I forget exactly when in the season it was, but I felt I was secure enough that I could play a little hardball. John Terry [who played Susan Lewis's love interest Div Cvetic in the first season] was cut, but I knew they needed me to complete the story arc of the love triangle to the end. I didn't feel I was valued enough. John Wells called and asked me what I wanted. I of course told him of my gratitude for the opportunity and how the show had pulled me from a low spot, but I mean . . . $500 a day? I told him I wanted to be a regular! I knew that wasn't going to happen. And it probably wouldn't have worked for me, anyway. Acting is a total confidence game, and my confidence wasn't as high as it had been a decade earlier. He of course said no on joining the regular cast, but he tripled my pay, which was okay.

I'll say this: I was in the number one film of the year, a cultural landmark in 1986, and ten years later, I was on the number one TV show. Those are the highlights of my career. And I always say I let George have the girl in the end.

Mark Greene and Susan Lewis always had chemistry, but Sherry Stringfield's departure—and questions over where their relationship would ultimately go—kept the writers from fully consummating their obvious attraction to one another.

Carol Flint There may have been a little bit of trying everybody out at the beginning. Sometimes it's like, "Well, would *this* be good chemistry? Would *that* be good chemistry?"

Lydia Woodward We did at times get close to [bringing Susan and Mark together]. Then we always pulled back because it felt like once we went there, what were we going to do? Then of course, Sherry decided to leave the show. So, we were able to position it as this missed opportunity in their lives. But we always knew that putting two main characters together was going to be a limited thing. To move them along, at some point you're just going to have to break them up. And you don't want to do it with everybody. So, you kind of hold back a little bit.

The writers certainly milked the will-they-or-won't-they aspect of the relationship between John Carter and Abby Lockhart, but Luka Kovač ended up being a much better fit for the nurse turned doctor.

Jack Orman The addiction story continued with Carter's relationship with Abby, because she was a recovering alcoholic who started off as a sponsor. That was sort of the entrée into that rather long relationship. They had this mutual understanding that was the foundation to their relationship.

David Zabel Carter and Abby seemed like they could be a viable relationship, and that's why we pursued it. But it did seem like, in a way, sort of an "opposites attract" kind of situation, in that she carried a darkness and moodiness that made her a tough fit with him.

Maura Tierney In the writers' minds, it was a relationship out of need and not necessarily depth. It was interesting they wound up together, because they [were] both missing something—some part of their spirit is divided.

Noah Wyle Luka happened. Luka's what ruined it.

David Zabel She was better with Kovač. He was dark and moody.

Goran Visnjic Maura Tierney and I were really good friends from the beginning. We clicked. It was really easy. And Luka and Abby had been running together for so long. I think for fans, it was a nice ending, and I liked it personally.

Maura Tierney I thought it was unexpected for the audience and for us.

Eriq La Salle and Alex Kingston had a terrific connection, so it was no surprise that Benton's burgeoning romance with Corday was a big hit with the viewers. But La Salle grew increasingly uncomfortable with the interracial relationship, especially since his previous love connections with Jeanie Boulet and Carla were loaded with challenges.

Eriq La Salle As an African American man, it becomes a bit offensive if the negative things are all you're showing. Because in real life, we romance and get on each other's nerves and laugh and do all the things that any other race of people do. So if the only time you show a balanced relationship is in an interracial relationship, whether it's conscious or subconscious, it sends a message I'm not comfortable with. [The writers] were sending a message that I didn't want to be a part of, which was the only time that this man becomes human and tender and vulnerable and open is when he falls in love with a white woman. [Of] the two relationships that I had prior to Corday, one was an adulterous relationship with Jeanie Boulet and then the next relationship I got into was with Carla. And unfortunately, the writing there was, every time you see them, they're either fighting or [having sex].

Eventually, he asked the writers to break them up at the end of season 5. It didn't make Kingston happy.

Alex Kingston It was a positive relationship and generated a lot of positive feelings. I actually thought it was a wonderful thing to put out for America to see.

Lydia Woodward Peter and Elizabeth were both very, very strong-willed characters, and so I think they were a good match that way. As you know, we did break them up. Eriq, quite understandably, was interested in having Benton be involved in a relationship with an African American woman. And he was not initially against being involved with Alex's character. He wasn't against that at all. But as time went on, he became more interested in being involved with an African American character, and we agreed. We brought their relationship finally to a close.

Eriq La Salle It took quite a bit of convincing [for them to change it].

Carol Flint I don't know if it ever has been an easy time to be the minority character in an ensemble, but it was a time where you would want there to be diversity. As the show went along, there was pretty good representation. Eriq was sensitive to what his storylines and romances would feel like in his community—probably more sensitive than we were—even though we were trying hard to be. But we weren't him. We did have diversity in the writers' room as it went along, but we didn't right off the bat.

"The best sequence I had was an episode in season 1 that had a plotline of Carol and Tag going away for a romantic weekend trip. All the anticipation centered around the sex toys I had brought in my doctor's bag. This was the episode where I had to parade around naked. I had done plenty of partially nude love scenes in films and in movies like *Top Gun.* That gave me the bravado to walk onto the soundstage at Warner Bros. with a long black sock pulled over my private parts and laughing like hell. In today's world, I would be marched off the lot but back then, everyone had a good laugh, and the tension was broken because I had nothing but respect for Julianna Margulies. My intention was to take the pressure and attention off her and make me the butt of the joke before we had to film my butt."

—RICK ROSSOVICH

As an interesting postscript, Benton and Corday shared a nice moment in the series finale before saying goodbye for good.

Eriq La Salle Benton and Corday had such a palpable chemistry that people could read into a lot of their looks, because they were genuine.

Speaking of palpable chemistry, Lucy Knight and John Carter developed sparks, but their relationship never went beyond a brief kiss in season 5.

Jack Orman I think that was kind of a one-off. It just felt to us as we were watching it, it was more of a big brother, little sister sort of relationship.

Noah Wyle The script originally had us having sex in one of the exam rooms, and somebody walking in on us. I had a big problem with it. In fact, in the fifteen years I was on that show, the 260-some-odd episodes I did, I only wrote [executive producer] John Wells one letter asking him to change something that he had written, and it was about that episode. I just thought Carter wouldn't do it, he wouldn't do it at work, and he wouldn't do it with his student. So I made this huge passionate plea to John about how the character's ethical center is his core defining characteristic, and once you infringe upon that or you chip away at it, it's very difficult to get that back. I went through this whole thing, and he was so amused by my letter that he proposed a compromise of this kiss.

Kellie Martin (Lucy Knight) It would have been fun. And I think that they had intended for Lucy and Carter to be together in the beginning, but when you start a storyline, you don't know where it's going to end up. It's such a puzzle, and it's maybe those two people who were friends and should have gotten together, but they didn't. That happens in life so often, and it feels like that's how it was on *ER* with Lucy and Carter.

15

Outpatient Status

At any given time, the emergency room at County General was easily packed with sixty or seventy actors. Many would be extras, some of whom—if they were lucky enough—got to lie on a gurney all day and earn the same level of pay as those who were stuck twiddling their thumbs in the waiting room. Others were actors who were either at the start of their career or were cast to make a big impact during awards season. Either way, it's safe to say that a significant segment of Hollywood managed to spend a day inside the fictitious Chicago hospital.

Many actors over the years came in for short stints as doctors. Character actor Clancy Brown was one of them: He started in 1997 as Dr. Ellis West, a topical character who came in to "preach the gospel of corporate ERs."

Clancy Brown (Ellis West) Ellis West might've been a character that they wanted to carry into the next generation of *ER*, but I guess I didn't do a good enough job for that to happen. I think at that point, PPOs and HMOs were taking over hospitals. I liked that group so much. They were such good pals. I knew Paul McCrane from *The Shawshank Redemption*, I had worked with Anthony before, and I knew Laura Innes from Northwestern. My character became involved with Kerry Weaver. That was a dream come true for me because as I said, I've known of her since college. She was a little bit ahead of me, she was a terrific actress, and everybody was in love with Laura Innes at Northwestern.

Ellis and Kerry were involved romantically for a little bit. I think my wife remembers it more than I do. Maybe that's why Kerry became a lesbian. I have no idea. I don't remember very many specifics of the relationship, except that at one point I had to be shirtless in her boudoir.

The other thing I remember is how Warner Bros. had these little wooden constructed houses with a bed and maybe a fan and a desk in it. It was on wheels, and they could push it all around the studio. That's what your dressing room was, and you had to be cool with that. I think that the only thing my agents told me was, "You're getting paid, and the only thing that's going to suck is these dressing rooms. Are you okay with that?" And I was like, "Yeah, sure."

Martha Plimpton was cast as a pregnant drug addict named Meg Corwin, who was introduced in the season 6 episode called "Sins of the Father." She would go on to appear in three more episodes.

Martha Plimpton (Meg Corwin) There was a period there in the mid- to late '90s where I just played pregnant drug addicts over and over again. I do remember that I was playing a waitress in a diner, and I had to carry a tray with stuff on it, and one was a glass of orange juice. We were rehearsing, and they said, "Do you want to rehearse with all that stuff on your tray?" I was like, "Yeah, sure." So, I walked, and when I got to Julianna Margulies, I fumbled, and all the orange juice went over her gorgeous camel cashmere coat. She was like, "Glad you rehearsed with the orange juice?" I was so embarrassed. I felt horrible, and it was one of my first scenes. A great way to kick off that experience!

That's the main thing I remember, other than the fact that it was great fun to do the show and I really liked working on it. I loved being back on the Warner Bros. lot after so many years. I hadn't worked there since *The Goonies*.

In 2007, Joe Manganiello appeared in several episodes as Officer Litchman, who ends up falling for Nurse Samantha Taggart, played by Linda Cardellini.

Joe Manganiello (Officer Litchman) I went to the Carnegie Mellon School of Drama, and John Wells was a Carnegie Mellon guy. So, when I got out of school, John Levey, who cast *ER*, came to our showcases. There was some talk about me being on *ER*. I was offered a TV holding deal by Warner Bros. for them to develop shows for me. But I said no, I'm doing films. I'm a film actor. Then I wound up that week being brought in to test for *Spider-Man* for Sam Raimi. And then right after that, I screen-tested for *Training Day* for Antoine Fuqua and then for *Black Hawk Down*. I screen-tested twice for *Hart's War* to play the third lead. I mean, all the film stuff was happening for me right out of drama school.

A few years later, the climate started changing, and John Levey called me and said, "Hey, do you want to come in and play this character coming up?" I came in and got the part of Linda Cardellini's love interest. We remained friends, and funny enough, we both starred in *Nonnas* on Netflix in 2025. So of course, the two of us talked about being on *ER* together.

In 2005, Kat Dennings joined ER *for a five-episode arc as Zoe Butler, a brief love interest for Shane West's Dr. Ray Barnett.*

Kat Dennings (Zoe Butler) I must have been seventeen or nineteen or something like that. It was supposed to be one episode. I was very excited to work with Shane West because he was a big heartthrob at the time and probably still is. I was just so excited because they shot at Warner Bros., where they had a whole hospital built. It was the most in-depth, detailed set I've ever seen. I mean, everything was practical. It was just mind-blowing and amazing to feel like I was a part of this legendary show.

Was I a patient? Oh, no. Wait. I was dating Shane, and then he found out I was underage. It was a crazy storyline. I don't know how I ended up in the hospital. But I do remember they must have liked me, because they made it into a small arc, so I came back for a few episodes. And then they wrote that my dad was hitting me, which was bad. It was a very dramatic turn they put in there, and I had tearful scenes in the hospital. I was covered in fake bruises. I was like, *My God, how does this happen?* But I was just so excited they wanted me back. Everyone was lovely and super nice. I vividly remember some actors would write down their lines on their clipboards and on the computer screens. So, if you see a doctor holding a clipboard, their lines were written on that. I've taken that with me my entire career. If I'm holding a piece of paper, my lines are on it. I thank *ER* for that tip.

In 2008, journeyman actor Michael Gaston was called upon to play Rick, a federal agent in charge of watching over a guy in the witness protection program. That guy was Steve Buscemi.

Michael Gaston (Rick) David Zabel was an old friend of mine. We went to drama school together, and he was an actor who made his way out to LA. Over the course of six or seven years, he went from being an actor to executive producing *ER*. I think I just got thrown into that job. I don't think I auditioned for it. I remember sitting between shots and talking to Linda Cardellini, who was just delightful.

Steve's character was even attacked in the hospital because he ratted somebody out. The episode ends with us leaving the hospital and him being in our custody. We get into an ambulance to be transported somewhere. The very last frame of the episode is the ambulance exploding. So, we were all killed by the people who were going after him. That happens to me a lot.

Before he went on to break hearts as Denny Duquette on Grey's Anatomy, *Jeffrey Dean Morgan was cast as a firefighter on* ER *for one episode in 2001.*

Jeffrey Dean Morgan (Firefighter Larkin) It was a huge episode. It was about this train crash that derailed and many people died. I was a fireman who got trapped underneath and ended up having my legs amputated. I remember being buried under the ground for a couple nights. I was a big fan of that show, so I loved being able to do it. I loved John Wells and had known him for years. I had done a pilot with him in 1994 for ABC—the same year he did *ER*—called *Mystery Dance*, and it was with Peter Riegert, Jane Curtin, and William H. Macy. We shot it in Portland. But only one of Wells's pilots got picked up and that was *ER*. So, John eventually hired me for *ER*, and then he hired me for *Shameless*, but I ended up shooting only one episode for the Showtime comedy and couldn't go back to do it again because I was stuck in Mexico doing this never-ending Western miniseries.

My favorite story from *ER* involved my mother. I mean, this was kind of at the height of *ER*. Everybody was watching that show, and my mom had a big crush on Noah Wyle. I'm buried in the ground, I can't leave, I'm like literally buried there for fifteen hours, so I was talking to Noah and told him, "My mom just loves you." So, he's like, "You got your phone?" He tells me to call my mom.

I call her and say, "Hold on a second. Someone wants to talk to you." I gave the phone to Noah, and he just walked away. And I swear to God, he talked to my mom for an hour and a half. I could see him way over there still talking. It made my mom's life. She was the happiest person she's ever been, talking to Noah Wyle.

In 2004, Julianne Nicholson snagged a pair of episodes as a young mom named Jordan who comes into the ER after she fainted at home.

Julianne Nicholson (Jordan) It was exciting because that was such a huge show at the time, and it was early in my career, so it was probably scary. I remember a little of the storyline. Or maybe I don't, something about a dead baby. I think I had a previous child that had died or something. It was very sad, of course. Maura Tierney was so kind to me. We had a big scene, and she put me at ease.

I also remember there was some conversation because I was crying, and then makeup wanted to come in and pat my face with powder because I get very red when I cry. I asked, could they leave it? Could we not cover up to see more of what's happening? They were like, "Yeah, sure." When you start off, you don't have a voice. You don't know that you can even afford to have a voice, or that was my experience. It was one of the first places I remember raising my hand and saying, "Maybe we don't need to powder. Maybe we can just leave the redness that comes with crying."

One of the first guest actors to receive an Emmy nomination was Rosemary Clooney, George's aunt, who played a woman with Alzheimer's in the 1994 episode "Going Home." Her character, dubbed Madame X, shows up to the ER alone and begins singing to the doctors and patients. She would return later in the year in an episode titled "The Gift." Rosemary Clooney died in 2002.

George Clooney I had nothing to do with it. John Wells called me up one day and said, "I got a part for your aunt," and I was like, "Oh, okay," and then they called her up and asked her to do it. I wish I could take credit for it, but I had nothing to do with it.

Noah Wyle I had the great benefit of getting sort of all the older patients, so I got Sanford Meisner, I got Red Buttons, I got Eli Wallach, and I got Mickey Rooney, so I had an unbelievable embarrassment of riches with the people I got to work with. But Rosemary was one of the earliest sort of heavy-hitter guest stars that we had on the show, and I thought she was just amazing. It's very hard to play less intelligent than you are or more confused than you are, and she had an interesting quality. And then when she began to sing, the expectation was that she would fall into her old sort of performance rhythm, but she didn't, she found a sort of vocal quality that seemed much more pedestrian and less polished than a professional would be, which made it even more heartbreaking.

George Clooney Noah was the nephew she always wanted.

In 2006, James Woods received an Emmy nomination for playing Dr. Nate Lennox in the season 12 episode dubbed "Body & Soul," told through a series of flashbacks. Lennox was a biochemistry professor and mentor to Abby Lockhart who suffered from amyotrophic lateral sclerosis, more commonly known as Lou Gehrig's disease. There's even one point in the episode when Woods's character pays homage to Gehrig's 1939 "Luckiest Man" farewell speech.

James Woods (Nate Lennox) Back then, I was kind of in the peak of my career and doing mostly movies, and I had just been through a personal tragedy. I'd lost my beautiful brother, so I wasn't really interested in working. But they said, "Look, we'd really love to have you do this." It's really a beautiful story, and I played a doctor and a patient, which is what made the story so great. I knew a lot about ALS to begin with. One of the things they said about ALS is if you have a choice between Parkinson's disease, multiple sclerosis, or ALS, take the other two and thank

God you're only going to suffer a little compared to ALS. It is just absolutely the worst disease.

They said, "Would you come in on Saturday before we start shooting? We want you to meet some of the people who are suffering from this disease." So, I went in, and John Wells was there, as well as the director, Paul McCrane. We sit down in a ring like it was an AA meeting. I'm not in AA, but I played the founder of AA [in the 1989 TV movie *My Name Is Bill W.*]. Anyway, each person was there to tell their story. We start with a young woman on my left, who seems normal as can be. She's just been diagnosed with ALS. And then as we went around the circle, it got worse and worse until we got to the guy to my right who's in a puffer wheelchair that used a straw to communicate. He was with his wife.

To this day, it brings me to tears. His wife said it was difficult because among the things that are most disconcerting at his stage of the disease is that he can't function and he can't function as a man with his wife. I said, "He's here today helping me understand the gravity of this disease. He's willing to expose the terrible dilemma he's in. I don't think I could meet a braver man." He started bawling, crying. Boy, that to me was a key moment as an artist.

The episode was so beautifully written. They really got it. And don't forget, that was one of their last seasons, and they weren't dogging it, man. They weren't like, "Oh, okay, here's a disease-of-the-week kind of thing." It wasn't like that at all. They put everything into it. I got to be energetic in the beginning, and then you see me start to decay, to ossify really, to become almost a petrified person. How was it explained to me? A soul inside a corpse. It was a great way of understanding it.

You're completely aware of what's happening to you, and you can't do a thing about it.

During season 6, Alan Alda was recruited to play Dr. Gabriel Lawrence, a renowned physician that Dr. Kerry Weaver hires to serve as the senior attending in the ER. It doesn't take long before Dr. Mark Greene, who wanted the head job, notices that Lawrence is showing signs of poor judgment and forgetfulness. Alda ended up earning an Emmy nomination for the short arc.

Alan Alda (Gabriel Lawrence) I had my program, *Scientific American Frontiers,* that I did for eleven years on PBS. I interviewed an expert in Alzheimer's, and I think I got in touch with her again when I was doing the part on *ER* to get some more familiarity about the condition. When we were doing *M*A*S*H,* we didn't go through intensive training, but there was a doctor on the set, Walter Dishell, who later became a friend. During the pilot, I was accompanying a guy on a stretcher from the helicopter, and I was very concerned about him. Walter called me over and said, "You don't have to be so emotional about every patient. You do this all day long, every day." And that kind of insight from somebody who knows was really important because your first impression is a naïve one.

The people on *ER* were wonderful to work with, and the writing, as it always was with John Wells, was strong. The characters are in situations they are working to climb out of, so there's always an objective that's very clear. I remember my first day on the job, when Gabriel goes up to a desk and says his name. I remember thinking, *I'm new here myself,* and I was hoping the day would work out okay. On that first day, I encountered a patient who was agitated, and we had to take a sample of something from him. I don't know what it was. So, the character just started improvising. John said the next day that he was hoping I would bring energy to the scene. And I thought, I didn't just bring energy, I brought fright.

Did anyone say [I would get an Emmy nomination] for playing Gabriel? No. We had a director of photography on *M*A*S*H*, and if he liked the scene, he'd say, "Dust off your tuxedo." After a while, I had a dusty tuxedo.

In the final moment of his five-episode arc, a now-out-of-work Dr. Lawrence is pulled into action by Carter, who can't figure out why a new patient was having acidemia seizures. Dr. Lawrence prescribes the drug Pavulon and almost immediately, the patient stops shaking. "Score one for the absent-minded professor," Alda says, before realizing his time as a physician has come to an end. "Well, I gotta go."

Alan Alda It's been more than twenty-five years. Every once in a while, this pops into my head. The last line I spoke didn't quite come to me. The last line was supposed to be "Gotta run." And instead of that, I said, "Gotta go," which means the same thing, but doesn't have that irony where he's using a common phrase for such a big event. He's giving up his career. It always pisses me off that I couldn't remember "Gotta run." I couldn't redo the scene, because the whole take went well. It was a take in which I could remember things. So, I was totally on board!

In 2002, Mary McDonnell received an Emmy nomination for playing John Carter's icy mom, Eleanor. She was introduced at the funeral of Carter's grandfather in 2001.

Mary McDonnell (Eleanor Carter) They called me in and said, "Listen, we've got this role. She's a complicated woman, and it's Noah's mom." They said to me, "We don't have room, nor can we create another huge guest star arc." It was sort of right after Sally Field, right? I said, "That's okay! I love the show. Whatever. Show me what you're going to write." They did, and it was fabulous. This role was so beautiful because she got to [highlight] part of Noah's character that I always felt was kind of mysterious. Her feelings were frozen. That was the word I remember, that somewhere in the past with her other son and everything that had gone on, she was unable to continue whatever feelings she had for John. That's what happens to people who don't know how to process grief. Grief can kill you. She clearly was more involved in drinking her grief away. I just remembered that we went through an awful lot to get to something more, and that it was a process of unfreezing.

Of the multiple guest actors who were nominated over the years—Bob Newhart, Forest Whitaker, Ewan McGregor, and Stanley Tucci, among them—only two walked away with Emmys for their work on ER. *The late Ray Liotta was recognized for playing ex-con Charlie Metcalf in the 2004 episode "Time of Death," while Sally Field earned the second Emmy of her career for playing Abby Lockhart's mom, Maggie Wyczenski.*

The Oscar-winning actress first appeared on ER *in 2000 and ended up returning for multiple episodes so John Wells could give viewers a rare look at bipolar disorder and its devastating impact on family. Field would go on to win her second Emmy in 2001 for playing a character with a mental health condition; her first came in 1977 for portraying the title role in the made-for-TV film* Sybil *that also aired on NBC.*

Sally Field (Maggie Wyczenski) To have a long-term career that goes on for sixty-some-odd years, you must recognize the roller coaster that it is. You are up, up, up, and then you have a wave that goes down, and you must be able to recognize the opportunities that come along that may not be what has been voiced as the thing you should be doing. I was in my fifties, and as a woman at that time, that was a difficult age group. They didn't know what to do with you. I didn't have a production company.

John Wells approached me. It was a time where network television was at its height. I had watched *ER*—not religiously—and I had great regard for him. He talked to me on the phone and said what he wanted to do. And without any hesitation, I said, "I'm in." Being an actor, you get to go places you never would have gone. You get to literally visit places all over the world and spend time there to be a part of the community. This was an opportunity to travel to a different kind of country, and that was to understand a mental health issue. That was very unknown at that time. No one really talked about it or knew about what bipolarism was. It wasn't even called that back then. It was called *manic depressive behavior,* and it was underdiagnosed, under-medicated, and not understood at all. You would just call the family member a problem, sometimes a severe problem, who a lot of times would land in jail or on the streets or lost altogether. Evidently, John had a family member. I don't know if I remember exactly who close to him was manic depressive or bipolar. He wanted to give me six episodes. He said three would absolutely be [my] story, nothing else. And then maybe they would start to bring in other storylines of other characters.

"When we saw Sally Field's performance as this deeply troubled woman, it was so affecting. Once I saw what she was doing, I was like, *Oh, now I understand my character. Now I see what my character grew up with.* It informed all of these things to me about Abby being emotionally guarded and super tough, but kind of vulnerable in a lot of ways. I valued that a lot."

—MAURA TIERNEY

He set it up so I could do serious research at UCLA, where they were really trying to understand this mental disorder, and to try to perfect any kind of medications that could be given. Because it has become so well recognized as a condition, you could call anybody bipolar who has a big temper. At least it's out there in society, understanding that this is a treatable mental condition just like depression. So, I went to UCLA every day into the research center, and I talked to the doctors a lot. I was also allowed to meet up with real patients who were in this study. After I spent all that time, John presented me with these exceptional episodes, and he directed the first one.

Maura and I just sort of clung to each other because both roles were highly emotional and difficult to find, to land on the right spot. Maura played a character who was trying to find her own existence. Who's going to love her? What match does she make? And here comes this mother who's bigger than life and sort of takes over the whole room and wears her little clothes and acts like she's the cat's meow. Of course, Abby just wants to kill her. [In one episode,] Maura and I were completely drenched all night long, however many hours into the night we shot. As a matter of fact, John Wells sent me a great eight-by-ten glossy of Maura and I looking at each other like drowned rats. It was during a big fight and she's yelling at me or I'm yelling at her. It's a great photo. I am glad to have it.

I have been lucky enough in my career to play other people with mental conditions that were unknown, unrecognized, and still criticized . . . one of them being what was then called *multiple personalities*. Now it's called all sorts of different things, but it really is a disorder that exists. Because of *ER*, people have stopped me on the street to say thank you. They say things like, *My mother has this, and I didn't know it was an actual condition or that I could turn to somebody for help. She loses herself when she gets in these patterns.* It was like what John had said initially that this is a huge condition that has gone undiagnosed, unrecognized, and unappreciated for how difficult it really is. It was an amazing adventure into your own head and into how close we are as human beings to being diagnosed with any of these conditions.

16

Medical Minute

A Look Back at "The Storm," Parts 1 and 2

Season 5, Episodes 14 and 15 | February 11 and 18, 1999
Part 1: Written and Directed by John Wells
Part 2: Written by John Wells and Directed by Christopher Chulack

As much of a big deal as it was that George Clooney was leaving *ER*, he and just about everybody associated with the drama tried to downplay his 1999 departure. Clooney declined to do any goodbye interviews, while NBC's marketing guru John Miller said at the time, "We think of this not as a finale, but a transition." Even his costars tried to de-emphasize Clooney's importance to the medical drama. "We will miss George personally," said Anthony

Edwards to the *Los Angeles Times*, "but so much of watching *ER* is having a history with it. So, it's just part of the mosaic of being entertained for an hour." Added Gloria Reuben, "So much is being made of this before anything happens."

But Clooney couldn't escape the scrutiny of leaving TV's most popular show. When he began doing press for his role in the 1996 movie *From Dusk Till Dawn*, scads of reporters asked if was planning to "pull a David Caruso"—a snarky reference to the actor who infamously left *NYPD Blue* in 1994 after less than two seasons. But Clooney was no Caruso, whose film career took a nosedive after leaving the ABC cop drama. Clooney let Warner Bros. TV know early that he wanted to pursue a career in movies and went on to make *From Dusk Till Dawn*, *One Fine Day*, *Batman & Robin*, *The Peacemaker*, and *Three Kings*. But he never broke his five-year contract, though it certainly helped that John Wells was willing and able to work around his burgeoning film schedule. As Wells told *Entertainment Weekly* in 1996, "We have a large ensemble in which the work is evenly split. If George is on a movie set Tuesday through Saturday, we can slot his stuff for Mondays, at least for a while. I think I'm more reasonable accommodating George because I was able to be more reasonable. George is not the central figure Caruso was for *NYPD Blue*."

Anthony Edwards He probably could have, for a lot of good reasons, gotten out of his deal. He [did] a very heroic thing by staying on the show.

John Wells George stayed very grounded on set as his career took off, and he worked really hard at that.

Noah Wyle George is an extremely smart guy, a very political guy, and a very talented guy. It was no surprise to anybody that he got tapped for bigger and better things early on. Actually, I give him a tremendous amount of credit for staying for the full five years that he was contracted to do because he could have left a lot earlier. He was already making *Batman* while he was still under contract with us.

Ellen Crawford We were sometimes shooting two different episodes in the same day because George was shooting *Batman* at night. That meant they had to pay us double for each of those episodes because they were trying to work around his schedule. George always had a sense of humor about himself. He was vocal about not being sure how long this stretch will last. You got to take advantage while you got it. He remained a lovely human being.

Abraham Benrubi By the fourth, fifth season, the show got good. Clooney was Batman by now, and we knew he wasn't going to stick around forever. So, it was interesting to watch how they wrapped up his storyline. But George stayed cool, man.

Peter Roth (Warner Bros. TV Chairman) I joined the company on February 22, 1999, and George Clooney left the series on February 18, 1999. So, I'm walking in and losing the single most important and successful dramatic star on the lot, because that was when "The Storm: Part 2" aired. There was no panic, because I knew it was happening. George and I knew each other because when I was at Stephen J. Cannell Productions, the only talent holding deal that I made was with a then-unknown George Clooney in 1988. So, while nothing happened in the year that I had him in a holding deal, we became friends. When I joined Warner Bros., George was very good to me. I think I called him up and I said, "Is there any chance you might reconsider?" He said not a chance. But he did say, "Peter, I want you to know I've already talked to the rest of the cast. I told them you're a good guy and that they should be respectful." He helped me a lot in the transition, because there were issues from the moment that I started.

Jack Orman It was clear that George was not going to stay past his five years. He never asked for a renegotiation of his contract. I mean, he loved the show, and it also launched a huge movie career. But by the time I showed up in the fourth season, we were already carving out the schedule so that Warner Bros. could make these movies with George.

"George never came and asked us for more money, but the other people did with the understanding that, *Okay, we'll give you more money. But you've got to give us more time.* But George didn't want to do that. He said, 'I'll stay and do the show for five years, at my exact same salary.' Therefore, he was one of the lowest-paid people on *ER* in years four and five. He loved the show, loved everything about it, but didn't want to do the show. He said he had no hard feelings with Warner Bros. He just wanted to make movies. So, I said, 'Is there anything else, George? I feel guilty about you doing this.' He said, 'Yeah, make me a basketball court. I love playing basketball in between takes.' I said, 'Okay, we'll put a basketball court next to the stage.'"

—BOB DALY

Noah Wyle We had one outside the stage and it was blocking traffic and it was becoming problematic. So they built Mr. Clooney a court. We [couldn't] let the talent hurt themselves out there on the court. So it [was] like a psych ward. It [was] all padded in. They'd close us in there with a couple of balls so we [wouldn't] hurt each other.

Bob Daly Of course George honored his deal. He stayed on the show for five years. He even came back for the final season. He's a wonderful actor and wonderful guy, but he never got another cent.

In his going away two-parter, Clooney's character Doug Ross is threatened with a murder charge after he gives a lethal dose of narcotics to a boy who was in the last stages of adrenoleukodystrophy, or ALD. "I dedicated my life to pediatric medicine," Doug says at one point. "Ricky was going to die. Not in a month or a week, in hours, and nothing I did or could have done was going to change that. His mother already watched one son die from the disease she passed on to him." Though he ends up escaping prosecution, Ross decides to quit County General. He and Carol share one more emotional moment together in the hospital before he walks out of the ER for good. Doug's final scene is with Mark Greene in Chicago, where they sip beer outside before going to play basketball. Mark accuses him of always cheating.

Christopher Chulack I saved Julianna kissing George for the last shot of the day. That was a big deal. It was a very emotional day for both.

Jack Orman George could have gone all the way to the end of the fifth season. But John Wells thought ahead and said, "We don't want to dramatize George's exit as the season finale, because we don't want to give America a reason to go, 'That was a good run, so don't tune in the next fall!'" So, the idea was to write the exit arc during February sweeps so then everybody would still be in the habit of watching the show. This is something we then continued to do throughout the series, especially as we were handing off characters and introducing new ones. We built an overlap.

Lydia Woodward I think that that was a fitting, heroic end. He was the soldier who did the right thing but got kicked out of the military. I think it was a little dicey because Hathaway hadn't had the twins yet, for God's sake. I became so opposed to any character ever having a child because it just was such a drag on a character's energy, especially a female character. You can never lose track of that child.

George Clooney I got to be the guy that flirts with girls, but also likes kids and saves kids. And you know, whenever you can stick up for a kid as a character, you win.

Pam Morrison I left in the middle of season 5, right about the same time as George. Somebody at NBC asked me, "How can you leave George Clooney?" Well, I'm not actually leaving George Clooney. George is leaving the show, and George Clooney is not, as I recall, putting my kids through college.

Lily Mariye It wasn't like we were making a George Clooney movie where he was the star, and then there were the rest of us. We were a real ensemble. So, when George left, it felt like a piece of us left, but it wasn't like, "Oh, well, now we can't go on because the star of our show left." He was an important part of our show, but I really did feel like we were an ensemble in every variation of cast that we had over the years.

Jack Orman I remember both of those episodes as being powerful. I just loved the idea that it was consistent with his character. He has always been a rule-breaker. He applied values-based medicine, and he was going to do what he thought was right despite the rules. And in the end, it cost him his job.

John Wells George kept saying to me, "It's not going to matter [that he was leaving]. The show's too big of a hit. It's not going to matter." And I kept saying, "Yeah, easy for you to say. You're leaving." And then it didn't matter. The numbers didn't go down at all.

17

The Nurses' Station

In the history of *ER*, most of the attention was heaped on the doctors who clocked in and out of the hospital. But there was always a contingent of actors who never left their shifts: the nurses and desk clerks. While actors like Ellen Crawford, Yvette Freeman, Laura Cerón, Lily Mariye, Deezer D, Conni Marie Brazelton, Abraham Benrubi, and Troy Evans never achieved series regular status, their presence in the ER was both crucial and highly entertaining. Viewers grew accustomed to their omnipresence and came to enjoy their zingers and stink eyes whenever someone messed up. High-priced stars may have come and gone, but viewers could always count on the likes of Lydia, Haleh, Chuny, Lily, Jerry, and Frank to keep the IVs dripping and the phones answered over fifteen seasons.

Yvette Freeman I went to the *ER* audition in my red Pinto. It was awful. My Pinto blew up in the parking lot. Swear to God. I was living in New York, so I didn't have a car for a long time. So, the car was sitting there smoking in the parking lot when I'm auditioning with John Levey. There were four of us. There was the Black one, that was me. A white actor I didn't know, and a Latino and Asian. It was for the role of Haleh, which I changed when I got the job because it was some kind of Indian name. I pronounced it like my grandmother's first name, Hallie. I went in there when it was my turn, still thinking about that car smoking in the parking lot, trying to figure out how I'm going to get home. So, I was testy. I got through the audition, and my car did make it back to Santa Monica. By the time I got home, I had the job because I had the attitude they wanted for the Black nurse. They hired people who are like their characters because it's easier for them to learn their roles. It wasn't a stretch.

Laura Cerón They were looking for a Latina actor for the role of Nurse Chuny Marquez. Quentin Tarantino was directing my first episode. He apologized because the role was kind of small, but I made the best of it. Initially, I started as an OB-GYN nurse who was helping to deliver the baby of Susan's sister, Chloe. That's how they introduced me. Chicago comes with a little bit of a character, a little bit of sass, a no-nonsense kind of attitude. So, I felt like my character brought that to the table.

Ellen Crawford At that time I had already worked for John Wells on *China Beach*, and John Levey had cast me in that. John Levey knew my work and the work of my husband, Mike Genovese. There was a couple they planned on having who they call *frequent flyers*; there's always a problem when they come into the

ER as patients. It was a policeman and his wife, and she had accidentally shot him in the foot. So, originally, they called to see if we could come in for that couple. They did let us read the whole script, which was unusual. I read the script, and I thought this one nurse felt right to me. So, when I went in, I explained that my husband was off doing a pilot and I'd be happy to read for this other role of Lydia. Happily, John Levey and John Wells said, "What a good idea." They had named the character Lydia Wright, who was originally Lydia Woodward. That was kind of a joke, because she was, of course, a producer-writer.

Lily Mariye I auditioned for episode 4 in the first season because they needed a new nurse. I was sitting in this waiting room with thirty beautiful Asian American women and one man, and everybody was dressed up in nurses' uniforms. I had on a little pink suit, and I thought, *Oh, I'm not going to get cast.* I knew John Levey because he cast me on *China Beach*, and I had known John for a long time. So, I walked in the room and John Wells's assistant said, "I'd like you to meet Lily Mari . . . Mara . . . Maree-uh?" I said, "It doesn't matter. Just spell my name right on the paycheck." I swear to God, I think that's how I got this job, because I was being fun to be with, I guess.

Abraham Benrubi I had auditioned for *China Beach* quite a few times and never got the job, which was fine. When John Levey was casting the *ER* pilot, I don't know if he just got tired of auditioning people or at some point there were actors that he trusted. They just offered it to me, and I was thrilled to get that offer. It was super fun and unique at the time, and it really felt different. Jerry was in the very beginning and the very end when the shift changed. There was a funny moment with a paramedic that everybody always teases me about. *Ask him if he wants a cookie or a medal or something.*

Originally, Troy Evans began as a different character in the ER *pilot. He got the call from John Wells after working with him on* China Beach.

Troy Evans He said they were doing this pilot of this thing called *ER*, and one of the leads was this young, very inexperienced actor named Noah Wyle. In the original script, there was a policeman who came in and had a gunshot wound in his leg. In the course of the episode, you find out that his wife had shot him. But in the pilot, that part got swept out. But what they ended up with was a vivid scene of me in a hospital bed and John Carter trying to take a blood sample but completely botching it. He sprays my blood all over himself in the room and makes a big mess. It was an introduction of Carter as this really well-intentioned, kind of frantic, bumbling person who wasn't quite ready for the job that was in front of him.

Over the years, I've worked on a lot of TV series where one year I'll be in an episode as a cab driver, and the next year I'm the bartender. They bring you back every twelve or twenty-four months if they're on the air long enough, so you play these different parts. On *ER*, they nipped that in the bud. They said anybody who was on that show could only be on it as one person. In season 6, they called me at about 11:00 at night and said, "Would you be interested in being the desk clerk on *ER*?" I said, "Well, I'd have to think about that. Hell yes!" The way they got around their own rule is that my police officer character had retired, and his retirement job was working as the desk clerk in the emergency room.

"My husband was in a car accident and was taken to the ER in Long Beach, and it was a really crowded waiting room. They finally called our name, and when we went in, the triage nurse looked at me and said, 'I know you!' Suddenly, the line wasn't so long. She pushed us through. And yet we could walk around on the street and people wouldn't recognize us. I remember Noah Wyle was once talking about going to Honey Baked Ham for Thanksgiving. I said, 'Hey, me, too. Do you order it?' And he said, 'No, I'll just go stand in line. Nobody notices me.' But if I was in a hospital, like when I was visiting my grandfather, people would make that connection. I saw these girls running across a huge lobby toward me and one of them was crying. She said, 'You are the reason I'm going to nursing school.'"

—LILY MARIYE

Yvette Freeman John Wells told me he's going to use me, so *be ready*. I said, "Okay, all right." I didn't know it was going to be a series. I just thought it was a movie. I had no clue when I was auditioning. Nobody told me it was going to last fifteen years of my life.

Ellen Crawford I don't think anybody made any promises. We were brought in as guest stars to the end of the series. But I think one of the unique things about *ER* and maybe why it was so successful was it was focused on the people working in the hospital as the team. You got to know them through their work.

Abraham Benrubi I was a guest star the whole time. I never had any guarantee of episodes. I'm six foot seven, and the writers definitely used that. There were a couple of funny moments, one being any time there was a small animal to hold, Jerry was called upon to contrast the size. That makes me think of an episode where I was trying to catch an escaped kangaroo.

Yvette Freeman I never became a series regular. But no one left because they weren't series regulars. I understood why. They couldn't write for everybody and their mama. We were the supporters. Hold it a minute. They called us the *fabric*.

Laura Cerón We made a living, obviously nothing compared to the principals. The residuals were good, though. The '90s were great.

Troy Evans I was there 129 times and had 129 different contracts. If they'd have taken every nurse, every nurse's aide, all the people running around in scrubs and made us all series regulars, it would've been a gigantic amount of money and a huge headache. So they hired me in 1998 at top of show [which is roughly the day rate for an unknown guest star plus a small percentage]. But they held me at that. So when my friends were coming on the show ten years later, they were making almost $2,000 an episode more than I was. It bugged me a little bit, but it still paid off my house.

"The scene that I love more than anything else was when Abby leaves and is never coming back to the ER. She's going to a tango lesson and doesn't know what she's doing. I give her a thirty-second tango lesson. We dance a little, and then she walks out the door. It was so lovely they put that in. And they gave Frank that moment! That's pretty sweet."

—TROY EVANS

Lily Mariye I did have a meeting with John Wells where he said, "Look, I could sign you to be recurring, but then you wouldn't be able to go do anything else. I just promise I'll always bring you back. You can always take other jobs, and we can be flexible. So, it's up to you." I said, "Well, in that case, let's just shake hands." After a few seasons, it was pretty evident that I was going to be there a long time. In fact, I had once asked to take off to guest star on *Chicago Hope*, which was our competing medical show. John Wells said, "As long as you're not playing a nurse." I said, "No, I'm playing a patient who's not even from this country." He said it was okay.

Yvette Freeman I could come and go with *ER*. I did a show that I took off-Broadway and won an Obie award. *ER* was my bread-and-butter job while I did other things. If I got a movie or anything like that, I could go do it. Why not stay on this job? I mean, they weren't writing that much for Black women as it was. Now it's changed. Now it's a new world out here.

Ellen Crawford As we became more popular, they would give us raises, but we were always signing guest star contracts. I don't think any of us were ever hired on a yearly basis. But we were given an idea of how many episodes we were going to do out of this many of whatever. It was always show by show.

Like the series regulars, the actors who played the nurses were given special training by the doctors on staff. Real nurses were also brought in to both instruct and to fill up the background in those trauma room shots.

Lance Gentile I used real nurses from my practice. I figured they'd be much better than background artists who had no medical experience. I hired them all, a lot of my friends and nurses that I work with.

Ellen Crawford It's surprising how many people there are in this town that have both film degrees and are doctors.

Lily Mariye Each one of us would, individually, get our little time with the doctor to learn how to pronounce words and learn how to work these instruments. They would have us come in on Saturdays to rehearse.

Laura Cerón We had wonderful technical advisors. They were the ones who told us that sometimes the nurses knew more than the doctors in each situation because they're hands-on. They're right there all the time. That was the consensus with the real nurses. They gave us a little bit more confidence with our characters, too.

Ellen Crawford I remember one scene where Dr. Greene is advising John Carter and he says, "The key is to get smart nurses." We were like, "Oh, yeah." They established that, which was nice.

Lily Mariye People would tease me and say, "I bet we could call you in an emergency." And I said, "Yes, and I'll dial 911!" I can pronounce everything, and I can tell you what's happening, but I would not touch you. You would not want me to perform any sort of procedure on you.

However integral they were to the action, the nurses and clerks rarely—if ever—were given lives out of the hospital. If they did, they were oh-so-brief brief snapshots, like when Lydia married her cop beau during Susan Lewis's last day in season 3. (Even then, the audience didn't get to hear the vows.) Otherwise, the nurses mostly kept to their lane as the ER's sage and often stern caretakers.

Lydia Woodward We really loved the nurses, but they were a group on the show that did suffer from the size of the ensemble because we had our main characters. Most of the nurses weren't main characters. They were supporting characters. I don't think we could have legitimately given them much more than what we did, but we loved giving them whatever we could.

Jack Orman We had thirteen characters. It was already a lot. My recollection is that John loved writing for the nurses. When the nurses saw a script was written by John Wells, they would get excited. They weren't necessarily full-on stories with them, but more lounge mix, kind of side humor stories. John, more than anyone, did a lot of ER visits where he would shadow doctors, and he just saw that the nurses were the heartbeat of the ER. He would always gravitate to them. But it was hard. We just had forty-three minutes every week.

Yvette Freeman They were getting ready to give me a family, and John Levey showed me some pictures of some kids. I don't know exactly what happened, but then John Wells told me that this was as far as we were going to go. They weren't going to build any more stories about us.

Laura Cerón They gave me a couple romances, and that was kind of nice. It was this nice bite of the large pie, and then it was like, now back to the trenches. One was with Dr. Greene, which went on for a few episodes. You know what's funny? We never went to my house. We ended up in his house and in bed, and then another time on a motorcycle. We never had sex in the ER. And then I was with Luka. That wasn't long-lived. At one point, they wanted us to argue in our native languages, and we were like, *What?* Goran was like, "No, this is weird. We would never do that."

Lily Mariye At one point, they wanted me to be in a closet having sex with Dr. Jack Kayson [Sam Anderson, who recurred for several seasons], and then he has a heart attack and dies. I said, "I don't really want to do it, but thank you for thinking of me."

Yvette Freeman If I was in a scene, I would say something was wrong or I would tell somebody off. I was the flippant Black nurse. There's a category for that. Black women have always had my role. Alfre Woodard did it in *St. Elsewhere*. I would lay you out because you're not doing right. I would do that to poor Dr. Benton. That was my getting on him. He didn't like that at all. I don't think Eriq La Salle really liked being talked down by all the Black women who came through. That was a trope, and he didn't like that trope. I think he spoke up about it. He kept getting belittled by CCH Pounder and me, I guess. So, they stopped that.

Lily Mariye There were a lot of Christmas episodes or birthday episodes where people would break into a conga line. I don't know why, but suddenly, everybody would be in a conga line. And I always said to the director, "I'm not going to do the conga line because I feel like my character doesn't have time for that. Fun is fun after work, but while we're here, I have stuff to do." So, I never joined in on it. There were a couple of episodes where they made it a point to see me standing there watching the conga line go by.

Troy Evans They never said anything to me about what they wanted from Frank, but I think they knew the energy that I brought, which is that sort of low-key flat. *You want to know where the bathroom is? It's over there, where it says* bathroom.

"I think as the writers got to know the cast more, they would start throwing weird stuff at us. So my character, Jerry, wound up doing a Shakespearean monologue, chasing a mouse, and all kinds of weird, strange moments. I always thought, *How can this really be part of the life of a hospital?* But then you talk to people in regular life, and they're like, 'Oh, we had a big clown at our hospital who was just like you.' I was like, 'That's bizarre.'"

—ABRAHAM BENRUBI

Abraham Benrubi I know we met Jerry's mom a couple of times. We had some extracurricular stuff with Jerry. Every now and then he would go to the bar. Deezer D and I would often steal the golf carts that litter the lot at Warner Bros. One particular time, he and I went to John Wells's office and pitched this idea to him where Jerry and his character, Malik, have a poker party and take all the doctors' money. There was about a thirty-second pause, and John goes, "That's a great idea, guys. Keep working on it." He dismissed us with a smile.

Yvette Freeman I knew that I was integral to this show. I knew how good I was, and I knew all the writers liked me. They tried. They slipped the little things in there. I got some little stuff, and I was living a good life for a TV person.

For Ellen Crawford, her fifteen-year gig as Lydia Wright led to a part-time passion. She spent several years at conventions, where she got to know the real nurses who worked in the nation's hospitals. Even Julianna Margulies found herself defending the profession when the writers suggested that Carol go to medical school to become a doctor.

Ellen Crawford Neal Baer had a great relationship with the Emergency Nurses Association. And in fact, they invited Julianna and me to come to their convention in Texas. She and I went and mostly just listened and got a mini-massage in the mall. The next time we were invited to go, I spoke about how the show worked, how we tried to be as close as we could, given you can't do an entire twelve-lead EKG and just wait for it. You had to have shortcuts. But we were really trying to be authentic. From then on, I was invited to go for about three years. I spoke at different nursing places, nursing conventions, nurse meetings, whatever. And it kind of morphed into doing some research as a layperson about conditions in hospitals. It became very clear that nurses, when they go on strike, it's for the patients. I had such deep, deep respect for people who really, truly did the work.

Julianna Margulies I think it was our third or fourth season, where they decided they wanted Hathaway to go to med school. I took tremendous offense to that, because nurses are never represented properly in a hospital. All the nurses I followed around in a real hospital before we started the show said the doctors fix people, but they heal them. I never forgot that. I fought so hard. I said, "You can't make Hathaway a doctor. You just can't. It's not right. It's not fair to the nurses in this world. They've got to be seen." And [the actors who played the nurses on *ER*] all stood behind me for that. It was such a great force of nature, these incredible women and Deezer D, who passed away.

John Levey The people of *ER* were always the center of the star. I refer to them in my book as the trampoline, all those wonderful nurses and EMTs and desk clerks, all of those men and women who were so stable and steady and so talented. They always allowed the stars to leap higher than they could have without that trampoline to jump on.

Carol Flint One of the strengths of the show was everything came flooding through the doors and you couldn't guess in advance what was going to be a runner and what was going to be the A story. Somebody who had a silly little whatever, like an ingrown toenail or something, could end up being the patient with the big story, whereas something that seemed serious could become trivial. Because of that, the support staff and all the people on the desk fit with that kind of storytelling. Sometimes they could usher something in that got passed over to somebody else and became a bigger story. Also, the audience's interest in those minor characters fit the democratic ideals of the series. I think that's why the ER worked at that time, before Obamacare. I think it worked because there was so much anxiety about people not getting good healthcare. The emergency room was where everybody and anybody could show up. We humanized the second tier. They fit the ethos of the series.

Abraham Benrubi I think my favorite moment of being recognized was after an episode where Jerry spreads a staph disease because he didn't wash his hands after using the restroom. That's one of the lovely things that Jerry got to do. I was in the bookstore and there were two moms looking at me whispering, and one of them came up to me to say, "You are so gross. You didn't wash your hands after you peed." She was convinced that whatever was happening on TV was real. I'll never forget that lady in the bookstore.

18

Medical Minute

A Look Back at "Be Still My Heart" and "All in the Family"

Season 6, Episodes 13 and 14 | February 10 and 17, 2000
Episode 13: Written by Lydia Woodward and Directed by Laura Innes
Episode 14: Written by Jack Orman and Directed by Jonathan Kaplan

In this unforgettable two-parter, a twenty-three-year-old law student named Paul (David Krumholtz) comes into the ER complaining of a bad headache. His erratic behavior leads Lucy Knight (Kellie Martin) to believe he's suffering a mental breakdown, but he ends up stabbing both her and Carter before she ever gets a proper diagnosis from psych.

The episode, directed by first-time helmer Laura Innes, is chock-full of storylines: Romano asks Alex to help him operate on his Bouvier named Greta; Abby watches an old woman die; Greene and Corday have dinner with his dad and her mom; a very young Anton Yelchin plays a victim of a car accident that claimed the lives of his parents; and the staff throws a very loud Valentine's Day party, which is why they initially missed the stabbing that was happening just a few feet from their celebration.

But the primary mission of the episode was to send off Kellie Martin, who wanted her two-year run to come to an end for personal reasons. Her character was conscious in the subsequent episode, dubbed "All in the Family"—written by Jack Orman and directed by Jonathan Kaplan—but she ended up dying from a pulmonary embolism. The best line in the two-parter came from Weaver, who angrily utters, "People were having parties while these two were in there bleeding to death."

Lydia Woodward It's not that we wanted to off Lucy exactly. When you have characters joining your show and then leaving your show, you try to vary up how they come in and how they go out. Sometimes people go to take jobs in other cities and other hospitals, and sometimes they get married and sometimes you kill them. All of that was a setup for Carter becoming addicted to opioids. It's not just lowlifes and disadvantaged people who become addicted to drugs. It's your neighbors, it's your friends, it's your doctors. So, the whole thing with killing Lucy was part of the setup for getting stabbed and then continuing on to his story.

Eriq La Salle One of my favorite storylines was when [Carter] got addicted to drugs.

Noah Wyle John Wells said, "I want to make you a drug addict," and I said that seems like a bit of a stretch for John Carter. He says, "Let me tell you why, because I think drug addiction is a ubiquitous problem that has not just a face, or any face—it has every face. So, you're the least likely character to develop a drug addiction, and I think that is exactly why it should be you. The way we'll get into it will be, you'll be hurt, and in the course of your rehabilitation, you'll begin to self-medicate, and your desire to get back to work will make you sort of push your recovery faster than you probably should." I'm not sure why they decided to make Kellie's last episode as the catalyst for the storyline for me, but it was a really effective way of kicking the whole thing off, because not only was my character suffering from a physical pain, but there was a psychological component to his guilt that also compounded the problem, which made it that much more believable.

Jack Orman I remember in that episode, Carter finally wakes up after surgery. This is "All in the Family," after he's safe, and Lucy didn't make it. Benton's not addressing him directly, because he just wants him to recover. And Carter figures it out. But in about thirty seconds, there's dialogue like, "Oh, my back is killing me." Benton saying he's going to prescribe the morphine. And then Carter realizing and looking at him and saying, "Lucy's dead, isn't she?" Those are the three prongs of the Carter addiction story right there in that scene. It is a combination of survivor's guilt and what a lot of people go through in terms of personal addiction, but it's not uncommon among doctors.

Kellie Martin John Wells called me into his office, and we discussed them wanting to do something big with Lucy. They wanted to do something big for February sweeps, and Lucy was the character who got played out. So, that's how I found out. When I found out that's what they were going to do, I was happy, and honored, yet at the same time a little bit wondering what I had done to deserve such a big demise. I mean, it was pretty brutal. But I think if you have to leave a show, especially a show like *ER*, that's the way to go.

Lily Mariye We just heard lots of different things. Kellie wasn't happy, and her sister had been ill.

Kellie Martin My sister had passed away a week before I started *ER*. So, *ER* was all tangled up with a lot of bad times in my life. It was the right thing for me to leave that show at that time. But it didn't feel like it at the time, for sure.

Jack Orman These things can be prolonged auditions in a lot of ways, right? I mean, because you're putting them onto a moving train and seeing how the chemistry reacts to what's going on.

Lydia Woodward I knew exactly how that was going to play out. I had it completely in my head before I even knew what the rest of the script was going to be. I just didn't know how to get there. It took me a while to figure out how to get there.

Kellie Martin The cast found out when they read the script. People were coming up to me on set saying, "You're going to be all right, though, right?" And me saying, "Nope, turns out nope. Not going to be all right." My conversation with Noah, after he knew I was leaving, I'd say the best way to describe it was bittersweet because I think he was surprised, and I think he was sad to see me go.

I didn't think of it as an honor at the time. Lucy was always a little bit of a mystery to me, so I never felt comfortable in her shoes. So, it felt like a little bit of an unfinished job maybe, because I just never really found her.

David Krumholtz (Paul Sobriki) On my first day, Kellie came up to me and said, "Hey, look, I just recently found out about this and it's been hard for me, and if you'd be kind enough not to walk around making jokes about how they're killing my character off, that'd be great."

Kellie Martin I did keep telling David, "It's okay. Don't feel bad. It's your job."

Noah Wyle David Krumholtz comes up behind me and stabs me in the back. The very first thing I played was a sort of mild annoyance that somebody might be trying to play a joke on me or trying to distract me from what I'm trying to do in that moment.

David Krumholtz Noah wanted to make sure that it didn't look like a movie stab where it's just a quick jab, that my character being smaller and coming up behind him and wanting to do it quietly and not as quickly, would have trouble stabbing someone in that portion of their back easily. He didn't want it to come off fake.

Noah Wyle Laura was more interested in what was happening on my face than what could be interesting about the salaciousness of seeing a knife enter my body.

Kellie Martin The most indelible image is me and Noah lying on the ground in a pool of blood.

Noah Wyle That was Laura's choreography, to have her on the ground in this pool of blood and have me eventually fall into it and have the last shots just being these close-ups of these faces trying to see each other.

David Krumholtz That scene is so heartbreaking. I mean,

horrible. Really, for the time, certainly pushing the boundaries of what you could show on television.

Kellie Martin There was a lot of blood. In order for it to read on-camera, there's way more than you end up seeing. So, there was a ton of blood. It's very sticky; it's very unpleasant.

Lily Mariye Usually we're walking around with gowns on with fake blood on them while talking about what we're going to have for lunch, or whatever. It was not a big deal to have fake blood on you. But in this episode, because Kerry Weaver and I picked her up and held her close to us, they had to soak our gowns with blood in a way that we never had before. As soon as they did that, it became somber, and I could see people looking at me going, "Wow, that's a lot of blood." Suddenly, it wasn't just another day at work. It felt real.

Noah Wyle The way that we reveal Kellie under the bed, the way that Laura chose to shoot it, and the way that I chose to play it, was an interesting combination of factors that make that scene extremely harrowing for a lot of reasons.

Kellie Martin I actually had never died on television until then, so I was excited about that part of it.

Noah Wyle I didn't think it was going to look like that. I didn't think that soundtrack ["Battle Flag" by Lo Fidelity Allstars] was going to be thumping in my head, and I didn't think it was going to be revealed in a piecemeal fashion. So it took on an extra degree of intensity as it got cut together, that I didn't see on the page initially.

Kellie Martin In the second episode, I had to have a chest cast made so they could use the sternal saw. It was not fun to be the actor lying on the gurney with the chest thing over you that they're going to saw into you. It was not fun to be the patient, like at all. I would take being a doctor any day of the week.

Noah Wyle It was a well-made episode. You don't kill a regular character off—at least we didn't.

Jack Orman What really worked with that pair of episodes is it was the time before characters were being killed off left and right on medical shows. It was somewhat unexpected. Also, we felt that we'd already done a few episodes where doctors left for other opportunities or they were on a train to Phoenix or whatever. So we saw an opportunity to do something quite memorable for the characters.

Kellie Martin The scene that was unnerving to me was that scene at the end of the second episode where I'm lying on the slab, dead, and they cover me up. And that was my last scene on the show, so the director, Jonathan Kaplan, came up to me, and he whispered, "You're wrapped."

Noah Wyle It was horrible. I felt horrible for David. He killed America's sweetheart, he cut her throat. Then he stabbed America's other sweetheart, twice.

David Krumholtz Two days after it aired, I was in Burbank going to the movies and somebody in the movie theater got really disturbed by seeing me and said, "You're the guy that killed . . ." and I said, "Yeah, you're actually the first person to say anything about it." He's like, "Dude, that's really messed up." Ultimately, it was four days of work for me when I was twenty-one years old living in Burbank by myself. That's what makes it all the more charming.

"One of the funniest dynamics in *ER* was that people were always complaining and had something to say about how I treated Noah. Noah and

I were probably the closest guys out of the entire cast. So it was a testament to our chemistry. It was a testament to our commitment to the characters. I just made a decision that I'm not going to apologize for Benton."

—ERIQ La SALLE

Noah Wyle Surviving that experience and the drug addiction, and all the rest of it, was such a key point in defining Carter. It's difficult to imagine his trajectory without it.

Jack Orman In the second episode, you're almost rooting for Noah when he's denying and lying the whole time. And then they end up doing the intervention in the very room where he was stabbed. They invited Benton into this. He was briefed. He shows up. His very presence in that room, in that intervention, escalates the thing for Carter to another level. Benton was holding it together and didn't say a word until the very end, when someone said, "Is that it?" And Benton says no. He's going to take it into his own hands.

Benton follows Carter out of the ER, where a confrontation ensues. Though Noah Wyle was hesitant to throw a punch, La Salle encouraged his costar to keep it looking as real as possible.

Eriq La Salle Benton came in like a big brother and a father and took him to rehab. But before that happened, Noah and I got into a fistfight. Noah hit me and saw the first take. It was a polite hit. And I'm like, "Dude, you got to knock this out of me. If you throw it, I'll sell it." And he threw it, and it didn't make me look good, but that was the thing. It wasn't about my ego. A lot of actors, they want to take it and bounce back. I was like, "No, I want you to knock me the hell out." When he swung, which was timed perfectly, I went flailing. My job is not to make me look good. This is your story. This is about you. It's about your rage. It's about the fact that you're out of control, that you're high on drugs, that you're in denial, all of those things.

Jack Orman We had the great benefit of a long relationship. It rewarded the loyal viewer. If this was a movie, it wouldn't work. But when you know the history between those two, it worked really well.

Eriq La Salle Benton was not the warm and fuzzy "I love you" guy. He wasn't that guy with words, except for with his son, but he was that way with his actions. I think that people really got into it because it was such a great foundation for such a strong bromance, like these two men loved each other whether they could say it, or one could say it, or whatever. So, to me, that was a scene about love. And so that pan really captured, "If you have to go to hell, I'm coming to hell with you, and I will always be there for you." So I think that really came through.

19

Medical Minute

A Look Back at "Such Sweet Sorrow"

Season 6, Episode 21 | May 11, 2000
Written and Directed by John Wells

No thanks to social media, it's virtually impossible to keep a secret in Hollywood these days. But Facebook and Twitter weren't around in 2000, so *ER* was able to hide the mother of all twists from its insatiable fan base: Carol was going to reunite with her beloved Doug toward the end of season 6. It would take months and months of negotiations, however, before viewers would be treated to such a romantic and satisfying end to Julianna Margulies's six-year run on *ER*. Even though George Clooney had left the show in

1999, Warner Bros. wasn't ready to say goodbye to the actress who played America's favorite nurse.

Julianna Margulies In 2000, my contract was up on *ER*, and I was ready to move back to New York. Jon Robin Baitz had written a part for me in his new play to be performed at Lincoln Center with Jason Robards and Ethan Hawke. This is every actor's dream, to have such a well-respected playwright, someone you have admired for years, tell you they were thinking of you and they wrote their next play. It is the biggest compliment any actor can receive. I was dizzy with excitement, bowled over that somehow, he entrusted my talent with his words. I let him know before I even read the play that I had one more year on my contract and if they produced the play the following year, I would be able to do it.

Peter Roth Having not been able to keep George Clooney, I was really hoping I might be able to, at the end of season 6, keep Julianna. I said, "Julianna, you can't leave. You just absolutely can't leave." I took Julianna out to lunch, and I offered her a two-year, $27 million deal on behalf of John Wells and the company. I was using every ounce of my persuasiveness. I was begging her; I was cajoling.

Julianna Margulies I called [my father] from my home in Santa Monica. I told him of my dilemma, and there was a long pause before he spoke. "Here's how I see it, Juli. When is enough, enough? Don't you have money in the bank? The question you need to ask yourself is this: Do you want to spend two years of your life wishing for it to be over so you can live the life you really want?"

Peter Roth At one point, I said, "When you have an important decision to make, who helps you? Who's your advisor?" She says her father. I said, "I'm calling your father." I actually called her father in Chicago. I had a half-hour conversation with him. I begged him. I said, "Sir, you cannot let your daughter make this decision. This is $9 million per year. She's vital to the show. The audiences adore her. We can't lose her. You've got to help me persuade her to stay." To his credit, he said, "This is my daughter's decision. She's making this for creative reasons. She wants to move on. This is her decision." I could not convince her.

Julianna Margulies I felt confident in my choice; this was my decision, no one else's. After months of harrowing soul-searching, I decided the right choice for me was to go with my heart. The next day, with supreme clarity, I politely turned down the offer from *ER*, called Robbie, and signed on to do the play. What I hadn't anticipated was the backlash.

Peter Roth She did [get harassed], but not from Warner Bros. It might've been from other castmates and, more importantly, the audience, because the first series she did [after *ER*] was a bust.

Julianna Margulies One day I was at the gym, the TV was tuned in to the daily talk show *The View*, and I was mortified to find that I was their topic of conversation. Barbara Walters held up the cover of the *New York Post*, or the *Daily News*, I forget which one, with the headline *ER* ACTRESS TURNS DOWN $27 MILLION! "Who does she think she is?" Barbara exclaimed to the other hosts, perching on their stools, drooling to get in on the discussion. "I mean, this girl is already forty-three years old, not some spring chicken. Does she think she's going to be a big movie star?"

At a press event for ER *that year, Margulies was asked about turning down such a huge payday. "The whole thing is surreal,"* *she told reporters. "Six years and we're still the number one show and people are still interested? On top of that, that kind of money, that's not real money." Her costar Eriq La Salle, who, together with Noah Wyle, had just signed his own $27 million deal in 1999, quickly responded, "Oh, it's real."*

Eriq La Salle Yes, I remember. Clearly there was no question in my mind as to how real it felt.

Ellen Crawford I was glad for her. You could talk to Julianna about her leaving and all that. She gave us all lovely jackets to say goodbye. I think it was a perfect time for her to leave. She was the one actor to win an Emmy out of all of us.

"It always had to be Carol and Doug, in the end. George and I, to this day, still sign our personal emails to each other 'Love, Carol' or 'Doug.'"

—JULIANNA MARGULIES

Peter Roth Then of course, she went on to do *The Good Wife,* which was magnificent. She was just brilliant in that. Anyway, I was very disappointed. I knew that, ultimately, I couldn't control it. It was her decision, but I really tried. I pulled out every stop to keep her, and I was disappointed in myself that I couldn't convince her. Years later, I remember going to a party. I think it was Kevin Bacon's birthday party, and Julianna was there, and I said, "You have to reconsider." I think it was like 2008 or something like that. And every time I talk to Julianna, we laugh about that story.

Written by John Wells, "Such Sweet Sorrow" follows Carol in her final moments at the ER when she tells Kovač, who had begun to develop feelings for her, that she is still in love with Doug and needs to go find out if his feelings are mutual. As Don Henley's "Taking You Home" plays in the background, Carol is seen dashing through the airport to catch a plane to Seattle, where she finds a flannel-wearing Doug in a bucolic, waterside setting. But at the table read for her final episode, Margulies and the rest of the cast were kept in the dark about how the episode would actually end.

Julianna Margulies It didn't really have a farewell to Carol at all. So, after the table read, I got very emotional. I quickly got up and ran to the bathroom and just cried. Because I thought, *Oh my God, this character means so much to me. And I know she does to so many fans, and I can't believe they're not giving her a proper send-off.* And Noah, bless his soul, he saw me and let me cry on his shoulder.

John Wells didn't let Margulies suffer for long. He then went to her trailer and let her in on his big secret.

Julianna Margulies John said, "Look, we have the right ending for Carol. But we can't tell anyone. Because if it gets out, it won't be a surprise. So, here's what we're going to do.'" I was like, "I wish he had warned me before I went into that table read!"

Lydia Woodward We kind of understood that they were always going to be the star-crossed lovers who eventually crossed back together in the very end.

Julianna Margulies John said, "We're going to fly the two of you out [to Seattle] separately. A car will pick you up."

Peter Roth George is an incredible human being. I mean, he has more integrity and more character than almost anybody I'd ever worked with. There was never a doubt in George's mind that he would do John that service, that he would come back and with intention and with calculation. I knew George would do the right thing, and he did, and then came back again for the season finale and final season as well.

John Wells We knew we wanted to get them together at the end, but we wanted it to be a complete surprise. So, I convinced Warner Bros. to give us a private jet and talked to George, and we flew up to Seattle with a very small crew that all signed pledges that they wouldn't tell anybody.

Christopher Chulack John says, "Come on, go up there. Warner Bros. is going to give us the jet." I said, "John, I can't." I had something with my daughter and I couldn't go.

Lydia Woodward I mean, almost no one knew about that.

George Clooney We shot the scene in the back of a house that no one lived in anymore and got back on the plane. The rest of the cast didn't know. [Anthony] Edwards didn't know.

John Wells I kept [the film] in my refrigerator because I was worried about it going through the lab, where we couldn't control it. We didn't tell NBC. It was never in any scripts. They knew nothing about it. Then I processed [the film] two or three days before it was on the air, and we cut [the scene] very late at night when nobody was around.

NBC execs and the rest of the cast didn't see the full cut of the episode until it aired on the East Coast on May 11, 2000.

Barbara Tranchito (NBC Publicity) The morning of the episode, I got a call from Jeff Zucker, who was the president of NBC. He goes, "Barb, I'm hearing rumors that George is back." I said, "I don't know what you're talking about." I couldn't give it away.

George Clooney I was in Italy, and I started getting calls. People were going batshit over the idea that we'd pulled it off. Then I started getting calls from Noah Wyle going, "Are you fucking kidding me?" Eriq La Salle was like, "You could've told me!" It was very funny, but we kept the secret from everybody, because there's no other way to keep it. I don't know how you do it now.

Julianna Margulies Honestly, every now and then I'll catch it when I'm flipping channels or something. And I still—that music—I still get very emotional. And I remember my mom saying to me—she was so shocked because everyone knew George was off the show—my mother said she screamed, which I think was a lot of people's reaction. It was the right ending for them because Carol and Doug were destined to be together.

Jonathan Kaplan We'd have producers' meetings with the Warner Bros. marketing people. They all came and prepared us for what their research showed—that there was going to be about a 20 percent falloff in terms of viewership when George left. So, there was all this hand-wringing, but there was no drop-off at all. They were just wrong about that. It was the same when Julianna left. There was a little drop-off, but nothing like the sky was falling.

20

New Rotation

When George Clooney and Julianna Margulies followed Sherry Stringfield out the ER doors, John Wells talked of feeling "worried" about the drama's future. And it certainly didn't help when headlines talked of "fresh starts" while asking whether *ER* could be great again. But the show had already established a successful pattern of rotating in exciting new characters before the originals transitioned out. With Paul McCrane (1997), Maria Bello (1997), Goran Visnjic, Maura Tierney, Ming-Na Wen, Michael Michele, Erik Palladino (all in 1999), Angela Bassett (2008), and David Lyons (2008) joining the lineup, *ER* was more than ready for the eventual departures of Anthony Edwards, Eriq La Salle, and Noah Wyle.

John Wells We really didn't anticipate that we would be able to change casts, particularly after, with all due modesty, the extraordinary success we had at the beginning. I think people are tied into the world and the characters, and we were able, very successfully, to introduce characters slowly so that we didn't have to have actors who came in and had to replace someone.

Jack Orman One of the main creative thrusts of the time that I was there was this handoff from the original cast to a new cast. There was a lot of time and planning put into that. When I first showed up, we were introducing Corday, then we introduced Abby as a more junior character who was always going to be a series regular. But we asked her to come in like five episodes early and do a guest thing just to plant her in the environment. There's an example of where we planned. We knew that Julianna Margulies would eventually leave the show, but we didn't want to turn around and say, "Hey, here's a replacement. Invest in her please, audience." So, we made sure to overlap 'em in a way that by the time Julianna left, people were invested in Maura's character.

John Wells One of the great advantages to the series has been it's a teaching hospital, and consequently, people are coming through it constantly who are just there for their education. And at a reasonable time, they leave or have other opportunities for a career. I think the audience understands that as an intrinsic part of how the show works. So it actually [allowed] us to bring people in.

Noah Wyle I had a chip on my shoulder with anybody that came on that show. I've systematically gone to and apologized to everybody over the years about being the person that I was, which was, "You better come to play, you better bring your A game. This is pro ball, blah blah blah." It was not an easy environment to work in, because we didn't suffer fools. We were really hard on people, and I was hard on people who were coming into the show, like Erik Palladino or Michael Michele. Everybody had to earn their keep, in my opinion, especially poor Kellie Martin.

John Levey John Wells had a plan. We put Alan Alda in the first five or six episodes of the season, and that gave us a kind of wonderful cloud cover while we experimented with Goran Visnjic and Erik Palladino on the male side. George obviously brought that tremendous sexuality of a great leading man, but he also brought the heroic doctor as a pediatrician, an advocate for children. Michael Michele, being the pediatrician, filled that part of it. Erik and Goran in their own ways brought us the leading-man sexuality and the heroic doctor. It was a well-conceived plan that worked.

Ming-Na Wen Well, I was only a recurring character [in season 1] because they had so many regulars already, and I think that ensemble was kind of set. It was just one of those things where it was easier, I guess, for them to keep you on as a recurring and be able to put you in. There were scenes with Deb running around wide-eyed and not sure where she's going. That was literally me coming out to Hollywood, not knowing what the rules were and not knowing if I was doing the right thing or the wrong thing.

She then asked to leave after the first season but was invited back in 1999.

Ming-Na Wen I did get my first pilot with *The Single Guy,* and then I was continuously working on various projects and films.

Out of the blue, my agent said, "*ER* wants you back. It's a series regular role." I was like, "Oh, really? That's fantastic." I never questioned why they wanted me back. I was just happy to be back. John Wells was sort of almost godlike to me. I never questioned what he did or didn't do. He was the creator, and I am the person to fulfill that vision.

Goran Visnjic I didn't audition. My agent sent me for a few general meetings, and one of them was with John Wells Productions. And at the time, I wasn't even aware that they were people doing *ER*. I was just in LA for a few weeks during the premiere of the movie or something, and I ended up at the general meeting, talking about things I've done before, what I would like to do in the future. Then two days later, my agent called me and said, "Well, you remember one of those meetings? One of them was the people from *ER*." I was like, "Are we talking about the same *ER*, the TV show on NBC?" She was like, "Yeah, they would like you to be on a show for a year." Then during the first year, they extended it by two more years, so it was a three-year contract at the beginning.

John Levey We needed a sexy leading man to join the troop. Goran was a great-looking, talented guy who had brought another color because of his nationality and the accent. Alex Kingston was a success as an English doctor, and it's certainly true that the medical world is full of international doctors in our emergency rooms. So it was authentic.

Jack Orman Goran did get a lot of press. I think that people were saying that [he was a George Clooney replacement], but we tried not to just do a facsimile of Doug Ross.

Maura Tierney I was the first of the second wave. I did eight seasons, and people still thought of me as one of "the new ones."

I was sort of on a little bridge from all those characters departing the show and then the new characters coming. So, it was kind of gradual. So, to me, it didn't feel like, *Here's a new* ER*!* It was offered as a regular, but the way they did it, which was interesting, was I first appeared in it in October of 1999, and I played Julianna Margulies's OB nurse. And then several episodes go by, and then I come back as a med student. So they planted that sort of on purpose for the character; they wanted to show that she was a nurse who was transitioning into med school. So, it wasn't really a guest star; it was sort of like the way they introduced the character. I do believe that if Julianna left, I'd be a nurse, and if Julianna stayed, I'd be a med student.

John Wells Maura came in and stayed through for many more years and was fantastic. I kept thinking it was the end of the series, and it never was.

Lydia Woodward We brought Maria Bello onto the show, who was a wonderful actress, and we failed her miserably. We failed that actress. We did not solve her character. And it was a shame, really. It was really a huge shame. That's kind of always been a regret, at least of mine. We didn't find a good enough positioning for her character, a kind of good enough angle on her character. I feel that it was completely our failure as a writing group to really say, "Why are we here with this person?" And I don't think we ever answered that.

Jack Orman I do think she left her mark on the show. John Wells would always talk about following actors around in that space. The way the show worked is you have a scene between Carter and Greene, for instance. We as the storytellers decide to follow Carter out of the scene, but we're trying to give the impression that if you follow Greene, instead, you're going to run into a whole other world and storyline that's just as rich and just as interesting. Although Maria was a short-term physician on the show, the idea was that there were comings and goings of doctors and nurses all the time who have rich, full lives. Her time on the show helped to bolster that.

Erik Palladino I remember my audition was good, but I had a lot of physical things to do. It wasn't just me talking to another doctor. It was like me doing an operation basically in the middle of the room. And it wasn't [on] an operating table; it was supposed to be in the outside world. I run up to a guy at a construction site, and I had to start performing sort of an operation on a patient in the field. I only had the dialogue for two days, and it was a lot of medical jargon that I've never done before. I didn't walk out going, "Got that!"

Jack Orman Malucci came in as that disruptive, entertaining, and humorous guy.

Sharif Atkins and Mekhi Phifer joined in 2001 and 2002 as Dr. Michael Gallant and Dr. Gregory Pratt, respectively, while Linda Cardellini, Parminder Nagra, and Scott Grimes joined as Nurse Samantha Taggart, Dr. Neela Rasgotra, and Dr. Archie Morris in 2003.

David Zabel I do remember bringing on Sharif and Mekhi around the same time. That was a way of trying to be real and maintain the diversity of the workplace in the ER. It wasn't just a way of like, "Oh, we've lost one really great African American actor who played a doctor, so let's replace him with another." We found two different actors who brought very different things.

Mekhi Phifer Pratt was described in a lot of different ways.

He was described as a cocky, arrogant, no-holds-barred sort of guy who had a lot to prove. It would show in his actions and his abrasiveness, at least in the beginning until we got to really delve into who he was. You got to see all these different facets of his personality and his righteousness to healthcare. His Hippocratic oath, if you will.

Linda Cardellini (Samantha Taggart) When I first came to town, I auditioned for the show several times and never got a part. And then I felt it was like the girl with a broken arm. It wasn't even a good part. But then I did a few things, and I had just come off of the *Scooby-Doo* movie and *Freaks and Geeks*. John Wells hired me on a Wednesday, and I was working on Monday. I had no idea what I was getting into. The first day on that set, I was floored. You have all this movement and then the technical dialogue, which is like a foreign language. You could have three different sets of cues. The doctor on the set could also call cut. It was the only show where somebody besides the director could call cut. Some days we'd do twelve pages. When I shot the *Scooby-Doo* movie, we'd do one page a day.

David Zabel We felt like we needed another nurse at that point because Abby was becoming a doctor. We wanted kind of a young, feisty nurse to fill a gap that we felt in the overall ensemble of the show. Linda was someone I had always loved. I loved *Freaks and Geeks*. I loved her and Busy Philipps. We talked to both. We ended up creating another role for Busy Philipps separately. Samantha wasn't replacing Abby because she had a very different energy and quality. And that was just another way of trying to keep this show constantly renewed and reinvigorated by bringing new energies.

Linda Cardellini I really loved the role that he was talking about. John said, "There's this young nurse, and she had a baby when she was like fifteen, and she struggles to make ends meet." It was better than anything that I had read.

Parminder Nagra John Wells had gone to see *Bend It Like Beckham* in a screening. Apparently, he was only going to stay for about five minutes but then ended up watching the whole thing. Then he went into the writers' room and said, "We're going to hire the girl from *Beckham*." I don't think everyone was completely happy, because he just sort of went, "This is what we're doing."

John Levey I think Parminder is the only person that I've ever seen John offer the job to in the meeting. I was shocked, but it certainly turned out great. Again, I think the hallmark of *ER*'s success is that John created this beautiful community of people, and then all of the people who were successful in that community, in that collaborative environment, were people who shared his and my belief in the importance of collaboration and community.

David Zabel We'd always wanted to represent East Indian medical providers on the show, and we hadn't done it. It felt like a little bit of a gap to us. We have this big-city hospital and there's no Indian doctor; there's no Pakistani doctor. We basically created the role for Parminder. She really inspired the role to a large degree.

"The weirdest thing I ever did got cut out of episode 2, season 11. They were still trying to figure out my character. A guy came in with a shark that was attached to his leg, and I used a credit card or something to get the shark's teeth to let go of the man's calf. It was a baby shark,

of course. It was just this weird thing. I know Linda Cardellini was in the scene with me, because I was still trying to get to know everyone and people were still trying to figure me out. Anyway, I think that they realized how ridiculous it looked and cut it out. So, I didn't really get anything solid for quite a few episodes."

—SHANE WEST

Mekhi Phifer The thing I loved about doing the show was that each character got to have key episodes. Paul McCrane's character and mine were always clashing like crazy. There was an episode where he was going to write me up and I was going to be fired, essentially. And then he got killed by the helicopter. The helicopter crushed him! I thought that was a good episode. I really enjoyed that because not only did I survive, but I had to show up in this crisis. I loved those kinds of episodes where buildings collapsed or things like that where he had to grab the reins and be the lead on the floor, the go-to doctor, and handle multiple cases at once. When those types of things would come up, they would give that to me a lot, which I really appreciated, because they were confident that I could do it.

Sharif Atkins I did a guest star arc in the beginning before I became a series regular, and it was just this sort of magnificent set where I'm trying to jump over a live wire over a puddle of water into an ambulance to help Laura Innes with a patient. It was that kind of spectacular stuff. As much as we like to create stars, there really is no such thing as someone doing it by themselves. It is really a team, and *ER* fostered that kind of energy of getting it done as a group and being able to play your role.

Parminder Nagra I was a huge, huge fan. I remember walking past the set and seeing Noah Wyle and Goran Visnjic outside, and I was totally fangirling. My agent at the time was like, "Are you sure?" I joined in season 10, which is also insane now to think how long shows ran. Anyway, he said, "You've just had a film that's come out, are you sure?" I just said, "You know what? I really love this show, and I just think this is an important move for me."

Scott Grimes David Zabel told me later on that I was there to facilitate other people's characters, like, here's an inept doctor to make all the other good doctors look better. And so I never thought it would last, because nobody, including the public, wants a bad doctor. We don't want 'em in real life; we don't want 'em on TV shows. So I was basically the enemy. But as time went on and they started throwing all this bad stuff at me, like *Here's how you're going to annoy this person,* or *This person is not going to like you,* it just became almost endearing. The audience was kind of pulling for me instead of wanting me to get fired; it became like, *What's Archie Morris going to do this week?*

David Zabel Scott is what is part of what we used to call the Darwinism of the room. That was the idea. He was a secondary character, and he was largely there to be a funny character who was not entirely competent, which we felt also was a reflection of what you sometimes see. But because of his intelligence and his quality as an actor, we as writers were like, "Wow. Well, that's interesting. We should keep him around and see what he could develop into. How can we develop this character? How can he evolve and change?" We just liked what he was doing. And that's what I mean by the Darwinism of the room. Grimes survived because Grimes came in and did a great job on something that was relatively simple and got people kind of going, "Hey, I'm leaning into this."

Scott Grimes There's a scene in season 10 or 11, I don't remember, when I'm eating french fries at the beginning of the episode, and I start to choke. Linda Cardellini gives me the Heimlich maneuver and I cough up a french fry into the glass. I take a breath and I start eating the french fries again, and they cut to the opening credits. It's this kind of funny moment of, even though he just choked, he's still going to eat the french fries. Jonathan Kaplan was the director, and we went to lunch after we filmed that. He walked up to me with a big smile on his face. He said, "Call [the producers] up and tell them you want to be a regular or you'll move on. They will make you a regular." He kind of gave me this wink like, *Hey, man, they're seeing what you're doing. If you push 'em a little, they'll make you a regular.* I didn't have to push them. They came to me. But I always thought that was a very cool moment, somebody giving you the confidence and telling you, "Oh, you're going to be on this show for a while." I loved Jonathan. He didn't have to do that.

In 2004, Shane West joined the cast as Dr. Ray Barnett, followed by John Stamos as Dr. Tony Gates in 2005.

Shane West They were looking for another guy, so I took a general meeting with them. I had always played in bands in my personal life as well as in [roles]. I think they took interest in how, the night before my meeting, I had played a concert. When I saw them, this big room of people, I still had remnants of eyeliner from the musical performance. I didn't know how to get that off. Maybe I had nail polish. So I had remnants of the night before, and they were absolutely fascinated by that. They kept asking me questions. It made me very relaxed, and they were very welcoming. They kind of just threw the character of Ray together from that general meeting.

Peter Roth John Stamos wanted to play a doctor. He wanted to reverse some of the association that he had from *Full House.*

In fact, Stamos had auditioned for ER *twice—first for the role of Dave Malucci, which the actor described in his 2023 memoir* If You Would Have Told Me *as an "Italian tough guy and paramedic whose temperamental attitude gets in the way of his talent as a future doctor." Stamos explains "he shit the bed" during the audition; the role went to Erik Palladino instead.*

John Stamos (Tony Gates) Fast-forward a few years. September of 2006, I'm on the backlot of Warner Bros. I've been hired—without auditioning, by the way—to play Dr. Tony Gates, a regular on *ER*. I'm nowhere near as destroyed as I was after that first audition, but still battered, bloodied, and lying on a gurney when John Wells comes by to welcome me. I'm instantly apologizing; I haven't seen him since [the last audition]. "John, I've been meaning to apologize for my horrible audition a while back . . ." John says, "Oh, you're talking about when you came in for the Malucci character? Yeah, we sort of knew it might not work before you even walked into the room. The second you showed up, our thoughts were confirmed. You were too much like George. Same energy, swagger, charisma. George had just left, so before you even opened your mouth, I decided it wouldn't be fair to put that kind of pressure on you."

David Zabel The new people were always young, sort of

twenty-five-year-old, nervous guy or girl, who didn't really know what was going on. It [was] interesting to take on John's character, who's been through all this stuff, and put him through the same cases, but with a totally different attitude. It just [allowed] us to play different colors than what we've played before.

John Stamos I [was not] the same guy who walked into that audition years ago, thinking I'd use the show for a little exposure and toss it for the first film that comes along. I'm no longer on the Clooney track. I'm showing up as Stamos. That's good enough.

John Wells People leaving the show wound up contributing to our longevity.

21

Medical Minute

A Look Back at "I'll Be Home for Christmas"

Season 8, Episode 10 | December 13, 2001
Written by Dee Johnson and Meredith Stiehm
Directed by Jonathan Kaplan

Like George Clooney, Eriq La Salle didn't want to make a fuss when it became his turn to leave the show; he gave plenty of notice that he wanted to take up directing and producing after his three-year contract extension expired in season 8. Fortunately, there was plenty of story built up to send him on his way. For years, Benton struggled with balancing his work and home lives, especially when it came time to parent a deaf child. After finally gaining custody of his son, Reese, Benton attempts to negotiate for better hours at the hospital. Naturally, Romano refuses. "Are you gonna throw away your career so you can play Mr. Mom?" snaps Romano. The answer was, obviously, yes: He quits County General and takes an out-of-town job at a clinic to work alongside his girlfriend, Cleo Finch.

Eriq La Salle Michael Michele became what [Benton] was with Alex. We were silly together. We were tender together, we fought, we held each other, we touched each other. We held hands, we laughed. That is a multidimensional relationship, and that's the only thing I ever wanted.

Peter Roth I did try to convince him not to leave, but just like when Anthony Edwards left, it's time for this character to leave. And nothing was done without the sanctioned support and the approval of John Wells. So, with Eriq, I think I said to John, "Should I try to convince Eriq to stay?" He said, "You can, but I don't think you're going to be able to."

Lyn Paolo We played a prank on Eriq because his nickname on the show was "the Big Cheese." When he was leaving the show, we got some ladders, and the whole costume department got together and wrapped his trailer in yellow tissue paper to make it look like a giant block of cheese. He just fell down laughing. The whole crew came out and cheered because he couldn't get in his trailer. That was his going-away present from the costume department.

Gloria Reuben Eriq's a guy's guy. He's got major testosterone flowing through [him], and it's a beautiful thing. My character was introduced halfway through the first season. It's a little intimidating coming on only for what was going to be three episodes, and then it turned into six and then et cetera. Eriq really welcomed me, and it was in that cool Eriq La Salle way. I think our chemistry was pretty good. It was always great to play off of what was going on in his eyes and the intelligence, the seriousness there.

The episode ends with Benton out jogging on Christmas Day in Chicago. He runs into Carter, who gives back a train token that Benton had given him on his second week. "You gave me that. I can use it to go home, or I could convince you to come back the next day," remembers Carter, who adds, "I owe you." He tries to hug Benton, but the latter doctor gently pushes him away and punches him instead. As Benton jogs away, Carter yells, "Hey, Peter! I'm a good doctor because of you." Replies Peter, "No, you're not. But keep trying."

"We'd make these bizarre bets when we get bored. Eriq was interested in becoming a director and wanting to make a short film, and he was looking for financing for his short film. So he asked me for money, and I didn't have a lot at the time, but catering in the early days was pretty bare-bones. They would put out these big, gigantic blocks of sort of government cheese, cheddar cheese. And I said to him one night, late, 'I'll bet you two thousand dollars you can't eat all that cheese.' And he says, 'How long do I have to eat it?' I said, 'Thirty minutes.' He said, 'Can I have a cracker with it?' I said, 'You can have as many crackers as you want.' That grown man proceeded to eat that cheese, all seven pounds of it or however much there was, and I paid him. But to this day, the most memorable moment was when I followed him out to his trailer and I heard him call his girlfriend to say, 'Oh, baby, I think I did something

stupid.' There's a pause. He goes, 'I need you to go to the store. I need you to get some prune juice and a papaya.'"

—NOAH WYLE

Noah Wyle Eriq and I talked about this: Our relationship on *ER* was such a groundbreaking one in a lot of ways because the power dynamic was completely reversed. This young, white doctor was killing himself for the approval and affirmation of a Black surgeon. And that was the only opinion that mattered to him. That was novel. And we knew that was novel when we were doing it.

Eriq La Salle *ER* was very much about heroes. I think back to the African American community. I think they just appreciated seeing someone that they could call heroic, whatever level that's on, whether it speaks to them personally or whether they have never seen a Black man as the boss of a white man on television.

Jonathan Kaplan When Eriq left, that was a big drop-off in viewing, but [the studio] didn't even bother researching that. It's just typical because the only two shows that appeared in the top ten for white America and Black America were *ER* and pro football. *ER* had a big Black following, and when Eriq left, the Black audience said, *Well, there's nothing here for me anymore.* And that was the biggest drop-off.

Eriq La Salle I became aware of it after Jonathan told me. It wasn't so much that it felt good. It was a good episode. I liked that Benton left on his own terms with dignity and grace.

22

Pediatric Care

Children added a different dimension to the lives of the County General doctors, but two in particular made life all the more complicated for their frazzled dads—Peter Benton's son, Reese, and Mark Greene's daughter Rachel. For the former, a deaf baby by the name of Matthew Watkins was cast as Benton's son with Carla while two different girls—Yvonne Zima and Hallee Hirsh—took on the role of Mark's problematic daughter.

Watkins doesn't remember much from his experience; he was barely one when he began recurring on the series in 1999. But it was a far different experience for Zima and Hirsh. On-screen, it was an endless fusillade of road trips, domestic fights, and long stays in the waiting room, a roller coaster of a ride that producers ultimately decided was too much for Zima as Rachel entered her difficult teenage years. She was replaced by Hirsh, a change that not only took viewers by surprise but had a profound impact on both actresses.

Trinia Watkins (Matthew Watkins's mom) One of my coworkers told me about the *ER* auditions.

Matthew Watkins My mom was dubious but tried anyway, because there was nothing to lose, and so was pleasantly surprised that I passed. The reason, I believe, was because, unlike the other babies, I was comfortable being held by strangers.

Yvonne Zima I was five and had come off doing my first job in Michael Mann's *Heat*. I was a hostage girl in the arms of Tom Sizemore when he got shot. I had to be handpicked by Al Pacino. They gave me a coloring book, and it was like an interview. When I got cast in *ER*, it happened very fast. Usually, it's a little slower, but I think they were in a bind. I was barely a person. I was a sad-looking child but was [actually] very happy. That's why I was always cast as the tearful, endangered waif in action movies. I was literally always in peril.

Trinia Watkins What I remember about the first day on set is that we were so anxious to meet all the actors, especially Eriq La Salle.

Matthew Watkins My perspective toward it at that age was that it was just something to be done, so I didn't realize that it wasn't common.

"Even as a kid, I felt like I was a part of something special. When we flew out to Chicago, they would put us up in the Ritz-Carlton, which at the

time had these different color-themed rooms, and they were so gorgeous. After many times being flown there, I think I had gone through every different type of room. We'd fly out and film like an ice-skating scene or just grab exteriors when it was winter in Chicago. My mom was on set, but we had a lot of nannies in circulation because my two sisters were also on network shows at the time. My middle sister, Vanessa, was on *Murder One*, and then Madeline, my oldest sister, was on *The Nanny*. And I was on *ER*. I was either working or at home or at school. The kids didn't watch anything I was in, which I think helped me not get bullied. My sister, Madeline, really got bullied because she was on a show the girls knew about."

—YVONNE ZIMA

Trinia Watkins I can remember sometime later, George Clooney was playing basketball outside the studio. As we walked by, he saw us and rolled the basketball to us. We played with the basketball very briefly because Matthew wasn't two years old yet at the time.

Yvonne Zima I really loved working with Anthony Edwards and Christine Harnos. They're such sweet people. I felt like Anthony was a second dad. He was so affectionate and sweet, even though my storylines eventually became very dark and crazy. Rachel was always stepping in shit or getting into trouble, or she had preteen vibes. In one episode, I dyed my hair and it was all punky, and we took Polaroids of real hairdos of people who dyed their hair black and changed it drastically. There were conversations about how it was a little extreme. We opted for the temporary, spray-in hair dye because I was still only ten.

Trinia Watkins We received letters from SAG and access agencies with signatures from the writers, directors, and actors recognizing the significance of Matthew's participation. We also participated in a church event where they applauded something along the lines of "the significance of him being the first Black *and* young deaf actor." We bragged to a few people at first [about her son's role on *ER*]. We also invited our friends and family to watch the first episode at our home. But because the deaf community is small, the news spread too quickly and people started to not respect his space and overwhelmed him. He didn't have a bodyguard. After that, we didn't brag or talk about it too much. We didn't want to make a big deal about it; we wanted to remain a private family.

Matthew Watkins remained a part of the ER *family until the series finale, where he appeared alongside La Salle for a brief scene. Uninterested in pursuing a career in Hollywood, he went on to earn his bachelor's and master's degree at the Rochester Institute of Technology and now works as an engineer.*

Matthew Watkins I've been meaning to go back and watch, but life comes at you fast, doesn't it?

Zima was twelve when she found out her time on the series had come to an end.

Yvonne Zima I didn't ever know why I got recast. I feel like my agent asked for more money, and then I was replaced. I don't know if that's true. I was deeply saddened by this. I did write a letter. I don't think anyone received it, but I wrote a letter to the producers, and I remember signing it with a tombstone and the name *Rachel Greene No. 1.* I wrote the dates I played her, and in the letter, I was laying it on super thick. It was emotionally manipulative. *If I could do better, let me know how!* In retrospect, it was dramatic, but I wanted to know why. It caused me a world of pain at that age.

John Wells When you're casting child actors and they're growing faster than the story, you must put in age-appropriate actors since each year doesn't correlate as an extra year in the lives of the characters. That often happens with child actors.

> *Hirsh was thirteen when she joined* ER *but had already amassed multiple film and TV credits, including* The Young and the Restless, Law & Order, Judging Amy, *and* You've Got Mail.

Yvonne Zima Hallee Hirsh is such a different actress that maybe they wanted to age her up and make this character crazier and more rebellious, and maybe they didn't think I could do that or be that.

Hallee Hirsh (Rachel Greene) *ER* was always the show that as soon as I heard the opening titles, I was like, *Oh, I'm out.* I would not watch that show, because it was bedtime, and it was very into blood and I am not. I hate seeing blood on-screen, and that was too much for me. Since I hadn't been watching it, it was all news to me when I was auditioning that it was for a recast. It seemed normal to me. I've been on so many things where someone's playing me when I'm younger and someone's playing me when I'm older, especially when you're a kid. So, it was never odd [for me].

To make the transition less jarring for viewers, writer Jack Orman dropped an image of Hirsh in a "previously on ER*" promo.*

Jack Orman The first time we see Hirsh, the audience could be confused and pulled out of the drama for a second. What I decided to do instead was bring in the new Rachel and shoot her side of a scene that Yvonne had shot. It was probably from season 7. I think Mark was giving her a necklace by the river or something like that. We just shot her side of it and put it in the recap. I wanted viewers to have the bump in the recap and not when they first see her.

Hallee Hirsh To me, Rachel Greene was, aesthetically, not even that edgy of a kid but desired to be. She was flirting with trying on that edgy stuff to set herself apart and fill whatever hole she was experiencing from her family situation, while also defining herself as separate from the desires of her parents and their significant others. People hated my character. They hated her because she was so mean to Mark. She's so annoying and such a brat and so ungrateful. And why is she acting like this to this man who they loved so dearly who was dying? People would say they should not have recast her. It should have been the original actor. She would've been much nicer. There was lots of hate.

Jack Orman I think it's sometimes hard to differentiate between an audience having issues with the character and having issues with the actor. I mean, Romano was reviled, but that means Paul was doing a great job.

Hirsh recurred during seasons 8, 9, and 10 and returned for the finale in 2009. Within a few years, she transitioned out of the industry to become a small business owner. Zima went on to pursue a career as a TV writer.

Hallee Hirsh When I think about *ER*, I miss the industry. I absolutely loved the large ensemble and how everyone was on their feet with that Steadicam style and how it all moved so fast. And I love the structure and security of episodic TV as a career. It's fantastic for an actor to know that you've got regular work. It can be the worst thing to book a gig, and then you're like, *Cool, I'm going to be doing this movie for a few months.* But then what happens after that? I don't miss that. I left behind the industry because it did not offer me the security that I wanted for my livelihood. When I became pregnant, I really understood that. I really admire what Yvonne Zima has been up to and that she's making her own work. I wouldn't have been able to emotionally survive if I hadn't transitioned into making my own work. The juvenile experience of just being told when and where to show up and whether I'll be working was not for me.

Yvonne Zima I didn't watch *ER* when I was a kid because it was past my bedtime. I'm going to watch it now because it's something to be studied and dissected. It was groundbreaking with like thirty-five million live viewers. People really watched TV in a different way back then, when it was a monoculture. Tell John Wells I want a job in one of his writers' rooms. I'm a fancy writer now!

23

Medical Minute

A Look Back at "On the Beach"

Season 8, Episode 21 | May 9, 2002
Written and Directed by John Wells

Like all the major departures on *ER*, the writers had plenty of time to prepare for Anthony Edwards's—a year and a half, in fact. The planning began after January of 2001, when Edwards went public with the news that the 2001/02 season would be his last. "It has been a long time playing Dr. Greene," he told the Associated Press, adding that he would rather have his character go up "in flames" than die of brain cancer. "There are a lot of El trains in Chicago.

You could trip in front of any one of them." Unfortunately for him, Paul McCrane's Romano was the lucky dog who got the spectacular death; Edwards would have to settle for fading away at sunup in Hawaii. Unlike Romano, however, Greene's death was telegraphed over three tear-jerking episodes, starting with "Orion in the Sky," which aired on April 4, 2002, continuing with "The Letter" on May 2, 2002, and ending with "On the Beach," which primarily followed Greene and his daughter Rachel, with Corday and their baby joining them later.

John Wells Of course when George left after five seasons, I was really worried. [But] I thought the show was definitely going to end in year eight when Tony Edwards left.

Anthony Edwards Mark was a central enough character, it would be a little bit difficult for him to wander off to another hospital. It was eight years, and it was a family decision with no regrets. I knew, of course, the show wouldn't be hurt by me leaving or anybody leaving, because it really was a combination of very talented people in a lot of different places. Because they all worked together so well, it created something bigger.

Jack Orman Our thinking was, *Okay, he's going to go. How many bites of the apple are we going to get?* We had three major opportunities. One was his last day at the ER. His last patient had a splinter. We could have ended the show there with him just walking out of the ER, knowing that he wasn't going to make it. But we needed to do the episode in Hawaii, and because he was a part of the *ER* family, we also needed a reaction from all our other characters. So, I decided, let's do it this way: We'll jump over his actual death. I wrote an episode called "The Letter," where they get the news through a fax from Corday that Greene had passed, and we get everybody's reaction to that news, how important he was to them, and how they're going to move forward without him.

Noah Wyle That was a good acting day for me [on "The Letter"]. I was on fire that day. Take after take after take, every angle, that well never dried up for me that day. There was something so beautiful about the way the letter was written—the structure of the scene, the surprise element to it. Also, the fact that I got to see [the letter] before anybody else did—which meant that I had to both have the feeling and hide the feeling, which was impossible. It just made it very elegant.

Anthony Edwards They had two years to tell the story of someone going through this life transition. The first year was the medical part of it, and then the second year was really the emotional journey of someone transitioning.

Jonathan Kaplan I just know that Tony's deal when he left was that he was going to die. They couldn't bring him back. He wanted it to be like when he is done with the show, he was done with the show. They were all pretty much financially set, the main cast. So, it wasn't about money.

Jack Orman It was a little bit of when the doctor becomes the patient, but then the patient is still the doctor. That journey of getting married, having a kid, the cancer diagnosis, he thinks he beats it, goes away for a while, and comes back. It was just a lot.

Hallee Hirsh "On the Beach" was the only script I've saved. When you do the table reads, they've got the big whiteboard on the wall, and it marks which episodes are during sweeps week, the big episodes. And my character tended to show up on the sweeps week episodes, the high-stakes one. I think I knew in advance that they were planning the Hawaii trip.

Jack Orman John has a place in Hawaii, and that's where we would do our writers' retreats. And it was great to be somewhere else rather than just the apartment. It was much more visual.

Hallee Hirsh I think I was there for maybe two or three weeks. It was incredible. I got to learn how to surf and drive. I wore a small bathing suit, and I had a wedgie in the episode, which was unfortunate.

Jack Orman The episode wasn't about whether he was going to die or not. It was going to be how he's going to die and how he's going to reconcile it. The mystery, the tension in the episode is whether he's going to be able to reconcile with his father and get on the same page with his daughter to impart whatever before he passes.

> **"If *ER* does anything, it reminds you that life comes at you with surprises, and the only constant thing in life is change."**
>
> **—ANTHONY EDWARDS**

Jack Orman John Wells just nailed it when Mark gives advice to his daughter. I thought it was really moving.

Hallee Hirsh One of the biggest moments of my career was his death scene. During that scene, my vision changed. All I could see was him and a light around him and everything in my periphery was just totally dark. I feel like I went into a trance as he was giving his last words to Rachel when he says, "Be generous with your time, with your love, with your life." It was like all the sound and light just disappeared. It was just him and the most important words in the world.

Anthony Edwards It was a horrible way to go. But if you are going to go, they let Mark Greene go in a way that was kind of beautiful.

At the time of his departure from ER, *Edwards told Tribune Media Services that "I have been incredibly fortunate to be part of this show. This is the only interview I am doing and part of that is because I know the reaction of me leaving this show doesn't make people happy. It's a character they loved, and I don't want to trivialize it in the selfishness of my life."*

The final scene of "On the Beach" includes a graveside service featuring Alex Kingston and Hallee Hirsh, along with Eriq La Salle, Michael Michele, Noah Wyle, Maura Tierney, Goran Visnjic, Sherry Stringfield, Yvette Freeman, Michael Ironside, Abraham Benrubi, Sharif Atkins, Troy Evans, John Aylward, Paul McCrane, and Christine Harnos. The episode ends with Rachel releasing a purple balloon—a callback to the moment on Greene's deathbed when he tells Rachel how she used to immediately release balloons after he bought them.

Jack Orman I think John Wells came up with the balloon while he was writing. I always read it as a hello to her father, and how she was going to let go of her anger and grief. It was a cathartic release to leave on some kind of high note after a very emotionally draining arc and final episode.

Hallee Hirsh That final scene felt pretty real. I got to be with that whole cast. We were in a cemetery right next to Warner Bros.

Christine Harnos My last episode was the funeral, but the one that was more personal was with Anthony in a diner [in "Orion in the Sky"]. He's telling me that he's not going to make it, his brain tumor is getting worse and that his time is limited. That was a tough scene. The funeral was a nice, fun experience. I met a ton of new people because it was a new cast mixed with the old. But my daughter, Rachel, looked a lot different from the daughter that was originally cast!

Anthony Edwards There've been many people who said that their experience of losing a loved one or family member made [Greene's death] a little understandable. It's why we listen to music or why we watch TV shows . . . we still want to be told a story and have it relate somehow to our lives.

David Zabel One thing stands out: We did that episode where Mark couldn't stick his tongue out straight. It was a great scene between him and Sherry Stringfield. He can only do it crooked. Susan gets nervous and says, "You need to go see somebody about this," and it turns out to be a brain tumor. She basically diagnosed off of that scene. A year after that, we got a letter from a woman in Texas who couldn't stick her tongue out straight and went to her doctor. She had a brain tumor. You couldn't make it up. This woman was like, "Your show saved my life. Your show saved my life because of the scene in which Tony Edwards can't stick his tongue out straight."

24

Discharge Papers

In many ways, Noah Wyle's decision in season 11 to step away from *ER* telegraphed the end of the medical series. Though *ER* would go on for four more years, viewership took a predictable dip from 12.06 million in season 12 to 11.5 million in season 13, before dropping further to just over 9 million in season 14. Meanwhile, NBC was starting to hint about wanting to close the trauma doors for good.

"I will tell you that toward the last two years of the series, it was distinctly possible that the show might've been canceled after seasons 13 and 14," remembered Peter Roth. "I remember talking to [NBC Universal president] Jeff Zucker, saying, 'Why don't you wait, man?' He wanted to declare at the end of season 13 that season 14 will be the end of the show. And I said, 'Don't do that. First of all, you don't know that it's the end of the show. Secondly, there may be a resurgence that you're not aware of.' The show was a true winner, and so Jeff appropriately changed his mind, and we had a fifteenth and final season."

Wyle's desire to spend more time with his young children is what prompted the actor to want to hang up his scrubs. He would tell reporters about how his son was born on Thursday, and how he had to return to work the following Monday morning. "At about 10:30 in the morning, for the first time in [almost a decade] I looked at my watch, and I looked up from my watch, and I said, 'Come on, everybody. What are we doing? Let's go,'" Wyle said. "And I thought, *What are you doing? Where do you want to be?* And I thought, *You know where you want to be.* I just thought, *I can't be here for eighty hours a week and miss this.* And I quit. But I called it a divorce with visitation rights, because I didn't want to say goodbye, obviously, to the best job and experience I've ever had. And really, the family [on the show] had become more than just a surrogate family to me. I was about to make a real family that needed to take precedence."

John Stamos was brought in to help fill the void in season 13 while established pros like Stanley Tucci, Sara Gilbert, and Busy Philipps wore white coats and fancy guest stars like Armand Assante, Forest Whitaker, John Mahoney, and Annabella Sciorra made trauma room appearances. In season 14, David Lyons signed on to recur as Dr. Simon Brenner, while Gloria Reuben briefly returned as Jeanie Boulet. Other guest stars that year included Peter Fonda, Hal Holbrook, and Steve Buscemi.

In April of 2008, NBC made the decision to shutter *ER*

after fifteen seasons. In interviews, John Wells tried to temper expectations about the series finale and whether to expect a starry turnout. George Clooney and Julianna Margulies, for example, weren't going to show up at the end. Instead, they returned as old marrieds for the nineteenth episode dubbed "Old Times" in which Doug, now living in Seattle with Carol, meets Neela and Samantha as they wait to retrieve a donated organ. But there was still a much-anticipated reunion in the series finale featuring Eriq La Salle, Laura Innes, Alex Kingston, Sherry Stringfield, and Parminder Nagra. John Wells also triggered those Wyle visitation rights. "I didn't want to do something like somebody dying, or there is a celebration, or the hospital closes, so that's why everybody comes back," Wells once said. "I wanted it to be natural."

John Wells We had always planned that the end of the series would involve Noah returning, because he was so central as a character at the very beginning.

Noah Wyle John Wells had told me early on that he felt because John Carter was the eyes and ears of the audience that he needed to be part of the closing. I knew I'd be back at some point. I didn't come back at all for the thirteenth and fourteenth seasons, and then I think I ended up doing six of the fifteenth and final season, which was so great. Talk about closure. To not be on that show and have that show be on TV was horrible. It was like watching somebody else raise your kids. But I was raising my own, and that was amazing. I don't have any regrets. That is exactly what happened.

John Wells Noah stayed through year twelve and then kept coming back, primarily because Alan Alda had told him you'd be insane to leave when [he] was around. So I said, "Thank you, Alan."

Peter Roth Getting seasons 14 and 15 was such a win for our company and for John Wells to be able to properly say farewell to the audience. I think we all felt grateful that we had as long a run as we did.

John Wells [Former stars] contacted me and said, "Yeah, I'll come back [for the final season]." When we were getting towards the end, I called George and said, "I sort of feel like we want to catch up with what happened to everybody." He thought about it a lot and then said, "I think you're right. I still hear from people all the time about how much they love that character. Let's see if we can do something." I called Julianna, and she came back. Everybody came back in the end. It was a bit of a victory lap for us.

David Zabel When we got to the final season, it was really exciting, because we had all these kinds of special concept episodes. We brought characters back like it was old home week. I had been on the show a long time, but I had never worked with Mimi Leder as a director, and Mimi Leder was back directing, as was Rod Holcomb. So that last season was just a thrill, also because you don't usually get the luxury nowadays of knowing a full year in advance. *This is the last year, so let's shoot out the lights!* We could do what we thought was best and creatively most interesting to us. Nobody was breathing down our necks and nobody was bugging us about anything.

"John Wells directed the 'Old Times' episode in season 15 [which marked the return of George Clooney and Julianna Margulies]. He came to me

and Linda Cardellini and said, 'Now look, girls. I know it's George, but can you not smile so much?' He really said that. Swear to God. He goes, 'It's Doug Ross as far as you're concerned. You don't know this doctor.' And we went to each other, 'What? *Of course* we're totally professional. *Of course* we're not being like that, right? We're going to play it properly, like professionals.' And then I went back to watch the episode, and I literally phoned Linda. I went, 'Linda, oh my God. If that was us toning it down, what on earth did we do beforehand?'"

—PARMINDER NAGRA

Scott Grimes The director of the final episode was the director of the pilot. It made everybody step their game up a lot.

Noah Wyle I give a lot of credit to Rod Holcomb, who directed our pilot, the one hundredth episode, and the series finale, for which he won a well-deserved Emmy. He had a knack for taking basically what was a very technical, jargon-based script and infusing it with a lot of humanity, and creating relationships between looks and behavior that really fleshed out the storytelling.

John Wells I'd gone off to direct a movie. I was supposed to direct what was *supposed* to be the finale, which was episode 19, when George and Julianna came back. And then I got a call from NBC's Jeff Zucker, who has already negotiated with Warners [for more episodes]. And I said, "Well, I'll write it, but I won't be there to shoot it." I went back to the cast and said, "They want us to do four more. What do you want to do?" And they said, "We want to do it." So I wrote the two-parter. And then I called Rod Holcomb, who had directed the pilot, and asked him if he would come back and direct the finale, which he did.

Abraham Benrubi Funny story. Rod and I were walking to lunch, and it was raining and I had an umbrella. I popped it open, and it almost took his eye out. I said, "I hope you can finish the show without that one eye." It was great to have him back.

David Zabel I remember John literally had the very end of the show in his mind before we even knew what the exact story was. New patients are rolling into the ambulance bay, and as the camera pulls away, you feel like, okay, there are new doctors working there and there are new patients coming in, and it's just going to keep going on like that.

John Wells I really wanted to say to the audience, "This place is still here, and if you took the wrong off-ramp in Chicago, you'd end up in front of the hospital where these people have always worked."

Scott Grimes Noah and I were sitting in the ambulance bay just between takes, and I always wondered why he just kept coming back. So I turned to him in that last episode and said, "Hey, are you happy the show's ending?" And I remember he said in such a beautiful way, "I am very relieved the show is ending, Scott, because I would do this show forever because it's there and it's my baby and I'm its child as well. As long as it's on, I'm going to do it. And I'm just so happy to move on from it." He would've never moved on. If the show had kept going, he would've always come back. And I always loved that, because it was this relief of him going, "Okay, now I can rest and not worry about *ER* anymore. I can say goodbye to that chapter because it will be gone." I respected that a lot.

Yvette Freeman I was sad to see it go, but it was time. I was tired, personally.

Maura Tierney I had done eight seasons. When I left, it was time. I wasn't bummed I wasn't in the finale.

Neither was Ming-Na Wen.

Ming-Na Wen I don't think that way [about feeling sad]. I really don't. I mean, I'm always just grateful for everything that comes my way. And if it was meant to be, or if it served the story and it made sense, then I think, yeah, that would've been great. But if it didn't serve the story, then I'm okay with that, too.

Linda Cardellini I only wanted to stay for a year, because I don't like to stay too long doing one thing. And then as time went on, the community of people and the talent that I got to work with . . . it's one of my favorite experiences, working on that show. We laughed so hard. I ended up staying there until the show went off the air because I just loved it so much.

Parminder Nagra Initially, I wasn't going to be in the finale at all. I was actually very upset because I'd been on the show for six seasons by that point. I was quite pregnant, by the way. By that point, I was seven and a half months pregnant, and they were trying everything by the end to cover me up with gurneys and clipboards. But I was like, "Look, I don't care what it is, but I must finish this show. That was so important to me." David Zabel and [producer-writer] Lisa Zwerling both phoned me and said, "We've got an idea." It was a lovely way, because it tied up that story of a happily ever after for Neela. She went on with her life. I would've been devastated if I hadn't been in it at all. We were still on the lot. We were still filming on our main stage. They just built this room out, but we weren't remote.

Set over the course of twenty-four hours, the two-hour series finale kicked off with Tony Gates greeting an ambulance carrying a fifteen-year-old girl who was unconscious after participating in a slumber party drinking game. Elsewhere, Nurse Lydia wakes up a slumbering Archie Morris—a callback to the ER *pilot—to treat an altered old lady found wandering in the rain. Guest stars included Alexis Bledel as the new John Carter–like intern; Ernest Borgnine as a man named Paul Manning, a tribute to a former* ER *writer who died in 2005; Marilu Henner as a bride's mom; and Hallee Hirsh as Greene's daughter Rachel, who comes to County General to apply for an internship.*

While bedlam continued in the ER, many members of the old gang, including Kerry Weaver, Elizabeth Corday, Peter Benton, and Susan Lewis, came back to Chicago to celebrate the opening of John Carter's health center named after Joshua, the son he had with wife, Kem (Thandiwe Newton). She came to the opening, too, as did Benton's son, Reese.

Matthew Watkins That red drink they had me holding in the finale was the most delicious drink I've ever had up to that point. They had to tell me to stop drinking it since people would see the drink being suddenly depleted between cuts.

Marilu Henner (Linda) I got in right under the wire! I've played this kind of character three times. They keep casting me as the mother of the groom who can't stand her daughter-in-law. Although this time, it's *really* funny, because we somehow end up in the emergency room—me and the bride. There are a lot of mouths to feed [in the episode], and it's just a really fun and flashy part.

Hallee Hirsh When I found out that I was going to be in the finale, that was a real trip. I got to tell my mom on her birthday. What an honor. I was so happy for Rachel to be moving in her father's footsteps. And then also what a great relationship for her and Elizabeth Corday to be moving in that direction.

Scott Grimes I remember I had to leave a week early. I had gotten this movie called *Robin Hood,* so I didn't get to have that ending. I got to have my ending, my last scene where everybody clapped. It was so lovely because Stamos and all the people who weren't working that day came down. But I didn't get to do those final scenes, which still is heavy on my heart, and I still carry it with me because this business sucks. You spend all this time with all these people, and then bang, it's over like *that.* And you don't see them in that capacity anymore.

Marilu Henner When I asked people, they were like, "We're sad, but it's time to move on." Everybody was kind of resolute. My call time was at noon on the third-to-last day. I got there, and there were so many people there. I was like, "Wow!" Then I realized they were dedicating Stage 11 to *ER.* It was cool. I happened to be at the right place at the right time.

One of the story arcs was based on the real-life story of John Wells's niece Shelby Lyn Allen, who died of alcohol poisoning in 2008. In the episode, Gates calls the cops to arrest the father who allowed vodka to be served at his daughter's slumber party.

John Wells What seems like teenage fun can be warning signs for a significantly dangerous medical situation.

Debbie Allen (Shelby's mother) I have vowed to do whatever I can to educate teens, young adults, and parents to the dangers of alcohol poisoning. I want all of them to know that immediate medical intervention can save lives. It is my deepest desire that no other families or friends will have to endure the pain of loss that we experience every day of our lives.

Steve Allen (Shelby's father) We're just trying to make young people, teenagers—really, anyone—understand that they may be used to seeing someone throwing up at a party, but they need to be aware that if you can't rouse them, they may have crossed that line into a medical emergency.

Critics generally liked the send-off, with Entertainment Weekly*'s Ken Tucker writing that "the two-hour finale didn't go in for anything fancy—no dream sequences; no teases for a spin-off—but I liked the fact that the surprises were small but effective." Afterward, the cast partied and made away with artifacts from the set.*

Christopher Chulack It was very emotional. I reflect on it now, and I'm thinking to myself, *Wow, that fifteen seasons, that's a lot. Where did the time go?*

Abraham Benrubi It was fun to go in there after we finished the final episode. John Stamos took the ambulance bay doors, and Noah Wyle took a bunch of medical equipment. Rightly so. It was a huge part of people's lives. I have a stethoscope. I have a pen that George gave us. I also have one of those surgical clamps. It's an excellent roach clip, just FYI.

Laura Cerón When you enter the ER, you hit this square button to open the doors. I took one of those and I took my stethoscope and what else? Oh yes, my name tag.

Noah Wyle I have *everything*. I've got a room in my house where the door to the room is the County General's emergency swinging door that we used to bust through. I've got the Exit sign. I've got the floor plan. I took the CPR practice dummy that we all learned on. I've got two square panels of the trauma room floors. When they tore the set up, I asked for those. I'm a very sentimental man. I took it all. And I had to take it because if I didn't take it, [John] Stamos was going to take it. That guy was grabbing gurneys and operating room lights. He was shameless. I think he got the emergency room ambulance bay sign that was in the ambulance bay. I think that's in his backyard. We knew when they were going to demo the set, and I just gave them a laundry list of the pieces I wanted.

Scott Grimes Stamos got me a door of one of the emergency rooms that, by the way, is still at his house. I haven't picked it up. It's been years. He keeps calling me and saying, "Dude, I still have the fucking door." There's a great picture at John's house of me and Maura and Parminder and John behind the door looking through it. It's a cool shot.

Lily Mariye I think for us, there was a lot of weight. Each time we shot a scene, there was a certain sadness when you move on, because you think like, *I'll never do this scene again.*

John Wells I was in Boston directing a movie. It was very odd to not be there for the final wrap party.

Noah Wyle My first day on the set was March 17, 1994. My last day [was] March 18, 2009. In between there's been marriage and children. There was this tearful goodbye after my farewell episode after the eleventh season. I came back to the lot the next week because Clint Eastwood was casting for *Flags of Our Fathers.* I drove up and the guard, who I had seen every day for years, asked me for ID. After I told him why I was there, he sent me across the way to the visitors' lot. Then I went in and put my name on a long call sheet for actors. It just hit me: back to square one.

Scott Grimes I have the last line of *ER* because as that shot is pulling away and you see the train go by, you're hearing me barking out orders for the triage. It wasn't planned that way, that they would give Archie Morris the last line. But it just happened to be that way because I was the person running the emergency. That was an honor for me.

John Wells It's very odd to say, but it really was time to end.

ER closed out its fifteen-season run as the number one show that night, averaging 16.4 million viewers.

25

Long-Term Prognosis

ER may have been surpassed by *Grey's Anatomy* as TV's longest-running medical drama in 2020, but its legacy isn't just tied to how long it remained in prime time. It won more awards than any other hospital series, but more importantly, it attracted the kind of ratings—47.8 million viewers at its peak—that broadcast TV just doesn't see anymore. "We turned some attention on the Congo and on Darfur when nobody else was," John Wells once said about the show's Africa-based episodes in season 12. "We had a bigger audience than a nightly newscast will ever see, making 25 to 30 million people aware of what was going on in Africa. The show is not about telling people to eat their vegetables, but if we can do that in an entertaining context, then there's nothing better." Closer to home, the way

Wells ran his show made a lasting impact on television. His writers' room set a standard, while the drama became an invaluable stepping stone for many actors, producers, and directors.

Leslie Moonves At the time, *ER* was revolutionary. It was great storytelling, but there were also short scenes, and it was shot in an entirely different way. I think the reason it initially did better than *Chicago Hope* was because of how fast it went. That was John Wells, and it was also Rod Holcomb, the director, and what happened to him.

Jonathan Kaplan It was one of the first shows that took advantage of the Steadicam. But in terms of the content, it was real. Even today, if I happen to catch a rerun or something, it was realistic. What we were allowed to show! Sometimes they'd say, "This is too gross, but it really feels real."

Preston Beckman Friday mornings, we were just like, *We are the smartest people on the planet.* We were thrilled with the numbers. Sweeps months would start on a Thursday. So, the first night of the sweep, we would have this gigantic lead over the other guys, and then over the next six nights, that lead would shrink. Internally, we called it *the greasy pole.* Those were good times. Shows like that don't come along that often.

George Clooney People forget when our show came out, we were [averaging] ten million more people than *Friends,* which was an hour earlier than us. We were just a huge, huge television show. We knew how lucky we were, and we knew that that wouldn't happen again.

Noah Wyle I got terribly spoiled having this first big experience be the most incredible experience you can be in. And then the rest of your career is comparing everything to this once-in-a-lifetime opportunity.

Julianna Margulies *ER* is responsible for our careers. I will always be indebted to *ER*.

John Wells Nobody was more surprised than I was when our show took off. For those of us on the show, it took a couple of years to realize just how culturally pervasive *ER* had become. I hesitate to say that *ER* changed how dramas were done, but people did build other shows with this greater idea of reality. What we were doing was something much closer to what really happens in a hospital than other shows that came before it.

Eriq La Salle We were in Chicago shooting, and George and I were on our way to grab something to eat. It was lunchtime. We passed by an office building, and I just remember there were maybe two dozen women in the lobby or whatever. These women literally came out and started running after us. George and I [started] running, and we ducked into an alley. Literally, it was like a cartoon. This herd of women went by, and we just looked at each other like, *What?* It was the loss of innocence, and it was the beginning of a whole new chapter in our lives.

Anthony Edwards From the start, the series reflected the reality of the emergency room with a visual, writing, and acting style that pays respect to that. You felt like you were watching a real world, with people coming and going, and the audience rewarded that with longevity.

Eriq La Salle It gave me the opportunity to portray a talented, hardworking African American doctor. I miss the comradery of the cast and being able to bring to life such amazing scripts.

Christopher Chulack Anybody that was affiliated with *ER* had their professional life changed. There's no doubt about it. I was born and raised in East Los Angeles, in a working-class family, and I used to kick myself when I started in the business. I started off delivering film to the projection rooms on the Warner Bros. lot. And then I worked my way up and became an apprentice film editor and an assistant editor, and then a sound effects editor and blah, blah, blah. But when I got to *ER*, I would say, "How the hell did I get here?" I don't know how I got there. It just happened, and it was just a cool experience. It opened the door for me.

"When I think about *ER*, it's a beautiful, perfect, and pristine memory."

—NOAH WYLE

Troy Evans Look at the average actor's IMDb page. I've got almost 130 episodes, just with *ER*. Most actors don't get 130 episodes of anything *total*. There's also a tremendous psychological benefit to working on something that was always high quality to working on something where all the actors were just really good. I wouldn't trade it for anything.

Parminder Nagra I really loved being a part of it. Every now and again, we touch base with each other. I've nothing but fond memories of that show. I mean, it was tough, don't get me wrong. It was a tough show. There were days where I was going, "They've got the wrong person." Between me and Linda Cardellini, we had a lot of moments. We gravitated toward each other. There were good days and bad days, and we were doing the show for ten months of the year. But then there were days where it completely clicked. There was just nothing like it. And then the laughter between cuts and the pranks that were carried on? It was a lot of fun.

Mekhi Phifer What I loved about it was the comradery that I've very rarely felt. I mean, we were really friends. We would spend twelve, fourteen hours a day with each other and then go hang out after work. We would never be sick of each other. We traveled together. We would rent RVs and go to Lake Tahoe or to Vegas. We would fly places. I know Scott Grimes and myself, we took our ladies to Hawaii and spent ten days there [together]. There were no egos. We really all had each other's back. I mean, we were all family. When I had a party at my house, everybody from the principals to the extras to sound to the grips, props, writers, and producers were all invited. It was that kind of energy.

David Zabel It was just such a well-run show, and that goes across both the creative and the administrative parts. That's what John Wells is best at. I learned so much from him and from the way that show ran. I had only been on two other shows before that, and I had never been on a show that worked that well. If you can get efficiency and still get creative accomplishment, that's like a home run. That's what *ER* was. It was a model for what a well-run show can be, both creatively and in terms of lifestyle. In this business, that's few and far between. You find that you have that balance.

John Wells I think we made it harder to do [medical] shows that were inauthentic. I think that *St. Elsewhere* started it, and then *ER* took us into a place where if you're going to do a medical show, it either has to be fantastical in some way, where you're clearly stepping away from the reality of what medicine is, or you have to be accurate and specific.

Rick Rossovich It's funny, the afterlife of shows. *ER* has played for years in syndication, and a new generation of fans have kept it afloat. It's even weirder that the crap show I did after *ER* stayed viable. *Pacific Blue* [the USA Network drama that aired from 1996 to 2000] plays on a Swedish channel five days a week and has for years. Cops on bikes . . . what a way to finish my run.

Christine Harnos I remember John [Wells] was always so present and generous, even with my character or me as an actress. Obviously, I wasn't one of the regulars, but anytime I worked, I always got a handwritten note from him about how grateful he was with what I was doing with my character. That means so much to a young actor.

Lily Mariye Everyone I know who has worked on *ER*, no matter in what capacity, came out with such professionalism and a strong work ethic. It taught me how to be a director because of how the production was run. We all learned what a great production should look like. Every one of the directors—John Wells, Lesli Linka Glatter, Paris Barclay, Tommy Schlamme, among them—really set our bar high. There's a reason those four went on to be presidents of the Directors Guild of America.

Peter Roth John Wells is a very, very good writer. I've worked with writers who are even more acclaimed, but nobody was as effective or as powerful or as controlling in a good way as John Wells. I used to describe him as the General Eisenhower of producers.

Jack Orman I had the benefit of *ER* being my first real writers' room experience. John Wells was always there, and it became the model for the Writers Guild show writing program, just in terms of how to do it, so there was scheduled time for the writers' room. It wasn't simply, "Let's just be in a room all day." It was three times a week in the afternoon. It was focused. You did homework, so to speak, outside the room, so when you came, you weren't staring at each other. I find that nowadays, staff are just locked in a room for almost the entire week. That's not the way this operated.

David Zabel We had lots of letters from people who were sick. I remember one was from a kid who was dying in the hospital. She was probably like nine or ten years old. She loved the show and found it so inspiring and moving. She loved Jerry the desk clerk, whom we all loved. She found him so fun and sweet and charming. The show kept her going. She ended up not making it, which is why it's not a great story. But the fact that on her hardest days, the show that inspired her or motivated her was still something.

Yvonne Zima I remember a gal from Make-A-Wish Foundation visited the set, and we were about the same age. She was a young Irish girl with light brown hair and pale skin, a beautiful child. We would do wheelchair races and hang out all day. And then it really struck me. Why does this girl want to watch this show? I don't even watch this show. I'm a kid. I watch kids shows. So, I asked her, "Why of all the shows, do you want to visit the set of *ER*?" And she said, "Well, I spend most of my life in hospitals, so it makes me feel normal."

Laura Innes One of the things that was so great about the show was Friday mornings. They had some kind of way to evaluate the response to the storylines. The writers always tried to include some kind of information that was new about medical services or treatment. So, for example, if there was a show about domestic violence or HIV medications or a new heart procedure, they could evaluate the impact of that storyline on real behavior. People would respond to these storylines in a way that made their life better and healthier. It's hard to imagine anything more powerful than that.

Noah Wyle I don't think a day goes by where I don't get a message from somebody saying that they were inspired by our show to go into medicine. It's got to be the greatest thing I've ever done with my life, especially in 2020, realizing that all those first responders got their inoculation about what it is to be a first responder from our show. That's extremely gratifying.

Neal Baer There were watching groups of medical students. I've heard lots of stories. I'm sure there are papers. I think there were papers written on how people applied to residencies in emergency medicine after a year.

Gloria Reuben There was someone whom every viewer could connect to. There was always something they could connect to it. It doesn't matter where you're from, how much money you made, or what your religion is. If something brings you into an *ER*, you're going to be treated the same.

Maura Tierney There [were] moments on set, and you get this sort of glimpse that I was part of this huge sort of phenomenon on television.

Anthony Edwards We just had a synergy of people. I feel like I laughed and stayed in love for eight years. It's all of these people that I love and miss.

George Clooney The hardest part is that when you look at the show and its consistency over so many years . . . it would be hard to do it at the level that we did.

Yvette Freeman I had never been in anything this long. And I haven't been in anything that long since.

David Zabel I doubt that you'll ever have a network show that's in the public's attention the way *ER* was because the audience is fragmented and fractured now. People watch things at different times. You just can't unify an audience anymore.

Lori Openden Years later, when I worked at CW, Leslie Moonves was the head of CBS, which co-owned the CW. So I used to bring him pictures and tapes of actors we wanted to cast in our pilots. I'd walk in his office, and he would say, "Lori, *ER* and *Friends* in *the same year.* That'll never happen again." I'd go, "Nope. But we were there. We saw it happen."

Leslie Moonves Most of our new hits are streaming, and they're not achieving those kinds of numbers. And with *ER*, it happened almost overnight. It happened in two weeks. It was huge. And it obviously struck a chord. But you're never going to see those numbers again out of broadcast and out of cable or streaming.

Julianna Margulies You can't capture lightning in a bottle twice.

Laura Cerón It was just a great time in LA. And of course, when you're working, it's even better.

John Wells I miss my friends. We had a good time.

Epilogue

Several times in the last two decades, John Wells and members of the original ensemble have been asked whether *ER* could—or should—be revived or made into a spin-off. Wells certainly left the door open. In 2019, the prolific writer-producer told *Deadline* that "we made an awful lot of *ER*s, 331 episodes. That's a lot of hours, so I can't imagine that we would [reboot it], but if somebody came in with an interesting idea about how to do it, we might."

Some of the cast members, however, weren't so easily convinced. During a 2020 *ER* reunion online, George Clooney argued that "it would be hard to say that you could do it at the level that we did it," while Julianna Margulies added, "I think you must leave what was so beautiful and move on. . . . It feels like it would cheapen it for me." Even

Noah Wyle said, "It was classy of John not to franchise it and not to do *ER: New York* or *ER: LA.*"

And yet those talks did eventually happen. In 2025, Wyle revealed in press interviews that serious discussions had taken place between him, Wells, Warner Bros. TV, and Michael Crichton's estate about creating "a small character piece centered around Carter fifteen years later, dropping in on him wherever he was to make a jeremiad scream from the mountaintop about what was happening." Former *ER* executive producer R. Scott Gemmill would serve as the showrunner, and there was even talk about using old footage from *ER* to show Carter's journey since County General.

"I was somebody throughout the course of my career who never liked to replicate success," Peter Roth told me. "I didn't like remakes. I didn't like updated variations of the same theme. I liked to always try something different. But by the time this idea came around, television had changed so dramatically and there were so many remakes, so many updated variations, so I thought, why not? Why not this? And the idea of Noah reuniting with John? I thought it was a spectacular opportunity."

Though the reboot "got pretty close to being a reality," the plan fizzled when Warner Bros. couldn't make a deal with Sherri Crichton, the fifth wife of Michael Crichton (who died in 2008), who controls the estate. As a result, Wyle and Wells went back to the drawing board with Gemmill and came up with *The Pitt,* which was described as offering a "realistic examination of the challenges facing healthcare workers in today's America as seen through the lens of the frontline heroes working in a modern-day hospital in Pittsburgh."

The drama, which premiered in January of 2025, was an instant hit, and not just because Wyle was its star and the masterminds of *ER*—including prop master Rick Ladomade, costumer Lyn Paolo, and technical advisor Joe Sachs—were also behind it. Each episode represents one hour in a fifteen-hour shift at a Pittsburgh hospital, and the action never left the confines of the ER. *The Pitt* went on to earn five Emmys that year for Outstanding Drama Series, Outstanding Lead Actor in a Drama Series (Noah Wyle), Outstanding Supporting Actress in a Drama Series (Katherine LaNasa), Outstanding Guest Actor (Shawn Hatosy) and Outstanding Casting for a Drama Series (Cathy Sandrich Gelfond and Erica Berger). It returned for a second season in January of 2026.

ER stars like George Clooney reveled in *The Pitt*'s success. "It's so good," the actor told Seth Meyers in June of 2025. He added that he and Wyle have "been really dear friends since we did the pilot [for *ER*]. He is just the most honorable, talented young man. I get to say [that] because I'm an old man and I cannot be happier for his success on the show. The show is just a beautiful show, and he does a great job with it."

"It just says so much about John Wells and his eye for talent. He knew over thirty years ago what he saw in Noah Wyle, who had almost no track record," added Troy Evans while talking for this book. "He went, 'This is the guy.' And also, Noah Wyle is just a sensational human being."

Unfortunately, Crichton's widow didn't walk away

quietly from those initial negotiations. Five months before *The Pitt* launched on HBO Max, she sued Warner Bros., Wells, Wyle, and Gemmill for breach of contract, breach of implied covenant of good faith and fair dealing, and international interference with contractual relations. Essentially, she was accusing the team on *The Pitt* of attempting to make a new version of *ER* without the approval of the Crichton estate.

As of press time for this book, the case had yet to make it to court. But Wyle spoke publicly about the pall that it cast on *ER*'s thirtieth reunion, which was celebrated in 2024.

"The only thing that I can legally speak to is how I feel emotionally, which is just profoundly sad and disappointing," he told *Variety* in 2025. "This taints the legacy, and it shouldn't have. At one point, this could have been a partnership. And when it wasn't a partnership, it didn't need to turn acrimonious. But on the thirtieth anniversary of *ER*, I've never felt less celebratory of that achievement than I do this year."

Acknowledgments

Luckily for me, I happened to catch John Wells before he would go on to launch the huge success that is *The Pitt* for HBO Max. In a brief, encouraging phone call in 2024, he said something along the lines of, "I've spoken many times about *ER*, but my quotes have gotten better over the years" before agreeing to participate. In my reporting, I tried to get to the bottom of what makes John such a kind and generous soul. I concluded that there is no deep mystery: He's just a good egg. And TV is better for it.

Huge hug to Rebecca Marks, who made sure Warner Bros. executives like Channing Dungey were okay with me taking a trip back to County General.

I am so grateful for all the executives, writers, producers, crew members, actors, title creators, and the great James Newton Howard who took the time to chat. One person even agreed to an interview from his hospital bed.

Everyone spoke so passionately about how *ER* changed television and their lives. Even better, just about everyone had a good George Clooney story to share.

Tracking down those people was no easy task, so I'm forever indebted to Chris Ender, Nan Sumski, Heidi Schaeffer, Brenna Wolff, Beth McClinton, Paul McGuire, Phil Gonzales, Olivia Gafford, Barbara Tranchito, Steven J. Campeas, Marianne Romano, Richard Hoffman, Robert Pietranton, Susan Madore, Sky Beukers, Penni Wasserman, Claudia Russo, Jeff Tobler, Lynne Segall, and Pam Golum.

Thank you to *ER* mainstay Ellen Crawford, who not only agreed to multiple interviews but then served as a conduit to a bunch of other actors from the show. Nurse Lydia kept in touch with *everybody*!

Tip of the hat to Kristen Baldwin, my former *Entertainment Weekly* editor who is still there to answer such burning questions as whether something sounds stupid. And Dan Snierson, your early encouragement was exactly what I needed to continue.

I'm so grateful to my former editors Nellie Andreeva and Pete White, who never once questioned how I was spending my time when I was not writing about self-tapes, soaps, and Jeremy Allen White's hair for *Deadline*.

Doing this book was my agent Jon Michael Darga's idea. Somehow, he knew that I would enjoy getting to the bottom of George Clooney's pranks and those nifty *ER* titles. Thank you, pal.

Sources

I. Admissions

Neal Baer, Author Interview, October 28, 2024
Preston Beckman, Author Interview, August 21, 2024
Abraham Benrubi, Author Interview, January 24, 2025
Christopher Chulack, Author Interview, July 9, 2025
Ellen Crawford, Author Interview, November 7, 2024
Yvette Freeman, Author Interview, December 7, 2024
Lance Gentile, Author Interview, November 5, 2024
Christine Harnos, Author Interview, October 4, 2024
Eriq La Salle, Author Interview, May 1, 2025
John Levey, Author Interview, August 12, 2024
Leslie Moonves, Author Interview, January 16, 2025
Lori Openden, Author Interview, January 17, 2025
Rick Rossovich, Author Interview, March 17, 2025
Tommy Schlamme, Author Interview, April 16, 2025
Tony Thomopoulos, Author Interview, June 13, 2025
Lydia Woodward, Author Interview, November 13, 2024

"Anthony Edwards Reveals His Favorite Prank by George Clooney and the *ER* team," Maureen Lee Lenker, *Entertainment Weekly*, March 29, 2018
"ER: An Oral History," Lynette Rice, *Entertainment Weekly*, March 12, 2009
"ER Calls Its Time of Death," Scott Collins, *Los Angeles Times*, March 28, 2009
"ER Reunion: Stars in the House," streamed live via YouTube on April 22, 2021
"ER: The Doctors Unmasked," Kate Meyers, *Entertainment Weekly*, December 9, 1994
"ER's Noah Wyle on Meeting Michael Crichton and Appearing on *Friends* with George Clooney," Phil Pirrello, Television Academy, September 20, 2024

"John Wells on Making ER Realistic," Television Academy Interviews, November 28, 2016

Julianna Margulies appearance on *The Kelly Clarkson Show*, November 8, 2024

"Noah Wyle Talks New Series 'The Red Line' & Looks Back on His Best TV Roles," John Russell, *TV Insider*, April 17, 2019

"Noah Wyle: the Complete Pioneers of Television" via YouTube, July 23, 2022

"Post-Mortem: ER Is Remembered Fondly," Bill Carter, *New York Times*, March 19, 2009

Sunshine Girl: An Unexpected Life, Julianna Margulies, Ballantine Books, 2021

"Swooning over Clooney," Mark Schwed, *TV Guide*, February 25, 1995

"The Story Behind ER," Pop TV, April 4, 2017

Top of the Rock: Inside the Rise and Fall of Must See TV, Warren Littlefield & T. R. Pearson, Knopf Doubleday, 2013

2. Medical Records

Scott Grimes, Author Interview, July 12, 2025

Laura Innes, Author Interview, February 13, 2025

Jonathan Kaplan, Author Interview, April 23, 2025

Eriq La Salle, Author Interview, May 1, 2025

Paul McCrane, Author Interview, March 22, 2025

Parminder Nagra, Author Interview, April 1, 2025

Erik Palladino, Author Interview, February 20, 2025

Mekhi Phifer, Author Interview, March 14, 2025

Goran Visnjic, Author Interview, February 18, 2025

Ming-Na Wen, Author Interview, April 23, 2025

Shane West, Author Interview, April 4, 2025

Lydia Woodward, Author Interview, November 13, 2024

Yvonne Zima, Author Interview, March 6, 2025

"At the End of His Patients," Meghan Daum, *Los Angeles Times*, May 15, 2005

"British Actress Alex Kingston Leaving ER," Associated Press, June 19, 2004

"Checking In with Linda Cardellini," Jacqueline Cutler, Zap2It, November 28, 2007

"ER Actor Says Role in TV Movie Was Spark for His Career," David Bauder, Scripps Howard News Service, October 16, 2002

"ER Reunion: Stars in the House," streamed live via YouTube on April 22, 2021

"ER Star Anthony Edwards Remembers Dr. Greene's Death 15 Years Later," Ethan Alter, Yahoo! Entertainment, May 9, 2017

"ER's Extreme Makeover," Mary Murphy, *TV Guide*, February 14, 2004

"From Freaks to Dead: Linda Cardellini Breaks Down 10 of her Best Known Roles," Angie Martoccio, *Rolling Stone*, May 8, 2020

"Gloria Reuben Leaves ER to Tour with Tina Turner," Liz Smith, *Baltimore Sun*, September 9, 1999

"Gloria Reuben: The Complete Pioneers of Television" via YouTube, May 20, 2022

If You Would Have Told Me, John Stamos, Henry Holt and Co., 2023

John Wells, Television Academy Foundation Interviews, November 28, 2016

"Michael Michele Says Success on ER Meant 'I Could Step Away for a Little While' to Be a Single Mom," Christina Dugan Ramirez, *People*, August 6, 2021

"Noah Wyle: The Complete Pioneers of Television" via YouTube, July 23, 2022

"Post-Mortem: ER Is Remembered Fondly," Bill Carter, *New York Times*, March 19, 2009

"Prescription for Success: *ER* Star and Boston Native Maura Tierney Adds Villain to Her Résumé," Tamara Wieder, Phoenix.com, February 12, 2002

"Sharif Atkins Looks Back on ER, Shares Advice from Maura Tierney," Meredith Jacobs, *TV Insider*, June 13, 2025

"Sherry Stringfield Is Feeling at Home off ER," Richard Huff, *New York Daily News*, March 12, 2000

"Sherry Stringfield, The Goodbye Girl," Dana Kennedy, *Entertainment Weekly*, October 17, 1997

"Spotlight: John Stamos: The New ER Star Leaves His 80s Persona Behind for Serious Work," Lynette Rice, *Entertainment Weekly*, December 1, 2006

Sunshine Girl: An Unexpected Life, Julianna Margulies, Ballantine Books, 2021

"Tierney's Long Shift on ER Is Nearly Over," Scott D. Pierce, *Deseret News*, April 29, 2008

Top of the Rock: Inside the Rise and Fall of Must See TV, Warren Littlefield & T. R. Pearson, Knopf Doubleday, 2013

"Underutilized Star on ER Gets Exposure on TV Movie," Mike Duffy, Knight Ridder Newspapers, February 13, 1999

3. ER Entrance

Scott Grimes, Author Interview, July 12, 2025

James Newton Howard, Author Interview, November 13, 2024

Suzanne Kiley, Author Interview, December 10, 2024

Eriq La Salle, Author Interview, May 1, 2025

Billy Pittard, Author Interview, November 6, 2024

John Wells, Author Interview, April 1, 2025

4. Doctor Speak

Neal Baer, Author Interview, October 28, 2024

Ellen Crawford, Author Interview, November 7, 2024

Troy Evans, Author Interview, July 11, 2025

Carol Flint, Author Interview, December 4, 2024

Yvette Freeman, Author Interview, December 7, 2024
Lance Gentile, Author Interview, November 5, 2024
Scott Grimes, Author Interview, July 12, 2025
Laura Innes, Author Interview, February 13, 2025
Jonathan Kaplan, Author Interview, April 23, 2025
Parminder Nagra, Author Interview, April 1, 2025
Jack Orman, Author Interview, June 24, 2025
Erik Palladino, Author Interview, February 20, 2025
Lyn Paolo, Author Interview, January 31, 2025
Mekhi Phifer, Author Interview, March 14, 2025
CCH Pounder, Author Interview, March 7, 2025
Goran Visnjic, Author Interview, February 18, 2025
Emily Wagner, Author Interview, January 7, 2025
John Wells, Author Interview, April 1, 2025
Shane West, Author Interview, April 4, 2025
Lydia Woodward, Author Interview, November 13, 2024

"Doctor Who: Alex Kingston Talks Playing the Mysterious River Song," Clark Collis, *Entertainment Weekly*, April 21, 2011

"ER Reunion: Stars in the House," streamed live via YouTube on April 22, 2021

"ER's George Clooney Heats Up Prime Time," Marilyn Beck, Associated Press, June 26, 1995

"ER's Noah Wyle on Meeting Michael Crichton and Appearing on *Friends* with George Clooney," Phil Pirrello, Television Academy, September 20, 2024

"Noah Wyle: The Complete Pioneers of Television" via YouTube, July 23, 2022

"Post-Mortem: ER Is Remembered Fondly," Bill Carter, *New York Times*, March 19, 2009

"Prescription for Success: *ER* Star and Boston Native Maura Tierney Adds Villain to Her Résumé," Tamara Wieder, Phoenix.com, February 12, 2002

"Sharif Atkins Previews His *Chicago Med* Visit and Its *ER* Déjà Vu," Vlada Gelman, TVLine, October 2, 2024

5. Medical Minute: A Look Back at "Love's Labor Lost"

Neal Baer, Author Interview, October 28, 2024
Lance Gentile, Author Interview, November 5, 2024
Rick Ladomade, Author Interview, April 9, 2025
Ming-Na Wen, Author Interview, April 23, 2025

"ER: An Oral History of the Powerful, Groundbreaking 'Love's Labor Lost,'" Joyce Eng, *TV Guide*, March 8, 2015

6. Preoperative Work

Neal Baer, Author Interview, October 28, 2024
Guy Norman Bee, Author Interview, July 1, 2024
Abraham Benrubi, Author Interview, January 24, 2025
Christopher Chulack, Author Interview, July 9, 2025
Ellen Crawford, Author Interview, November 7, 2024
Troy Evans, Author Interview, July 10, 2025
Yvette Freeman, Author Interview, December 7, 2024
Lance Gentile, Author Interview, November 5, 2024
Scott Grimes, Author Interview, July 12, 2025
Jonathan Kaplan, Author Interview, April 23, 2025
Rick Ladomade, Author Interview, April 9, 2025
Lily Mariye, Author Interview, June 24, 2025
Pam Morrison, Author Interview, August 9, 2024
Parminder Nagra, Author Interview, April 1, 2025
Jack Orman, Author Interview, June 24, 2025
Lyn Paolo, Author Interview, January 31, 2025
CCH Pounder, Author Interview, March 7, 2025
Tommy Schlamme, Author Interview, April 16, 2025
Goran Visnjic, Author Interview, February 18, 2025
Ming-Na Wen, Author Interview, April 23, 2025
John Wells, Author Interview, April 1, 2025
Shane West, Author Interview, April 4, 2025

"ER Calls Its Time of Death," Scott Collins, *Los Angeles Times*, March 28, 2009
"ER Reunion: Stars in the House," streamed live via YouTube on April 22, 2021
ER's 300th Celebration at the Paley Center via YouTube, December 2007
"John Wells on Making ER Realistic," Television Academy Interviews via YouTube, November 28, 2016
"Noah Wyle: The Complete Pioneers of Television" via YouTube, July 23, 2022
"Post-Mortem: ER Is Remembered Fondly," Bill Carter, *New York Times*, March 19, 2009
"Prescription for Success: *ER* Star and Boston Native Maura Tierney Adds Villain to Her Résumé," Tamara Wieder, Phoenix.com, February 12, 2002

7. Medical Minute: A Look Back at "Motherhood"

Abraham Benrubi, Author Interview, January 24, 2025
Christopher Chulack, Author Interview, July 9, 2025

Chris Haston, Author Interview, March 12, 2025
Rick Rossovich, Author Interview, March 17, 2025
Lydia Woodward, Author Interview, November 13, 2024

"ER Reunion: Stars in the House," streamed live via YouTube on April 22, 2021
"That Time Quentin Tarantino Directed an ER Episode," Phil Pirrello, Television Academy, September 20, 2024

8. Pain Management

Scott Grimes, Author Interview, July 12, 2025
Laura Innes, Author Interview, February 13, 2025
John Levey, Author Interview, August 12, 2024
Lily Mariye, Author Interview, June 24, 2025
Paul McCrane, Author Interview, March 22, 2025
Jack Orman, Author Interview, June 24, 2025
John Wells, Author Interview, April 1, 2025
David Zabel, Author Interview, June 26, 2025

"ER Reunion: Stars in the House," streamed live via YouTube on April 22, 2021

9. Medical Minute: A Look Back at "Hell and High Water"

Neal Baer, Author Interview, October 28, 2024
Christopher Chulack, Author Interview, July 9, 2025
Lyn Paolo, Author Interview, January 31, 2025

"A Pair of Survivors Who Throw Off Sparks," Steve Vineberg, *New York Times*, October 21, 2001
"Doctor, Doctor Give Us the News," Staci Sturrock, *Palm Beach Post*, February 17, 2001
"ER: Here's the Real Reason Carter and Lucy Never Got Together," Natalie Abrams, *Entertainment Weekly*, April 2, 2018
"ER Reunion: Stars in the House," streamed live via YouTube on April 22, 2021
"ER: The Story Behind 'Hell and High Water,'" Joyce Eng, *TV Guide*, November 8, 2015
"Noah Wyle on Quitting ER and Falling in Love With Acting (Again) on CBS' Red Line," Jean Bentley, *Hollywood Reporter*, April 23, 2019

10. Funny Bone Specialist

Guy Norman Bee, Author Interview, July 1, 2024
Abraham Benrubi, Author Interview, January 24, 2025

Laura Cerón, Author Interview, January 16, 2025
Christopher Chulack, Author Interview, July 9, 2025
Ellen Crawford, Author Interview, November 7, 2024
Carol Flint, Author Interview, December 4, 2024
Lance Gentile, Author Interview, November 5, 2024
Laura Innes, Author Interview, February 13, 2025
Jonathan Kaplan, Author Interview, April 23, 2025
Rick Ladomade, Author Interview, April 9, 2025
John Levey, Author Interview, August 12, 2024
Lily Mariye, Author Interview, June 24, 2025
Pam Morrison, Author Interview, August 9, 2024
Parminder Nagra, Author Interview, April 1, 2025
Lyn Paolo, Author Interview, January 31, 2025
Rick Rossovich, Author Interview, March 17, 2025
Emily Wagner, Author Interview, January 7, 2025
John Wells, Author Interview, April 1, 2025
Yvonne Zima, Author Interview, March 6, 2025

"Anthony Edwards Reveals His Favorite Prank by George Clooney and the ER Team," Maureen Lee Lenker, *Entertainment Weekly*, March 29, 2018

"ER Reunion: Stars in the House," streamed live via YouTube on April 22, 2021

"George Clooney Pranked Noah Wyle into Pranking Steven Spielberg," *Conan* on TBS, July 18, 2013

"George Clooney, the ER Heartthrob Works from Dusk to Dawn, but Will He Give Up His Day Job?," *Entertainment Weekly*, January 26, 1996

"Gloria Reuben: The Complete Pioneers of Television" via YouTube, May 20, 2022

"Maura Tierney Breaks Down Her Career with ER, The Affair, The Report & More," *People TV*, December 11, 2019

Top of the Rock: Inside the Rise and Fall of Must See TV, Warren Littlefield & T. R. Pearson, Knopf Doubleday, 2013

11. Medical Minute: A Look Back at "Union Station"

Neal Baer, Author Interview, October 28, 2024
Abraham Benrubi, Author Interview, January 24, 2025
Ellen Crawford, Author Interview, November 7, 2024
Carol Flint, Author Interview, December 4, 2024
Mike Genovese, Author Interview, February 11, 2025
Lance Gentile, Author Interview, November 5, 2024
John Levey, Author Interview, August 12, 2024

Lily Mariye, Author Interview, June 24, 2025
Pam Morrison, Author Interview, August 9, 2024
Lori Openden, Author Interview, January 17, 2025
David Zabel, Author Interview, June 26, 2025

"A Farewell to Blood, Guts and Fame," Bill Carter, *New York Times*, November 21, 1996
"Anthony Edwards: The Complete Pioneers of Television" via YouTube, July 2, 2022
"Secrets Behind ER: A Look Back at the NBC Medical Drama," E! News, July 12, 2018
"Sherry Stringfield Is Feeling at Home off ER," *New York Daily News*, March 12, 2000
"Sherry Stringfield, The Goodbye Girl," Dana Kennedy, *Entertainment Weekly*, October 17, 1997
"The Story Behind ER," Pop TV, April 4, 2017
Top of the Rock: Inside the Rise and Fall of Must See TV, Warren Littlefield & T. R. Pearson, Knopf Doubleday, 2013
"Why Sherry Stringfield Has Returned to the ER," *Chicago Tribune*, October 19, 2001

12. Medical Minute: A Look Back at "Ambush"

Neal Baer, Author Interview, October 28, 2024
Preston Beckman, Author Interview, August 21, 2024
Christopher Chulack, Author Interview, July 9, 2025
Carol Flint, Author Interview, December 4, 2024
Lily Mariye, Author Interview, June 24, 2025
Pam Morrison, Author Interview, August 9, 2024
Jack Orman, Author Interview, June 24, 2025
Lyn Paolo, Author Interview, January 31, 2025
Tommy Schlamme, Author Interview, April 16, 2025
Lydia Woodward, Author Interview, November 13, 2024

"Alex Kingston Shakes Up ER," Dan Snierson, *Entertainment Weekly*, April 24, 1998
"ER Cast Performs Without a Net in Season Premiere," Diane Werts, *Newsday*, September 25, 1997
"Going Live Gives ER a Shot in the Arm," Don Aucoin, *Boston Globe*, September 24, 1997
"Live TV: Kick for Audience," Graham Jefferson, *USA Today*, September 25, 1997
"NBC's ER Prepares for Unprecedented Live Season Premiere," Eric Deggans, *Tampa Bay Times*, September 21, 1997
"Prepping for a Tricky Operation: A Live ER," Richard Huff, *New York Daily News*, September 22, 1997
Top of the Rock: Inside the Rise and Fall of Must See TV, Warren Littlefield & T. R. Pearson, Knopf Doubleday, 2013

13. The High Price of Healthcare

Christopher Chulack, Author Interview, July 9, 2025
Bob Daly, Author Interview, March 11, 2025
Leslie Moonves, Author Interview, January 16, 2025
Jack Orman, Author Interview, June 24, 2025

"Heart-Stopping ER Deal," Jenny Hontz, *Variety*, January 14, 1998
"Operating Funds: ER Surgeons Anthony Edwards, Noah Wyle Cut Huge Deals," Michael Fleming, *Variety*, August 4, 1998
"The Thursday-Night Massacre," Bill Carter, *New York Times*, September 20, 1998
Top of the Rock: Inside the Rise and Fall of Must See TV, Warren Littlefield & T. R. Pearson, Knopf Doubleday, 2013

14. Irregular Heartbeats

Carol Flint, Author Interview, December 4, 2024
Eriq La Salle, Author Interview, May 1, 2025
Jack Orman, Author Interview, June 24, 2025
Rick Rossovich, Author Interview, March 17, 2025
Lydia Woodward, Author Interview, November 13, 2024
David Zabel, Author Interview, June 26, 2025

"A Pair of Survivors Who Throw Off Sparks," Steve Vineberg, *New York Times*, October 21, 2001
"Doctor, Doctor Give Us the News," Staci Sturrock, *Palm Beach Post*, February 17, 2001
"ER: Here's the Real Reason Carter and Lucy Never Got Together," Natalie Abrams, *Entertainment Weekly*, April 2, 2018
"Noah Wyle on Quitting ER and Falling in Love with Acting (Again) on CBS' Red Line," Jean Bentley, *Hollywood Reporter*, April 23, 2019
"Why Eriq La Salle Asked the ER Producers to Break Up Benton and Corday," Brian Cronin, Comic Book Resources, October 14, 2021

15. Outpatient Status

Alan Alda, Author Interview, June 20, 2025
Clancy Brown, Author Interview, June 17, 2025
Kat Dennings, Author Interview, March 14, 2025
Sally Field, Author Interview, May 22, 2025

Michael Gaston, Author Interview, June 16, 2025
Joe Manganiello, Author Interview, March 24, 2025
Mary McDonnell, Author Interview, June 25, 2025
Jeffrey Dean Morgan, Author Interview, April 30, 2025
Julianne Nicholson, Author Interview, June 13, 2025
Martha Plimpton, Author Interview, March 3, 2025
James Woods, Author Interview, June 18, 2025

"ER Reunion: Stars in the House," streamed live via YouTube on April 22, 2021

16. Medical Minute: A Look Back at "The Storm," Parts 1 and 2

Abraham Benrubi, Author Interview, January 24, 2025
Christopher Chulack, Author Interview, July 9, 2025
Ellen Crawford, Author Interview, November 7, 2024
Bob Daly, Author Interview, March 11, 2025
Lily Mariye, Author Interview, June 24, 2025
Pam Morrison, Author Interview, August 9, 2024
Jack Orman, Author Interview, June 24, 2025
Peter Roth, Author Interview, January 7, 2025
Lydia Woodward, Author Interview, November 13, 2024

"A Not-So-Long Goodbye: Clooney Leaves ER," John Kiesewetter, *Cincinnati Enquirer*, February 18, 1999
"George Clooney on What ER Did for His Career, 46th AFI Life Achievement Award," TNT, June 19, 2018
John Wells, Television Academy Foundation Interviews, November 28, 2016
"Noah Wyle: The Complete Pioneers of Television" via YouTube, July 23, 2022
"Noah Wyle: Warner Bros. Built the ER Cast a Basketball Court," *Conan* on TBS, June 13, 2011
"The Story Behind ER," Pop TV, April 4, 2017

17. The Nurses' Station

Abraham Benrubi, Author Interview, July 9, 2025
Laura Cerón, Author Interview, January 16, 2025
Ellen Crawford, Author Interview, November 7, 2024
Troy Evans, Author Interview, July 10, 2025
Carol Flint, Author Interview, December 4, 2024

Yvette Freeman, Author Interview, December 7, 2024
Lance Gentile, Author Interview, November 5, 2024
John Levey, Author Interview, August 12, 2024
Lily Mariye, Author Interview, June 24, 2025
Jack Orman, Author Interview, June 24, 2025
Lydia Woodward, Author Interview, November 13, 2024

"ER Reunion: Stars in the House," streamed live via YouTube on April 22, 2021

18. Medical Minute: A Look Back at "Be Still My Heart" and "All in the Family"

Lily Mariye, Author Interview, June 24, 2025
Jack Orman, Author Interview, June 24, 2025
Lydia Woodward, Author Interview, November 13, 2024

"ER Alum Eriq La Salle Looks Back on The Benton–Carter Rehab Moment 25 Years Later: 'If You Have to Go to Hell, I'm Coming to Hell with You'," Joyce Eng, Gold Derby, May 16, 2025

"ER Oral History: Behind the Shocking Stabbing of Carter and Lucy," Natalie Abrams, *Entertainment Weekly*, March 30, 2018

"Eriq La Salle: The Complete Pioneers of Television" via YouTube, July 16, 2022

"Noah Wyle Shares Why Lucy Knight's Death Was Such a 'Revelatory' Moment for John Carter on ER," Stacy Lambe, *People*, March 28, 2025

19. Medical Minute: A Look Back at "Such Sweet Sorrow"

Christopher Chulack, Author Interview, July 9, 2025
Ellen Crawford, Author Interview, November 7, 2024
Jonathan Kaplan, Author Interview, April 23, 2025
Eriq La Salle, Author Interview, May 1, 2025
Peter Roth, Author Interview, January 7, 2025
Barbara Tranchito, Author Interview, February 27, 2025
Lydia Woodward, Author Interview, November 13, 2024

"George Clooney Reveals How They Kept His ER Return a Secret," Samantha Highfill, *Entertainment Weekly*, May 31, 2019

"How ER Kept George Clooney's Return a Secret," Phil Pirrello, Television Academy, September 16, 2024

"Julianna Margulies Has No Regrets She's Still Leaving ER Despite $27 Million Offer," Scott D. Pierce, *Deseret News*, February 3, 2000

20. New Rotation

Scott Grimes, Author Interview, July 12, 2025

Parminder Nagra, Author Interview, April 1, 2025

Jack Orman, Author Interview, June 24, 2025

Erik Palladino, Author Interview, February 20, 2025

Mekhi Phifer, Author Interview, March 14, 2025

Peter Roth, Author Interview, January 7, 2025

Maura Tierney, Author Interview, April 16, 2025

Goran Visnjic, Author Interview, February 18, 2025

Ming-Na Wen, Author Interview, April 23, 2025

Shane West, Author Interview, April 4, 2025

Lydia Woodward, Author Interview, November 13, 2024

David Zabel, Author Interview, June 26, 2025

"A Delicate Balance: ER's Casting Director John Levey Must Consider All the Possible Ailments While Keeping the Series Alive," Behnoosh Khalili, *Backstage*, November 4, 2019

"ER Finale Keeps Hope Alive," Rob Owen, *Pittsburgh Post-Gazette*, March 24, 2009

ER's 300th celebration at the Paley Center via YouTube, December 2007

"ER's John Stamos on Playing Doctor," Eric Goldman, IGN, November 1, 2006

"From Freaks to Dead: Linda Cardellini Breaks Down 10 of Her Best-Known Roles," Angie Martoccio, *Rolling Stone*, May 8, 2020

John Wells, Television Academy Foundation Interviews, November 28, 2016

"Maura Tierney Interview 2023: From ER to The Iron Claw," Collider Ladies Night via YouTube, December 23, 2023

"Ming-Na Wen on Why She Left (and Came Back) to ER," Phil Pirrello and Mara Reinstein, Television Academy, September 17, 2024

"Post-Mortem: ER Is Remembered Fondly," Bill Carter, *New York Times*, March 19, 2009

"Sharif Atkins Finally Finds His Niche," *Chicago Tribune*, June 17, 2018

"Sharif Atkins Looks Back on ER, Shares Advice from Maura Tierney," Meredith Jacobs, *TV Insider*, June 13, 2025

"Spotlight: John Stamos," Lynette Rice, *Entertainment Weekly*, December 1, 2006

21. Medical Minute: A Look Back at "I'll Be Home for Christmas"

Jonathan Kaplan, Author Interview, April 23, 2025

Eriq La Salle, Author Interview, May 1, 2025

Lyn Paolo, Author Interview, January 31, 2025

Peter Roth, Author Interview, January 7, 2025

"ER Actors Noah Wyle, Maura Tierney Looking to the Future," Todd Hill, *Staten Island Advance*, May 26, 2002

"ER Reunion: Stars in the House," streamed live via YouTube on April 22, 2021

"Gloria Reuben: The Complete Pioneers of Television" via YouTube, May 20, 2022

"What the Original ER Stars Think About Grey's Anatomy Beating Their Record," Jean Bentley, *Hollywood Reporter*, February 28, 2019

22. Pediatric Care

Hallee Hirsh, Author Interview, March 18, 2025

Jack Orman, Author Interview, June 24, 2025

Matthew Watkins, Author Interview, August 30, 2025

Trinia Watkins, Author Interview, August 30, 2025

John Wells, Author Interview, April 1, 2025

Yvonne Zima, Author Interview, March 6, 2025

23. Medical Minute: A Look Back at "On the Beach"

Christine Harnos, Author Interview, October 4, 2024

Hallee Hirsh, Author Interview, March 18, 2025

Jonathan Kaplan, Author Interview, April 23, 2025

Jack Orman, Author Interview, June 24, 2025

"Anthony Edwards: The Complete Pioneers of Television" via YouTube, July 2, 2022

"ER Star Anthony Edwards Remembers Dr. Greene's Death 15 Years Later," Ethan Alter, Yahoo! Entertainment, May 9, 2017

"ER's Noah Wyle on Meeting Michael Crichton and Appearing on *Friends* with George Clooney," Phil Pirrello, Television Academy, September 20, 2024

"Grateful for ER, Edwards Buries Dr. Mark Greene," Jacqueline Cutler, Tribune Media Services, May 9, 2002

"Hidden in Plain Sight: Anthony Edwards Is the Quiet Man Who Anchors ER's Cast," David Bauder, Associated Press, March 15, 2001

"Post-Mortem: ER Is Remembered Fondly," Bill Carter, *New York Times*, March 19, 2009

"The Story Behind ER," Pop TV, April 4, 2017

Top of the Rock: Inside the Rise and Fall of Must See TV, Warren Littlefield & T. R. Pearson, Knopf Doubleday, 2013

24. Discharge Papers

Abraham Benrubi, Author Interview, January 24, 2025

Laura Cerón, Author Interview, January 16, 2025

Christopher Chulack, Author Interview, July 9, 2025
Yvette Freeman, Author Interview, December 7, 2024
Scott Grimes, Author Interview, July 12, 2025
Hallee Hirsh, Author Interview, March 18, 2025
Lily Mariye, Author Interview, June 24, 2025
Parminder Nagra, Author Interview, April 1, 2025
Peter Roth, Author Interview, January 7, 2025
Maura Tierney, Author Interview, April 16, 2025
Ming-Na Wen, Author Interview, April 23, 2025
David Zabel, Author Interview, June 26, 2025

"ER Admits Last Patient: Marilu Henner," Joyce Eng, *TV Guide*, April 1, 2009

"ER Final Episodes: Doug Reunites with CAROL . . . and Dr. Benton?," *Entertainment Weekly*, 2005

"ER Finale Based on Death of Producer's 17-Year-Old Niece," Fox News, April 2, 2009

"ER Finale Keeps Hope Alive," Rob Owen, *Pittsburgh Post-Gazette*, March 24, 2009

"ER's Noah Wyle on Meeting Michael Crichton and Appearing on *Friends* with George Clooney," Phil Pirrello, Television Academy, September 20, 2024

"From Freaks to Dead: Linda Cardellini Breaks Down 10 of Her Best-Known Roles," Angie Martoccio, *Rolling Stone*, May 8, 2020

"How ER Kept George Clooney's Return a Secret," Phil Pirrello, Television Academy, September 16, 2024

John Wells, Television Academy Interviews, November 28, 2016

"Noah Wyle on Quitting ER and Falling in Love with Acting (Again) on CBS' Red Line," Jean Bentley, *Hollywood Reporter*, April 23, 2019

"Noah Wyle: The Complete Pioneers of Television" via YouTube July 23, 2022

25. Long-Term Prognosis

Neal Baer, Author Interview, October 28, 2024
Preston Beckman, Author Interview, August 21, 2024
Laura Cerón, Author Interview, January 16, 2025
Christopher Chulack, Author Interview, July 9, 2025
Troy Evans, Author Interview, June 10, 2025
Yvette Freeman, Author Interview, December 7, 2024
Hallee Hirsh, Author Interview, March 18, 2025
Laura Innes, Author Interview, February 13, 2025
Jonathan Kaplan, Author Interview, April 23, 2025
Eriq La Salle, Author Interview, May 1, 2025
Lily Mariye, Author Interview, June 24, 2025

Leslie Moonves, Author Interview, January 16, 2025
Parminder Nagra, Author Interview, April 1, 2025
Lori Openden, Author Interview, January 17, 2025
Jack Orman, Author Interview, June 24, 2025
Mekhi Phifer, Author Interview, March 14, 2025
Rick Rossovich, Author Interview, March 17, 2025
John Wells, Author Interview, April 1, 2025
David Zabel, Author Interview, June 26, 2025
Yvonne Zima, Author Interview, March 6, 2025

"ER Closes Doors, Leaves Satisfying Legacy," Susan C. Young, *Today*, March 2, 2014
"ER Reunion: Stars in the House," streamed live via YouTube on April 22, 2021
"Eriq La Salle: The Complete Pioneers of Television" via YouTube, July 16, 2022
"Gloria Reuben: The Complete Pioneers of Television" via YouTube, May 20, 2022
John Wells, Television Academy Interviews, November 28, 2016
"Maura Tierney's Long Shift on ER Is Nearly Over," Scott D. Pierce, *Deseret News*, April 29, 2008
"Post-Mortem: ER Is Remembered Fondly," Bill Carter, *New York Times*, March 19, 2009

Quote Boxes

1. Anthony Edwards, "Anthony Edwards: The Complete Pioneers of Television" via YouTube, July 2, 2022
2. Julianna Margulies, "ER Reunion: Stars in the House," streamed live via YouTube on April 22, 2021
3. Gloria Reuben, "Gloria Reuben: The Complete Pioneers of Television" via YouTube, May 20, 2022
4. John Stamos, *If You Would Have Told Me*, Henry Holt and Co., 2023
5. Billy Pittard, Author Interview, November 6, 2024
6. Lance Gentile, Author Interview, November 5, 2024
7. Neal Baer, Author Interview, October 28, 2024
8. Laura Innes, Author Interview, February 13, 2025
9. Mekhi Phifer, Author Interview, March 14, 2025
10. Julianna Margulies, "That Time Quentin Tarantino Directed an ER Episode," Phil Pirrello, Television Academy, September 20, 2024
11. Paul McCrane, Author Interview, March 22, 2025
12. Neal Baer, Author Interview, October 28, 2024
13. George Clooney, "ER Reunion: Stars in the House," streamed live via YouTube on April 22, 2021

14. Carol Flint, Author Interview, December 4, 2024
15. Mike Genovese, Author Interview, February 11, 2025
16. Goran Visnjic, Author Interview, February 18, 2025
17. Rick Rossovich, Author Interview, March 17, 2025
18. Maura Tierney, Author Interview, April 16, 2025
19. Bob Daly, Author Interview, March 11, 2025
20. Lily Mariye, Author Interview, June 24, 2025
21. Troy Evans, Author Interview, July 10, 2025
22. Abraham Benrubi, Author Interview, January 24, 2025
23. Eriq La Salle, "Eriq La Salle: The Complete Pioneers of Television" via YouTube, July 16, 2022
24. Julianna Margulies, "How ER Kept George Clooney's Return a Secret," Samantha Highfill, *Entertainment Weekly*, September 16, 2024
25. Shane West, Author Interview, April 4, 2025
26. Noah Wyle, "Noah Wyle: The Complete Pioneers of TV" via YouTube, July 23, 2023
27. Yvonne Zima, Author Interview, March 6, 2025
28. Anthony Edwards, "ER Star Anthony Edwards Remembers Dr. Greene's Death 15 Years Later," Ethan Alter, Yahoo! Entertainment, May 9, 2017
29. Parminder Nagra, Author Interview, April 1, 2025
30. Noah Wyle, Author Interview, April 2, 2025

Index

Names of actors and real people are **boldfaced**.

About the Author

Hyun Park

LYNETTE RICE is the *New York Times* bestselling author of *How to Save a Life*, her oral history of the hit medical show *Grey's Anatomy*. Previously, she was a senior writer at *Deadline*, as well as an editor-at-large for *Entertainment Weekly* and a writer covering TV for *The Hollywood Reporter*. Lynette wrote about *ER* during its heyday and forged many relationships with some of the most important players on the drama, both behind the scenes and in front of the camera. She lives in Los Angeles, California.